MARK MORRIS

Farrar Straus Giroux · New York

MARK

JOAN ACOCELLA

MORRIS

Library of Congress Cataloging-in-Publication Data
Acocella, Joan Ross.
Mark Morris / Joan Acocella.—1st ed.
p. cm.
Chronology of M. Morris's work.
Includes index.
1. Morris, Mark, 1956– . 2. Choreographers—United States—
Biography.   I. Morris, Mark, 1956– . II. Title.
GV1785.M635A27   1993
792.8′2′092—dc20   [B]
93-13697   CIP

Grateful acknowledgment is made to the following for permission to reprint previously
published material: lyrics from *Soap-Powders and Detergents* by Herschel Garfein, copy-
right © 1993 by Herschel Garfein, courtesy of the author; excerpt from Charles Siebert's
"Morris Dances," in *Vanity Fair*, April 1989, courtesy of the author; excerpt from John
Gruen's "Mark Morris: He's Here" in *Dance Magazine*, September 1986, copyright © 1993
Dance Magazine, used with permission.

TITLE PAGE PHOTO:
The company in Championship Wrestling, from Mythologies (Danièle Pierre)

TO BART

Author's Note

This book is in no way authorized. Mark Morris read the manuscript before it went to the printer and corrected a few factual errors. Beyond that, he had no direct involvement in the making of the book. Indeed, from what I could tell, he was largely indifferent to it, which was a great relief to me. My goal was to provide an account of his life and a guide to his work, but what I wanted most was to give a portrait of his imagination—an idea of how he thinks, or how he thinks the thoughts that lead to his dances. About this, there was only so much he could tell me. I had to turn to his dances and speculate on what I saw there—a necessity he took for granted. So the book is my view, not his; any statement that is not in quotation marks with his name on it is not his fault. Still, he gave me everything I said I needed—above all, a long series of interviews. He is a wonderful talker, and he likes to talk about dance. This was a help, needless to say. He was also honest, patient, and a lot of fun. For all that, and for the sheer pleasure it was, for two and a half years, to sit and think about his work, I am more grateful to him than I can say.

Aside from Morris, the two anchors of this book were Morris's family and his company. Barry Alterman, the general director of the Mark Morris Dance Group, was indispensable to me. He lent me files, told me stories, saw me through problems. He is also an excellent dance critic. The rest of the administrative staff—Nancy Umanoff, the managing director; Tom Geyer, her assistant; Karen Hershey, the development director; Johan Henckens, the technical director—

helped me in every way they could. Tom Geyer was on the phone with me almost every day.

Morris comes from a small, tight-knit family. His mother, Maxine, and his sister Maureen still live in the house where he grew up in Seattle. His other sister, Marianne Johnson, lives nearby with her husband, Keith, and their children, Tyler and Amanda. The family was very good to me. Maxine Morris, over four days of interview, supplied much of what the book has to say about Morris's childhood; she also lent me her programs and photographs. Maureen Morris not only told me about her brother's childhood, but it was she, more than anyone else, who gave me a sense of the *tone* of the family, and of Morris's relationship with his father. Marianne Johnson told me about the family's games and theatricals. Outside the family circle, but not far outside, stands Verla Flowers, Morris's first and most important dance teacher. Flowers helped me to understand what kind of child artist Morris was, and what kind of child. She too let me walk off with her programs and photographs.

Much of the rest of my information came from interviews with Lynda Barry, Mikhail Baryshnikov, Rob Besserer, Robert Bordo, Ruth Davidson, Linda Dowdell, Tina Fehlandt, Herschel Garfein, Susan Hadley, Peter Wing Healey, Chad Henry, Mary Hoagland, Penny Hutchinson, Jill Johnson, Hannah Kahn, Clarice Marshall, Erin Matthiessen, Jon Mensinger, Gérard Mortier, Keith Sabado, Peter Sellars, Page Smith, Teri Weksler, and David White—an unusually candid, thoughtful, and quotable group of people. Many others answered questions for me: Maren Erikson, Joan Goldberg, Eve Green, Terrence Grizzell, Doris Hering, Speight Jenkins, Eric Johnson, Judy Kinberg, Seymour Kleinberg, Sali Ann Kriegsman, Sandra Kurtz, Norman Langill, W. McNeil Lowry, Lodi McClellan, Bruce Marks, Luisa Moffett, Mark Murphy, Paul Nicholas, Norton Owen, Kay Pratt, Janet Soares, Phyllis Stonebrook, Yannick Vermeirsch, Jennifer Carroll Walker. Johan Henckens, Richard Howard, Rudi Oeding-Erdel, and Ernst Pawel helped me translate the European reviews. The chronology of works that comes at the end of this book was built on the base of an earlier chronology compiled by William James Lawson. I am grateful to Lawson for the work he saved me; to Nancy Umanoff and Tina Fehlandt for providing facts that could not be supplied by the records, only by superb memory; and to David Vaughan for lending his practiced eye to the reviewing of this long catalogue.

Many of my quotations of Morris and his collegues come from articles by others. Published sources are credited in the notes at the end of the book, but since I have stolen some of their best quotes, I want to thank the writers here: Janice Berman, Laurence Bertels, Pope Brock, Lori Brungard, Rupert Christiansen, Michael Corsetino, Michael Crabb, Debra Craine, Nancy Dalva, David Daniel, Roger

Downey, Jennifer Dunning, Joan Dupont, Iris Fanger, Robert Greskovic, John Gruen, Deborah Jowitt, Daryl Jung, Rudy Kikel, Alan Kriegsman, Thierry Lassence, Alastair Macaulay, Luisa Moffett, Allen Robertson, Tobias Schneebaum, Laura Shapiro, Charles Siebert, Thea Singer, Christine Temin, Tobi Tobias, David Vaughan, Yannick Vermeirsch. I have also picked up quotations from two television programs, *Mark Morris*, produced by Judy Kinberg and Thomas Grimm and directed by Grimm for PBS, and *The Hidden Soul of Harmony*, produced and directed by Nigel Wattis for London Weekend Television. Many of the ideas, and some of the words, in this book have already appeared in articles by me in *Art in America*, *Dance Magazine*, *The Guardian*, *Parkett*, *7 Days*, *The Village Voice*, and *Vogue*.

Most of the first draft of the book was written at the MacDowell Colony in New Hampshire in the summers of 1991 and 1992. Had the Colony not taken me in, the project would have been far harder and longer, as it would have been without a generous grant from the JCT Foundation.

Parts of the book have benefited from the reading and advice of Elizabeth Baker, Sally Banes, Deborah Drier, and Deborah Jowitt. Robert Gottlieb read the entire manuscript; he also helped me choose the photos. Robert Cornfield, my agent, not only read each chapter as it was written and rewritten, but watched over the project from the time the proposal was hatched. To all of them and to the staff of Farrar, Straus and Giroux—Cynthia Krupat, who designed the book; Phyllida Burlingame, who saw it through editing and production; and above all my editor, Jonathan Galassi—thank you.

Contents

MARK MORRIS

Mark Morris, 1989 *(Pierre Radisic)*

MARK MORRIS

In September 1988, Belgium's state opera house, the Théâtre Royal de la Monnaie, called a special press conference so that local journalists could speak to the man who had just taken over as the house's director of dance: Mark Morris. It was a tense moment. For more than a quarter of a century the dance director of the Monnaie had been Maurice Béjart, whose sexy, up-to-date ballets, full of existential brooding, were revered by the Belgian people. But in 1987 Béjart had quarreled with the opera house and walked out, and now the Monnaie had appointed this thirty-two-year-old American in his place. Most of the Brussels press had never heard of Morris until he landed Béjart's job. Furthermore, he didn't look like an opera-house dance director. He had long, shaggy hair, and he wore a cowboy shirt. When he told a story, he made funny faces to go with it. One of the journalists, trying to get some fix on who he was, asked him to share with them his philosophy of dance, a question that would have been a natural for Béjart and that would no doubt have elicited from him a long, handsomely worded statement on the nature of dance, the conundrum of modern history, and other matters. Morris listened to the question, paused, mumbled around a bit, and then said, "My philosophy of dance? I make it up, and you watch it. End of philosophy."

This response, while it did nothing to smooth his entry into the

Belgian dance community, was nevertheless an accurate description of Morris's attitude toward his work, and also of his work. Punk though he may look, he is an old-fashioned artist. He has been making dances since he was fourteen, and he no more questions that activity than a baker would question the making of a pie. Consequently, he doesn't feel he needs a philosophy of dance, only a way of making it. Nor does he have any problem with the usual way of making it, simply out of movement and music. A jump, a landing, the way that jump relates to another jump on the other side of the stage, the way both of them relate to the musical beat: to him this is a perfectly decent mode of communication, an eloquent language, and the one he speaks most naturally. Accordingly, his dances show no self-consciousness, or no self-consciousness about being dance.

But if Morris's answer to the Belgian journalist was a good description of his artistic philosophy, it was also, in its cheerful effrontery, a good sample of his personality. Morris in his early years had a reputation as Mr. Outrageous, and he did much to earn it. He took curtain calls in Bermudas and flip-flops. He swigged beer at meet-the-choreographer symposia. He seemed unable to get through an interview without pointing out that he was homosexual. Not that the interviewers needed to be told this. There was much about him that was effeminate, and he had the usual fun with this. (During his first season in Brussels, Belgium's Queen Fabiola attended one of his performances. "*Vive la reine!*" people shouted as she came through the foyer. "I thought they meant me," Morris later said to a reporter.) At the same time, rather unnervingly, he was also very butch—a big hairy guy who lumbered around noisily and waved a beer bottle at you as he spoke. As a French journalist once put it, he was part diva, part truck driver.

But what really earned him his *enfant terrible* reputation was his mouth. Morris was constantly saying what was on his mind, particularly, it seemed, whatever courtesy or expediency would require him not to say. For years people wondered why Peter Martins, the director of New York City Ballet, did not invite Morris to make a dance for that company, but in view of the fact that in a 1988 interview with *Newsweek* he called New York City Ballet's American Music Festival "the Peter Martins record collection festival"—and also described one of Martins's contributions to the festival as "that lecture-demonstration for the seventh grade"—there was little cause for wonder that Martins hadn't rushed out to hire him.

Nor did those who hired him get much better treatment. In an interview he gave while preparing a work for the Brooklyn Academy of Music, a longtime supporter of his work, he exclaimed, "Wonderful BAM!" and then said that BAM's president, Harvey Lichtenstein, had told him to be sure to call it that. ("He can be a real pain in the neck," Lichtenstein said in a separate interview.) In Brussels, during the early, tense months of his stay there, he was asked what he thought of Anne Teresa de Keersmaeker, the leader of Belgium's young, anguish-ridden dance-theater movement. "All you have to do here," he said, "is not wash your hair for a week and then sit on stage and act depressed and you've got it. 'Magnifique! Formidable!' "

Invariably, the day after an interview with Morris hit the stands, Barry Alterman, the general director of the Mark Morris Dance Group, would receive rather more phone calls than usual. ("Sometimes I feel like the man who walks around with the shovel behind the elephant," Alterman once said.) But as many enemies as Morris made with his big mouth, he probably made more friends. Amid the dry hum of intramural *politesse* that governs dance, as it governs most artistic fields, many people were grateful, now and then, to hear a squawk of candor. And however much trouble Morris may have won with his outspokenness, he certainly didn't fail to win publicity.

It wasn't publicity seeking, though. Nor was it simply truthfulness or rudeness, though Morris has large reserves of both. More than anything, his outspokenness is the product of his extroversion. Morris was a child who was loved by his mother. In a given situation, he does not necessarily ask himself whether the thing he wants to say or do is going to accord with the needs of those around him. Whatever is in him, out it comes. This goes for his dances—he creates with extraordinary ease—and for everything he does. Even when he is working, especially when he is working, he is always cracking jokes, teasing people, trying on various foreign accents, laughing, singing. "In work and in life, he is very much full of joy," as his friend Mikhail Baryshnikov has said of him. Occasionally, in Europe, where matters of hierarchy and decorum are more strictly observed, his revels have confused people. As he has said, he had some difficulties getting the dancers of the Paris Opera Ballet to pay attention to him when he created a work on them in 1990. No doubt the Parisian dancers, accustomed to strict hierarchy, were asking themselves whether the nut case in the Bermudas was actually the choreographer.

At the same time, he is a completely serious person, even something of a stick-in-the-mud. Morris is a quiet-living man who spends most of his waking hours making dances and, when he is finished with a job

and has time off, generally goes home to visit his family in Seattle. His practical skills are poor, on the whole. He is not good with money, and his personal finances are handled by his company's managing director, Nancy Umanoff: "I hand out money to him, and he spends it, whatever it is—$100 or $10. He shares a credit card with his mother and pays the bills; the trouble is, he's always losing it." For a year and a half after his company moved back to the United States from Belgium, he had no home. He lived out of a suitcase in Baryshnikov's New York apartment. He has one concern in life, his work, and he pursues it with a single-mindedness that shuts out most other considerations. Though he has had great success, he would probably still be making dances if he had had no success whatsoever. "If he can't do it in an opera house," says Alterman, "he'll do it in a church basement."

In a curious way, his concerts show this same mix of playfulness and

Morris and dancers in
rehearsal, Brussels,
1990 (*Danièle Pierre*)

seriousness. A good example was his 1992 New York spring season, which took place at the Manhattan Center Grand Ballroom. This was a space such as only the Mark Morris Dance Group could have chosen. Upstairs from the old Manhattan Opera House, in what is now a rather seedy part of town—the building is currently owned by the Unification Church of the Reverend Sun Myung Moon—the ballroom is normally used for such things as beauty pageants and MTV New Year's specials. Everything about it is exuberantly tacky. Franco-Italo-Moorish decoration hangs from the ceiling. Dance-of-all-nations murals cover the walls. And during its occupation by the Mark Morris Dance Group it became rather funkier. In the bar Barry Alterman installed a musician, Jay Bailey, whom he had discovered on a subway platform. Bailey sang and played the washtub bass, and he had with him a colleague who played brushes on the washtub. The bartenders were sweet; the drinks were cheap; the ushers let you

bring your drink into the theater. Many people, once they got in, strolled around the room, sipping their beers, greeting their friends, and exclaiming over the decor. This was not your normal modern dance concert. It was more like a party. At the same time, installed in the front of the theater was $11,000 (per night) worth of live classical musicians, instruments in hand—an impressive display of seriousness. And once the dancing started, it was completely straight.

But Morris's dances too are straight in a slightly crooked way. Some of them are quite shocking. In one of his better-known pieces, a vampire seduces a little girl and she goes off with him happily. In another, set to a suite of old parlor songs, a man dances in his underpants with a brown paper bag over his head. But in most cases what is shocking—or surprising, unexpected—is simply the quality of the dancing, which is often slightly awkward or, in most cases, just very deliberate. Even when the dancers are doing something beautifully, you can still see their intention, their effort. You can see the exact thing they are doing; it doesn't elide into a nice smear of dancing. This deliberateness gives the movement a disturbingly direct quality. It is a little too close to physical reality, and hence to certain emotional realities. As Morris has said, there is always something "a little uncomfortable" about his work. Many people find this funny. Audiences laugh out loud not just at his comic dances but also at his most sober-minded work. Then, the next time they come, they wonder why the other people are laughing.

In that 1992 concert he revived an old work, *Prelude and Prelude*, to a duet for violin and harpsichord by Henry Cowell. As the piece opens, a line of dancers stands facing forward, with golden fans in their hands. The harpsichord begins to play, and the dancers begin moving the fans from position to position, trying, it seems, to cover their bodies, but never covering everything they want to. Now the violin starts up, and when it does, a lone woman breaks away from the lineup, moving out onto the floor in a solo full of inelegant steps: sumo wrestler squats, backward falls that leave her with her legs splayed in the air. She is undaunted, though—very dignified. She goes on with the dance, and the sight of this lonely figure journeying out, away from the group—the bodily image of the violin's lonely voice rising out of the machine-like threshings of the harpsichord—soon becomes piercing. Everything is strange, "uncomfortable": the golden fans, the embarrassed bodies, the woman's struggle. Then slowly the whole thing tips over, and it is no longer strange.

CHILDHOOD

Mark Morris was born in 1956, in Seattle, to William Morris, a high-school teacher, and Maxine Critten-den Morris, who stayed home with the children. Their ancestry was North-ern European, their religion Presbyterian. They lived in a six-room house, white with blue trim, on a quiet street in the Mt. Baker section of Seattle. Their block was mostly Italian-American and Jewish, mostly working-class. "A couple of the fathers sold insurance," says Morris's sister Mau-reen. "One was a jeweler, one was a garbage collector, one was a mortician. One ran a brothel, but it was called a hotel."

Some of the family's ancestors had been on this continent for cen-turies. Maxine Morris's father was descended from English Quakers who settled in Salem, Massachusetts, in 1630. Her mother's stock was Irish and German. Her German grandfather, Johann Zimmerman, had traveled from his native Pennsylvania to the West in a covered wagon in 1876. Eventually he settled in Montana, where he established a large sheep farm. His daughter Mabel married Bill Crittenden, also from a farming clan, and their daughter Maxine, Mark Morris's mother, was born on the family farm in Fairfield, Montana, in 1917. That same year, Morris's father, William Morris, born in 1913, moved with his family from Ohio to a farm in Fort Benton, Montana, on the west bank of the Missouri River. So both of Mark Morris's parents spent their early years on Montana farms.

In both cases they were unprosperous farms. Bill Morris's father hated farming. He went into politics and left his sons to scratch a living out of their dryland plot. Maxine's father, Bill Crittenden, also disliked farming, but he got out. At age twenty-six he moved his family to Helena, the state capital, and thence from town to town as he worked first in a grocery store, then in a wholesale warehouse, then as a feed salesman. Once the Depression hit, he did whatever work he could get.

But Bill Crittenden took hardship lightly. He was a character, a card, a man full of fantasy and joy. He adored chickens—wherever the family lived, they always had a chicken coop—and one way he hit upon to make money in the early thirties was to have a radio program where, as "Chicken Bill," he answered questions that people sent in about their chickens. For the first program, he of course had no letters from listeners yet, so the family made up the questions. One was "Which came first, the chicken or the egg?" To answer this, Bill got out the Bible and pointed out that while it said that God created the fowl of the air, it didn't say anything about eggs. So that was it: the chicken came first. According to family history, Bill's answer to this longstanding question was a big hit with the radio audience and his program became very popular.

But what Bill loved even better than chickens was dancing and music. In Bozeman, Montana, where he grew up, he attended every vaudeville show that came through, and after the shows he would invite his friends over and teach them the tap-dance routines he had seen. Once he married, he acquired an accompanist: Mabel Crittenden played the piano, and she knew a lot of ragtime tunes. At every party and picnic, Bill always led off the dancing. He also loved to dress up in costumes. His favorite trick was to put on a disguise and then appear at a party, or even just at the neighbors' house, and see how long it took them to recognize him. (Presumably, they obliged him by taking a long time.) Sometimes he came as a hobo, often as a woman, complete with dress, hat, and high heels. Wherever Bill went, there was always a show, and this quality of his, together with his passion for dancing and his freedom of fantasy, unquestionably left its imprint on his grandson Mark.

In between, however, came Maxine, who inherited her father's love of dancing. When she was a young woman in Helena, she and her friends would go every Saturday night to whatever dance pavilion had a good band playing. "I always picked my boyfriends for how they danced," Maxine Morris says. "I guess they weren't ugly, but I never looked at their faces. I just danced with them. That's how I got together with Bill."

13

Though they grew up about 150 miles apart in Montana, Maxine
Crittenden and Bill Morris didn't meet until they both had moved to
Seattle in search of work. Bill had had a hard youth. He was the youngest
of seven children, and as each of them went off to school or work, more
and more of the responsibility for the farm fell on him, until at last he
was carrying it alone, and very unhappily. He too hated farming, and
wheat gave him asthma attacks. Finally the Depression came and the
family lost the farm. Bill moved to Seattle, and there he took various jobs,
slowly working his way through the University of Washington. In 1940
he was doing clerical work at the Puget Sound Naval Shipyard, outside
Seattle, when he met Maxine, who had just moved there from Helena and
was working as a secretary.

Bill's family was Welsh, so they sang all the time, and as a boy he
had learned piano and also drums, which he played with his high-school
band. He loved to dance, and his courtship of Maxine took place on the
dance floor. On their first date, they danced all night to Henry Bussey's
band. After they were married in 1941, they went every Saturday night
to the Trianon Ballroom on the Seattle waterfront to dance to the big bands
that came through—Artie Shaw, Harry James. In 1947 their nights out

were curtailed by the arrival of their first child, Marianne. A second daughter, Maureen, was born in 1951. By now, Bill had taken a job teaching at Franklin High School in Seattle, and in 1952, to accommodate their growing family, they bought the white house in the Mt. Baker district, near the school. On August 29, 1956, their third and last child, Mark William Morris, was born, into a dancing family.

In most respects the Morrises were an ordinary middle-class household—they watched *Lawrence Welk*, they went to McDonald's, they pinned their Christmas cards over the mantel—but there were at least two unusual things about them. One was the extraordinary rate of amateur art making in the house. No one in the immediate or extended family had ever been a professional artist, and only one became an artist, but they were constantly producing art, simply by way of amusing themselves. Bill had a large double organ in the living room, and playing it was his joy and relaxation, so there was always music in the house. Mark danced before he could walk, pulling himself up by the edge of the coffee table and yanking himself around to whatever tune was playing in the living room. The children sang for their father while he played. He taught them his favorites: "Sweet Sue," "Sentimental Journey." When the family took car trips to California or Montana to visit their relatives, they sang all the way, all five of them.

Everyone in the house was always involved in some kind of show. Bill played the organ at local fairs. The children were continually rehearsing for performances in school talent shows, Campfire Girl jamborees, Christmas pageants, PTA suppers. Big family dinners also included theatricals. Marianne took ballet lessons; Maureen was in her school chorus. Both girls studied piano.

They even made films. This was the special project of Maxine's brother Jim, Grandpa Bill's only son and the primary inheritor of his nutty exuberance. Uncle Jim smoked big cigars; he drove a big red Cadillac, and turned the radio up loud and sang along. He had a glamorous wife, Audrey, who dyed her hair a different color every year. (One year she dyed it a pink that came out so nice she dyed her poodle to match.) Jim was a beer distributor, and because he set up store displays, he always had a garage full of excellent theatrical materials: sombreros, leis, bolts of cloth to make sarongs and turbans. Every summer Jim's family and Maxine's family would converge for several weeks on the home of their sister Eva, who had remained in Helena, where she had a big house filled with eight children. The treat for the cousins on these Montana vacations was to go with Uncle Jim into the countryside and make films, with the children as the actors and Uncle Jim as the director and cameraman. These were serious projects, with scenarios and scripts and elaborate costumes that

Theatricals at Uncle Jim's, c. 1959. Left to right: Maureen Morris, cousin Carolyn Crittenden, Marianne Morris, Mark

the aunts and uncles helped the children make. Over the years Uncle Jim and his crew made a Robin Hood movie, a Mexican desperadoes movie, a ballerina movie, several cowboy movies, and a Saharan adventure movie called *Safari to Irafas*. (Irafas is "safari" spelled backward.) The age range of the cousins was about twenty years, but Uncle Jim used everyone. Mark's sister Marianne Johnson remembers that in *Safari to Irafas* Mark was about six years old. He and two other small cousins played a posse of desert tribesmen whose job it was, in the final scene of the movie, to come and arrest the villains. "When the villains stood up, they were twice as large as the desert tribesmen, but they got arrested anyway, and they all marched off into the sunset." Uncle Jim filmed the movies, then spliced them and added silent-movie captions and music. The final product was screened with a great deal of fanfare and popcorn.

Grandpa ("Chicken") Bill and Grandma Mabel were also catalysts for fantasy. In the early forties they had settled in Seattle, and Mark and his two sisters were with them often. Their house, Morris remembers, "was like a spell." Grandpa Bill was a devotee of joke novelty items, and the house was full of these things: bottle openers in the shape of false teeth, rubber Frankenstein-monster hands wedged into door jambs. Grandma

The nomad tribesmen of "Safari to Irafas," c. 1963. Left to right: Morris and his cousins Steve and Jim Munzenrider

17

Mabel was an avid gardener, and in the back yard there were fifty rose-bushes and a birdbath. There was also a patch of woods—the children pretended to go camping there—and a toolshed that was turned into a dolls' playhouse, with beautiful doll furniture made by Grandpa Bill. The grandmother played the piano for the children and taught them songs: "Ragtime Cowboy Joe," "Redwing," old parlor songs. There were chipmunks who came to the house. The grandmother had named them, and she made up stories about their adventures for the children. When she baked cookies for the children, she always left some out for the chipmunks too.

At home Mark and his sisters supplied their own entertainment. Mark built cascades with piles of dishes in the kitchen sink. He organized the neighbor children into shows. When he and Maureen got bored, they mashed flowers in clay pots in the garage and dyed their clothes. "We had the feeling that we could do just about anything we wanted," says Maureen. "We had much more freedom than the other kids on the block." For this reason, and also because most of the other mothers on the block worked while Maxine Morris did not, the other children were often at their house.

The second remarkable thing about the Morris family was its ethical seriousness. They were good Samaritans, always doing for others, taking in strays, setting an extra place at the table. In part, this was simply a matter of character—both parents were extraordinarily kind-hearted—but it was also the product of social forces. When Mark was in grade school the population in the neighborhood began to shift. Black and Asian families moved in, and as they did, the white families moved out, with some exceptions, including the Morrises. Mark's best friend in grade school, Peter Tudor, was from a Barbadian family. Soon there were so many Japanese families in the neighborhood that they staged an annual Bon Odori festival. (Mark danced in it.) By the time Mark was a teenager there were enough Samoan students in his high school to field a Samoan dance ensemble; it performed at assemblies.

Many of these families had difficulties, as the Morrises were well aware. In 1960, Franklin High School set up a special-education program for students designated as "potential dropouts," and Bill Morris was assigned to this program, in which he taught English and social studies. "A lot of the students in the program were just black kids that the other teachers didn't want, because they were behavior problems," says Maureen. One boy, she remembers, had a big scar around his neck where his father had tried to cut his throat. Bill took his responsibility for these

students very seriously, and he looked after them outside school as well, throwing parties for them and giving them jobs so that they could make pocket money. The Morris children rarely came home from school without finding a teenager in a leather jacket mowing their lawn or fixing their car. The family also took in other young people. Penny Hutchinson, one of Mark's best friends during his adolescence and later a member of his company, would sleep at the Morris house when she wasn't getting along with her parents. The family was so generous that Mark, when he was a teenager, sometimes felt he couldn't stand it: "I didn't want everybody to be so nice, because it seemed to me to distort the facts. Nobody could say, 'I don't want to go to dinner at those people's house, because I don't like them.' " So they always ended up going to the dinner.

Throughout Mark's childhood, the Morrises had little money. High-school teachers made a poor living in the fifties and sixties. At times Bill felt that somehow he had missed the boat. All his brothers had better jobs and bigger houses and golf-club memberships. They chided him for falling behind, and this pained him. But he was not ambitious, and he didn't like golf, so he went his own way and, however ambivalently, taught his children to do the same.

Mark started dancing merely by way of playing. When Marianne danced in the living room in her point shoes, he jammed his feet into plastic orange-juice cups and danced on point too. He made up solos for himself to the *1812 Overture, Carnival of the Animals, Danse Macabre,* and performed them draped in sheets and towels. Then, when he was eight, Maxine took him to a performance of Jose Greco's flamenco troupe. Watching Greco and his company, Mark decided that he too would like to be a dancer—a flamenco dancer. He pestered Maxine to take him for lessons, so she looked through the ads in the paper and finally found a studio that offered Spanish dance: Verla Flowers Dance Arts.

Verla Flowers (this was her real name) was the kind of person who would fascinate a child. She wore floral-print muumuus and silver tap shoes that jingled as she walked. She had copper-colored hair mounted in a beehive hairdo that got done on weekends and then descended gradually in the course of the week. (According to one of her students, you could tell what day of the week it was by consulting Flowers's hair.) She was warmhearted, vivacious, and slightly eccentric. In 1965, when Mark Morris arrived at her door, she was fifty-two.

A Seattle native, the daughter of a ballroom dance teacher, Flowers had had the kind of eclectic training typical for a young woman who wanted to be a dancer in the twenties and thirties. She had studied not just ballet but also jazz dance, acrobatics, tap, ballroom, Hawaiian, and Spanish dance—skills that she was able to use when, in her teens, she danced in nightclubs and in movie-house shows. "We did cowboy numbers with lariats," she recalls, "and dances in big chiffon skirts like Loie Fuller." As a young woman she studied and taught for a number of years at Seattle's highly respected Cornish School of the Arts. Then, in the late thirties, she opened her own dance studio, where she offered the same range of dance styles that she herself had studied. In 1965, Verla Flowers Dance Arts had a faculty of seven and taught ballet, tap, acrobatics, Hawaiian, Tahitian, Spanish, jazz, "creative," ballroom, and baton twirling. (Fencing was added the following year.) Still, it was not an atypical suburban dance studio. "I was a small-time dance teacher who worked with small children mainly," Flowers says. Once a year, in June, the school had a big recital, with numbers ranging from "Me and My Teddy Bear" to accurately staged flamenco dances. Every child had a part.

All the Spanish dancing at the school was taught by Flowers herself, so it was she who became Mark Morris's teacher. She took him as a private pupil, and they liked each other immediately. She soon realized that he was an unusual student. Within the limits of a child's body, he could do almost anything she asked him to, but what seemed to her most extraordinary was his power of concentration. "At the end of our half hour, he was still completely intent, ready to go on, and I was completely exhausted. When he got home, his mother told me, he would go up to his room and practice what he had learned until she made him come down to dinner. Then he would go back up and practice until he had to go to bed." The other unusual thing about him was his rhythmic intelligence. Spanish dance has extremely complicated rhythms, often twelve-count phrases with complex internal accents, but he picked up everything immediately and wanted to go on to the next thing.

He was voracious—"a brain like a sponge," Flowers says. Originally she had intended to shift him to a group class once he learned the fundamentals, but this became impossible: "No class could have kept up with him. He really intended to be a professional Spanish dancer, as soon as possible. It didn't matter to him that he was nine." When things went too slowly for him, he became bored and disruptive. "His mother talked to me," Flowers remembers, "and she said, 'Verla, we've got to keep him busy.' "

What Flowers came up with to keep him busy was ballet. To her way of thinking, ballet was the basic form of dance training. Mark had already been hanging around in the back of the school's ballet classes, trying out the steps. He was clearly interested. So Flowers spoke to Maxine Morris. Maxine said she thought it was a fine idea, but that Verla would have to be the one to convince Mark's father. Then, even more than now, ballet for men was regarded as effeminate. In the end, however, Bill Morris was not hard to convince. Flowers made her argument to him on financial grounds. Mark might intend to be a Spanish dancer, she said, but he needed ballet training too, so that if he was laid off or couldn't get work—common problems for Spanish dancers—he wouldn't have to wait tables. He could switch to a different style of dance, a versatility that only ballet could give him. Flowers also assured Bill, in her words, "that as for effeminacy, I would work against that with every breath in my body. I said, 'I know the word ballet is scary, but I really feel that if we look ahead to his future, he should have it.' " Bill said okay, and Mark began ballet lessons at age ten.

Flowers planned his ballet studies carefully. She *was* looking to his future. She found him a small, well-trained partner, so that he would not injure his back in lifts. She also saw to it that in addition to ballet he learned hearty, foot-stomping character dances: a Mexican hat dance, cowboy dances, a Ukrainian trepak, with lots of leaping and squatting. She had him take fencing. She was not concerned about his sexual orientation; she didn't feel she had any control over that. She was concerned about his artistic orientation. She wanted him to be able to see himself and show himself in many different ways. When recital time came and he was the prince in the ballet (as he was often to be), she wanted him to be able to lead the hoedown as well. "There was almost no question that he was going somewhere," she says, "and it was a responsibility—a little frightening."

At the same time, she was simply trying to find outlets for his energy. She taught him a Russian dance so that he could get a job with Seattle's Russian Balalaika Orchestra. (He danced with this group regularly for three years, for pay, starting at age eleven.) When the Bolshoi Ballet came to Oregon in 1967 and needed children for one of their pieces, she drove him to Portland to audition. (He was accepted, and danced with the Bolshoi for a week.) When Jose Greco came to Seattle to audition dancers for scholarship study, she took him to the audition even though he was way below the age limit. Again he was accepted, and at age eleven went to study for a week at Greco's summer school in Indiana. In the late sixties,

"He really intended to be a professional Spanish dancer, as soon as possible. It didn't matter to him that he was nine." Morris, age ten, in a Spanish cape dance at a Verla Flowers Dance Arts recital (Courtesy of Verla Flowers)

when Jillana, of New York City Ballet, came to the studio scouting for students to receive Ford Foundation ballet scholarships, Flowers put Mark in the front of the class and was disappointed when he wasn't chosen.

Flowers featured Mark in all her recitals. When he was only thirteen, she put him on her faculty to teach character dance. When he was fourteen, she let him teach Spanish dance, her own specialty, at the studio. (Later he taught ballet there as well.) She invited him to choreograph; many of his earliest dances were made for her recitals. When he was fifteen, she sent him in her place to a dance congress in New York so that he would learn how to set a dance from notation. She put him on scholarship almost from the moment he arrived at the studio—he paid no fees whatsoever. She also laid out the money for some of his costumes, and when, some years later, he went to Spain to study flamenco, she gave him $500 to help with his travel expenses. "He was the son I never had," she says.

Mark was a born performer. From early childhood, he had always been a theatrical character; once he found his way onto a stage, he was completely at home. Even when he was nine, performing for PTA dinners, he was utterly self-assured. "He knew what to do to interact with an audience," says his sister Marianne. "He held his head up and looked at the audience and danced to them." He was self-assured offstage as well, and this was a good thing, for by the time he entered his early teenage years, he was not your average child. "He looked like a junior vampire," says the musical-comedy writer Chad Henry, who became friends with him around this time. "He was thin, small, very intense, with big dark circles under his eyes. He was outrageous—very verbal, a blabbermouth." Furthermore, he was already effeminate, a fact that of course drew comments from the other children and probably confused him for a while as well. Years later, in 1982, he made a piece, jr high, that he says was inspired by his experiences at Asa Mercer Junior High in Seattle. In one part, four boys inspect their nails, three of them holding their palms up and curling their fingers inward, the masculine way, the fourth (played by Morris) holding his fingers out as if inspecting a manicure. In another section, less funny, he cups his hands over his chest as if looking for breasts.

But while he was different, he had a kind of confidence and sophistication that spared him the treatment normally meted out to nonconforming children. The cartoonist Lynda Barry, who knew him in junior high, remembers:

At Mercer if you were weird and you were white it was very easy to get beat up. I was always trying not to get beat up. But Mark seemed to walk right through it. It was like he had some sort of song playing in his head that no one else could hear, but it made him strong in the center of what was then called weirdness. I remember, once, being in the hall when these two bad-asses tried to give him trouble. Maybe they were calling him a fag. One said, "Hey, you a boy or a girl?" I got nervous. I thought there was going to be a fight. But Mark didn't even break stride. He said, "Follow me to the bathroom and see which door I go into."

He was also very outgoing, always organizing projects and directing things and making people laugh. "We were in a play together," Lynda Barry recalls:

I can't remember if Mark and I wrote the play or adapted it from a story, but I was a princess and he was a prince, and we were on stage presenting it during assembly in our school auditorium. I gave my cue line and turned to where Mark was supposed to enter from, and he wasn't there. I gave it again, and no Mark, but the audience was screaming. I couldn't figure out what the hell was going on. I kept looking around and they were laughing and screaming, and finally I looked up and saw that Mark

Opposite:
Ad for Verla Flowers
Dance Arts (From the
scrapbook of Maxine
Morris)

25

had decided to make his entrance by lowering himself from the ceiling on a rope. The teacher liked it. She gave him an A.

Once he threw a Bastille Day party and I was invited. How did he even know what Bastille Day was? Anyway, we were supposed to come as our favorite French personality. People came as the Eiffel Tower, as Marat, as Chef Boyardee. Another time he had a square dance where he called all the actions for us to do, like lie on the floor, go out the door, kick your partner in the ass, and we all did whatever he said and he would laugh his head off and fall on the ground. For ninth-grade graduation he got voted loudest laugh. I got that vote too, for the girls. I think we also both got voted weirdest.

Even at thirteen it was clear that he was staying up way too late. You could see it in his face. He looked like he never slept. And it looked like the thing that was keeping him up was exciting.

In fact, at thirteen he *was* staying up too late, and the thing keeping him up was a folk dance group. Folk dance groups are common in America. Any city that still has a substantial German or Russian or Croatian population is likely to have at least one folk dance ensemble. In the sixties and seventies, however, the folk dance movement underwent a temporary expansion, fed by the utopian ideals of the period. Community, universal harmony, the quest for "roots," the longing for innocence, the search for a popular art rather than a high art: these aspirations, together with allied movements in the music world—folk singing and ethnomusicology—produced a folk dance renaissance, and the West Coast, where utopianism always runs high, and ran highest in those years, contributed heavily to this trend. In many cities and college towns, new folk dance groups sprang up. The Koleda Folk Ensemble was one of them.

It was founded by a man named Dennis Boxell. Boxell had learned folk dancing while growing up in the Midwest. Then, in the early sixties, when he was stationed in Europe with the army, he fell in love with Balkan folk culture. He traveled from village to village in Yugoslavia and Bulgaria, and also worked with the dance troupes of the region, learning their dances and recording their music. He eventually moved to Seattle, where he taught dances to various folk dance troupes and finally, in 1967, founded his own group.

Koleda's membership, which over the years numbered between thirty and fifty, consisted in part of ordinary middle-class citizens who simply made Balkan dance their hobby. But this was the late sixties, the height of the hippie movement, and most of Koleda's members were counter-culture types. According to Chad Henry, who was one of the Koleda musicians, "It was about ninety percent misfits and spiritual homeless" —"a very wild bunch indeed," as Morris later put it. For a time the group was attached to a *kafana*, or Balkan coffee shop. (They rehearsed in the back.) Later they had other headquarters. The organization was chaotic and its finances often in disarray. Boxell was not an ideal administrator. He was unreliable in business dealings and autocratic with the troupe. At the same time, he was immensely charismatic. In a small way, he had a sort of cult-leader status. "He was a sleazebag," says Mary Hoagland, who was his assistant artistic director, "but he was an inspirational sleaze-bag." He was passionately serious about Balkan dance and music, and he inspired that seriousness in others. Furthermore, he made them feel that their dance- and music-making was serving a higher ideal. "Koleda was like a little village," says one of its former singers, Jill Johnson. "Dennis wanted to create a family, the family that he never really had, and the villages of Eastern Europe became his model. What he had in mind was a group of happy, singing, dancing peasants, with everybody filling in and supporting the others."

Koleda met five or six nights a week, but many of its members recall that it absorbed their entire lives. Balkan music has extremely complicated rhythms—7/8, 11/16—difficult and thrilling to master. In recent years this musical style has become familiar to Americans through the recordings of the Bulgarian State Radio and Television Female Vocal Choir under the title *Le Mystère des Voix Bulgares*. But in the late sixties it was still highly exotic, and the members of Koleda regarded it as their secret, their private joy. Night after night they practiced and rehearsed, with Boxell combining steps from various traditional dances into new routines. The rehearsals were aimed at performances—the group danced at schools and colleges, they did benefits, they went twice to Eastern Europe, in 1968 and 1970, to perform and learn—but the members of Koleda seem to have enjoyed the rehearsals more than the performances. They would dance till four in the morning, then perform the next day, then dance all night again. Sometimes, on a weekend, they would go out of town on retreat and spend two or three days completely caught up in Romanian or Bulgarian or Macedonian dancing.

They didn't just work. "I remember one infamous weekend," says Chad Henry: "We went to rehearse for three days at a Jewish summer camp. At the end of the three days they had to bring in a rabbi to re-

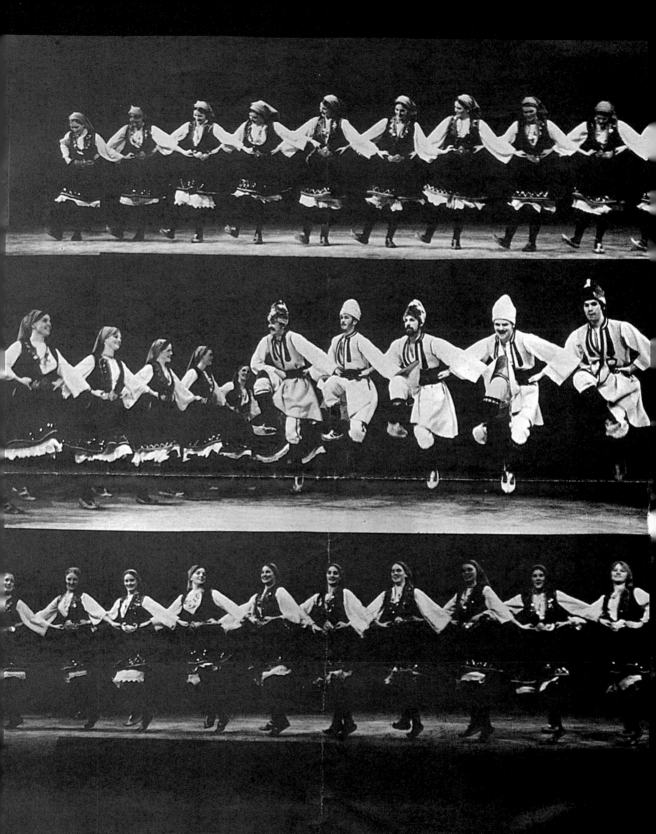

THE KOLEDA FOLK ENSEMBLE

303 NORTHEAST NORTHLAKE • SEATTLE, WASHINGTON 98105 • TEL: 206 634-3266

Morris in a Koleda
performance, c. 1971
(Bihoa Tsai)

kosherize the kitchen. The second night there was this party, and everyone got ripped. They broke the lock on the swimming pool, and everyone was swimming nude and going wild. I think there were a lot of new relationships that night." Short of the members' living together—actually, some of them did live together—Koleda was like a sixties commune, and the project on which they were embarked was itself a symbol of community. Holding hands in a circle, dancing and singing in harmony, they made art out of friendship and love, and friendship and love out of art.

In 1970, at age thirteen, Morris was taken to a Koleda rehearsal by a friend, and for the next three years he more or less never left. To him, Koleda was a dream come true. First, it was dancing, all the time—the thing he most liked to do—and dancing to complicated rhythms, which, as a flamenco student, he was able to master, and loved to master. Furthermore, Koleda offered him the first social environment in which he wasn't an odd duck. However well he handled being "weird" in school, it can't have been that easy. The members of Koleda, on the other hand, were as

Opposite:
Koleda Folk Ensemble
flier, c. 1973

29

weird as he, and this was liberating to him. "He was able to let his hair down and be completely wild," says Chad Henry, "because he had this safety net of people around him who were all doing the same thing." Finally, the members of Koleda were adults, and they treated him like an adult. Almost all of them were at least ten years older than he, but because he was such a wonderful dancer and, as usual, took the work so seriously and was so good at directing things (by this time he was already teaching for Verla Flowers), they listened to him and made him one of them. For all these blessings—the respect of adults, the chance to go wild, the feeling of community, the mental pleasure of mastering the difficult, game-like Balkan rhythms, the physical pleasure of doing the hearty Balkan dances —he adored Koleda. He spent every weekend with the group. He slept over at their houses. "We sang and drank slivovitz and danced until we dropped," he said in a 1984 interview. "It was marvelous."

Koleda was to have a profound influence on Morris's choreographic style. From the Balkan dances he learned how he wanted the dancing body to look, with the weight held low and the feet flat against the floor. He also learned the habit of combining complicated rhythms with simple steps, and he took some of those simple steps—chain dances, circle dances, certain hopping and bouncing steps—directly from Koleda's routines. From Koleda's dances and from its ideals, he also learned how he wanted an ensemble to look: like ordinary human beings, full of variety. In Balkan villages, everyone dances, the fat and the thin, the grandmothers and the grandchildren. There were no grandmothers in Koleda, nor are there any in the Mark Morris Dance Group, but the community ideal remained in Morris's mind. The dancing ensemble was not to be a sleek, high-bred group, different from the world, but rather an image of the world: human beings joining hands and dancing together.

The lessons that Morris learned from Koleda were absorbed all the more deeply by virtue of the fact that he took them in at such an impressionable age, when he was developing his adult artistic intelligence, his adult emotions, and also his adult sexual feelings. He had heterosexual experiences before he had homosexual experiences, but the latter came to him first in Koleda, and they were powerful. Before, he had known he was "different." Now he realized he was homosexual. That for him this was a reasonably benign discovery was due in part to his family, but it was also due to the nature of Koleda. In terms of sexual orientation, the group was mixed; about a third of the men were homosexual. It was also mixed in terms of sexual license. While some people, both homosexual and heterosexual, went in for the kind of promiscuity popular in those years, others were stable married couples or conservative-minded single people who were just interested in friendship and dancing. This great range of sexual habits led to and was supported by a philosophy of extreme tolerance. "You could do anything you wanted," says Mary Hoagland, "as long as you danced or sang." Sexual variety, then, was a product of group feeling: people went to bed with each other because they fell in love within the group, and those who didn't tolerated those who did.

It was within this communal atmosphere that Morris had his sexual awakening: "I fell in love with the group. I fell in love with several individuals in sequence, and they fell in love with each other." The fact that the majority of the people in Koleda were not homosexual was probably critical to his view of this experience, for what he seems to have developed was a sense not so much that he was different, or even a member of a group that was different, but merely that he was part of the world's variety. Koleda's group-centered philosophy supported his sexual discovery; in return, he embraced that philosophy and never forgot it. Not just sexual acceptance, though, but all the forms of happiness that he found in Koleda—artistic, social, emotional, physical—reinforced the communal vision. Utopianism is a constant theme of Morris's work, and that utopianism comes from Koleda.

Thenceforth, dancing became his life. When he wasn't dancing with Koleda, he was dancing somewhere else. He went to folk dance nights at the University of Washington. He went out social dancing with friends such as Penny Hutchinson. "We wanted to be anywhere where there was live music and we could dance," Hutchinson says. "When there wasn't a dance at one of our schools, we'd go to dances at other schools and dance until we got kicked out." Meanwhile, Morris was studying and teaching several afternoons a week at Verla Flowers's studio. From 1972 through 1974 he went every summer for five weeks to a dance camp on the Olympic peninsula run by First Chamber Dance Company, a small Seattle ballet troupe. The students took five classes a day, in ballet, mime, Spanish dance, jazz dance, and modern dance, including the Martha Graham technique. (This was the first time that Morris studied modern dance.) But as with Koleda, the work took place in an atmosphere of elation. The setting was idyllic—"I saw the aurora borealis for the first time," Morris remembers, "and there was the beautiful ocean, and mist all the time"— and for some of the students, including Morris, the nights were one long party, with dancing, drinking, and considerable bed crawling.

He didn't just dance; he went to dance concerts. Many important
troupes—the Paul Taylor company, the Martha Graham company—came
though Seattle during his early teenage years. He saw them all, and loved
them. He and his friends also traveled to Vancouver, sleeping three and
four to a motel room, to see troupes appearing there. The company he
knew best, though, was the Joffrey Ballet. Founded by Robert Joffrey, a
native of Seattle, the Joffrey company had long summer residencies in
Washington in the late sixties, and when they came to Seattle, Morris and
his friends would sneak in to their performances. In all the companies that

he saw, the pieces he liked best were those that seemed to him most modern—Joffrey's *Astarte*, with its steamy erotic duet, or Twyla Tharp's *Deuce Coupe*, with its bebopping to the Beach Boys—and those that seemed to take on life's great questions, such as Graham's *Clytemnestra*, which he declared his favorite dance. Probably for these same reasons, the appearance of modernity and the appearance of profundity, he also loved Maurice Béjart's Ballet of the 20th Century, the company that his own troupe was to replace at the Théâtre Royal de la Monnaie in Brussels some fifteen years later.

Another thing that the teenage Morris admired in dance, as one might predict from his Spanish and Balkan studies, was musical subtlety. He first saw the work of George Balanchine in a performance by the Pennsylvania Ballet. On the program was Balanchine's *Concerto Barocco*, which is set to Bach's double violin concerto and brilliantly mirrors the internal workings of the music. There is a famous moment in *Concerto Barocco* where, in imitation of Bach's counterpoint, half the dancers move their arms on the count of three, the other half on the count of four, at the same time that all of them are hopping on point in unison. It is like a fantastic machine. When Morris saw this, he burst out laughing, he was so thrilled.

By now he had also begun to make dances of his own. At age fourteen he created his first modern dance piece; at fifteen, his first ballet, on point—a piece called *Renaissance*. This is an early start for a choreographer, but he set out, as usual, with complete confidence. Most of the dancers in *Renaissance* were in their twenties, but they seem to have had no problem taking direction from a fifteen-year-old choreographer. "I worked with him again later, when he was older," says one of them, Jennifer Carroll Walker, "but when he was fifteen, he was exactly the same, just skinnier. He knew what he was doing. He knew what he could ask, and couldn't ask, from each dancer. And the piece he made was very hard." From 1971 to 1976, the remaining years of his youth in Seattle, he created some twenty dances—for Verla Flowers's recitals, for the plays at his high school, for local children's theater productions, for any enterprise that would hire him. In these jobs he didn't just supply the choreography. He often chose the music and found the musicians as well, to say nothing of running the rehearsals and getting everybody to do what he wanted. In other words, he wasn't just a fledgling choreographer; he was a fledgling company director.

A number of Morris's earliest pieces still exist on videotape. Two of them—*Barstow*, which he made at age sixteen, and *Ženska*, made at seventeen—are especially interesting, because he liked them enough to reset them, years later, on his own company. Both are young, tentative works, but already they have certain traits that were to become central to his mature style. To start with, *Barstow* uses vocal music, with lyrics—an unusual choice for a teenage choreographer—and its steps mimic the lyrics, in a strange sort of mime dance that looks both naïve and sophisticated at the same time. The steps also mimic the music, the very thing that Morris had so admired in *Concerto Barocco*. Finally, in both pieces, the dancing is very unbuttoned. The dancers hurl themselves into the air. They dive into turns from odd angles and keep pumping the turn until it can go no further. "You couldn't look beautiful in that dance," Penny Hutchinson says of *Ženska*. (It was made on her.) The reason you couldn't look beautiful was that Morris wanted everything pushed past grace. The result was more visceral than most stage dancing and also more informal-looking, because it was untidy and showed the body's limits. All these peculiarities—text illustration, music visualization, recklessness—were signs of things to come.

Even more prophetic was the music Morris chose for his early pieces. He did not use Chopin, Mozart, rock 'n' roll—music that would have automatically pleased the audience and the dancers. Instead, he chose out-of-the-way things: Renaissance crumhorn duets, music by experimental composers such as Harry Partch and Conlon Nancarrow. For *Mourning without Clouds*, a dance he made at age fifteen for a Verla Flowers recital, he wrote the music himself. Scored for a seven-piece chamber orchestra and mixed chorus, it is a brainy little composition, short on melody, but with a rigorously structured fugue. For *in pruning my roses*, another piece for a Verla Flowers recital, he again used a musical composition of his own, combining it with Shostakovich's Sonata in D. Also, by age fifteen Morris had already begun trying to arrange things so that the music for his dances could be played live. To make this possible, he chose pieces for small ensembles and persuaded his friends to play them. Verla Flowers got around union regulations by placing the musicians onstage. (A few years later, when the musicians' union forced Pacific Northwest Ballet to dance his *Brummagem* to a tape of its Beethoven score, he registered his protest by having three radios play, on different channels, at the same time as the tape. One reviewer found the effect very interesting.)

In fact, aside from dance, the other thing that occupied his life was music. When he was seven or eight, his father had taught him to read music, and thereafter he spent hours every day playing the family piano. "I didn't know enough to know that I couldn't play the piano," he says, "because I could read the music and figure it out, and I had endless patience for this. So I would work through things that were way, way too hard for me—even today they would be too hard—and play them for hours and hours, with running eyes and burning shoulders." When he was experimenting with percussion for his musical compositions, he would string a rope across the den and hang various things from it—bells, juice glasses—which he would then bang while he played the piano. As the family had done in their shows and movies, he used whatever he had at hand. He was a fearless improviser.

Morris never took a piano lesson until he was sixteen, and he quit after five or six sessions. By then he had been playing, however badly, for a number of years, and to go back to fingering was frustrating to him. (Also, there was no money for lessons.) He had the same frustration in his high-school music-theory class. The teacher would assign the class a melody which they were to harmonize according to rules derived from the Bach chorale preludes. Morris would take the melody home and orchestrate it with hair-raisingly dissonant chords. He liked this; it sounded Bulgarian to him. The teacher liked it less, but Morris still made it through music theory and enjoyed the class very much. He also belonged to the school's regular chorus and its honors chorus. He dragged himself to school at 7 a.m. three times a week for honors chorus practice.

Music became the basis of his social life—the thing he did with his friends. When he was a young teenager, one of his closest companions was Page Smith, a girl who lived down the block and was a serious cello student. (Today Page Smith is a principal cellist with the Northwest Chamber Orchestra and the Pacific Northwest Ballet Orchestra.) Smith remembers that in junior high she and Mark often spent all recess playing rhythm games: "He would stamp out one rhythm with his feet and another with his hands. Or I would be the drone, keeping a steady rhythm, and he would try out things over it—a four to a three, or something like that. So we'd just walk around the playground, stamping and clapping, until recess was over."

At age fifteen Mark and Page moved over to Franklin High School, where Bill Morris taught. The school was only a half block from the Morris home, and almost every afternoon they went directly from school to Mark's house to play music. Either Mark would play the piano and Page the cello, or they would both play the piano. Since neither of them was a good pianist, they split up the hands, one taking the right, the other the left; that way, they figured, they could get through the harder pieces. Mark shopped for sheet music at the music store and the Salvation Army. They played a great grab bag of things—Tcherepnin, Fauré, Shostakovich, Hindemith, C.P.E. Bach, Gottschalk, Walton, Satie. They taught themselves to whistle Bach's two-part Inventions. A number of Morris's later works were set to pieces that he worked on with Page, such as Gershwin's Three Preludes and Tcherepnin's *Bagatelles*. Likewise, Vivaldi's Gloria in D, to which he set his *Gloria*, was a piece he sang in Franklin High School's honors chorus. The parlor songs that his grandmother taught him, the country-western songs he listened to on the radio—these too became scores for his dances. He is now at work on a piece to Bach's two-part Inventions. He has a long memory.

When he wasn't playing music, he was singing it, and though he had been singing from childhood, the songs now became more complicated. With Page, Chad Henry, and Maureen, he sang Balkan songs, rounds, four-part madrigals, Appalachian Sacred Harp songs. "We liked things that had a puzzle element to them," says Henry. Henry was as interested as Mark was in out-of-the-way music—pieces with odd tones, shifting rhythms, uneven phrase lengths—and they swapped finds: Indian music, Polynesian music. Avant-garde music Mark found out about by himself, by rifling the record shelves in the public library and the local music stores. One day he opened an album he had just bought and found inside its wrapping a bonus introductory record containing selections from Harry Partch and Conlon Nancarrow. He fell in love with them and bought every record of theirs he could find. Though music was his way of socializing, it was also the matrix of his inner life. "For him music was truly hypnotic," says Chad Henry. "By the time he told you about a piece of music, he had already been inside it, thinking about it, for days, weeks. So in his mind it had already collected all this back-story, this subterranean stuff, from his emotional response. That part is what came out in the dances."

Between dancing and music, Morris had little time for school, and little patience for it. Already in elementary school he was often removed from class for being disruptive. High school he seems largely to have ignored. "Anything creative, like the school plays, he would work like crazy," says Paul Nicholas, who was his drama teacher and the director of the school plays. "But anything routine, which was so much of the classwork, he just couldn't focus on. Really, he almost wasn't there. He was already well into a career, and everyone knew it." The school authorities coped with him as well as they could. They put him in honors classes, where the teachers were more tolerant. They excused him from gym on the grounds that his dance training was gym enough. Finally they put him on a work-study program whereby he received academic credit for studying and teaching dance. As a result, he was able to graduate a year early, at age sixteen.

In high school he was no longer teased for being different. He was too authoritative, too independent. There was an artistic crowd in the school, and he hung out with them. "We were pretend-bohemian," he remembers. "I would buy ancient, old men's overcoats, and on the coat, every day, I would wear a big, beautiful jeweled brooch, with rhinestones, from the Salvation Army. I changed the brooch pretty much daily." With his long hair and his dark-circled eyes, this gave him a sort of louche glamour. By his last year of high school, he had separated himself even from the artistic crowd. His friends were mostly older people: musicians, actors, people from Koleda. He never had any doubt that he would be an artist, or even saw this as a choice. The thing he was doing—choreography—he had been doing from childhood. Eventually, he started getting paid for it, but that was the only change.

Maxine Morris, a woman of completely conventional appearance and manners, was absolutely unswerving in her support of this unconventional child. "His teachers would call me up every now and then," she remembers, "and say he had been bad. Then they would tell me the thing that he had done, and it was usually so clever, so funny, that I had an awful time trying to talk to them and keep myself from laughing." Once he began performing, she did everything she could to ease his way. When he won the scholarship to the Jose Greco school, she packed her bag and went with him to Indiana for a week. When he got his job with the Russian Balalaika Orchestra, she was the one who engineered this. (She had heard that the troupe needed a dancer, so she asked Verla Flowers to teach Mark a Russian dance and then took him to audition.) When he began staging dances, she tie-dyed backcloths and sewed costumes. Until Mark was grown, she never took a full-time job. She drove him to Verla Flowers's studio—a long trip across town—and waited while he took class. She drove him to his folk dance nights and other engagements. It was also she who suggested to Franklin High that he be put on a work-study program. Maxine was not exactly a stage mother; she didn't push him. "I just let him decide what he wanted to do," she says, "because he knew more about it." But whatever he decided to do, she was there with the car keys.

A dancing career was something she respected, and she did not wish he had chosen something more usual.

Bill Morris did wish this. Those brothers of his who nagged him about his lack of ambition also nagged him about Mark. To them Mark's peculiarities were merely a subdivision of Bill's fecklessness. "They said to him, 'Tell Mark to go play basketball. Don't let him take ballet,' " Maureen remembers. "They were worried that Mark would be gay." Bill was undoubtedly worried about this too. Penny Hutchinson remembers an evening when she and Mark were going to a dance and Bill was to drive them. As usual for a dance, they dressed in the most outré clothes they could find, often thrift-shop items. "Flamingo-colored shirts, with vinyl trim on the pockets—that sort of thing," says Hutchinson. "So we went out to get in the car, and Mark's father saw him and started yelling at him, 'You're not going anywhere dressed like that. You look like a homo!' Mark got very upset."

But Bill had mixed feelings. Mark was not just an unconventional child; he was also, by now, a very accomplished one. Bill was proud of Mark's achievements, particularly his piano-playing, and defended him to the uncles. He also enjoyed Mark. "He got a kick out of him," says Maureen—a kick that was probably based in part on vicarious satisfaction. Torn himself between doing what he wanted and doing what others expected of him, he cannot have helped admiring this child who did exactly what he wanted. Maureen remembers: "Dad would yell at Mark, 'Don't wear that. Go upstairs and change.' Mark would turn around and walk out the back door, and my dad just thought it was funny. He had an image of what a father was supposed to be—how you put your foot down—but it wasn't really him."

Unlike Maxine, Bill was straitlaced. He made the family go to church; he gave lectures on duty; he allowed no alcohol in the house. At the same time, he had that sort of obliviousness that fathers sometimes have, at least in the eyes of their adolescent children. He talked out loud at the movies. (He was hard-of-hearing and didn't like to wear his hearing aid.) He played corny old songs on his corny-sounding organ. Some of what Mark felt about this can be read in a solo, *Dad's Charts*, that he made for himself in 1980, for his company's first concert. The title refers to the chord charts that Bill Morris, like other amateur jazz players, used in structuring his improvisations. *Dad's Charts* is likewise an improvisation, structured by certain movements to which Morris keeps returning, movements that were his father's. There is a bowling move, because Bill bowled;

there is a falling-asleep movement, because Bill was always falling asleep at inopportune times; there is a typing movement, because Bill taught typing (and was always after his children to learn typing, so they could make a living). There is a movement where Morris slaps himself in the face, because a student once slapped Bill in the face, a thing that greatly shocked him. There is a gut-out stance that is Morris's memory of seeing his father standing naked in a sauna, with his belly out. And the music for *Dad's Charts* is a roller-rink-type organ tune, the kind of music that Bill liked to play.

What is interesting about the dance, however, is that it is not just the father but the father and the son in one body. In between the solid, fuddy-duddy "father" poses, Morris becomes the runaway son, leaping, flying, scooting across the floor, out of reach. When he does the "sauna stance," for example, Morris keeps alternating it with a ballet stance. The effect is like a card being flipped back to front: on one side the big, heavy father, with his stomach out, spied on in his nakedness; on the other side the agile son, escaping from his father and his father's life, and escaping by *dancing*. The piece is a declaration of independence, with a nasty little edge.

At the end of *Dad's Charts* Morris falls to the floor, writhing. Around 1969 there was a race riot of sorts at Franklin High. A number of black students locked the principal up and then began invading classrooms, including Bill Morris's, and in the melee one of the students hit Bill in the face, knocking off his glasses and his hearing aid. (This is the slap in *Dad's Charts*.) Bill was very disturbed by this episode, and his doctor told him to slow down for a while. So in 1971 he left his special-education class at Franklin and went to work as a consultant at the education district's main headquarters. But he was still nervous and unwell. Page Smith remembers one night in January of 1973 when Bill came home from work very tired. "Mark asked him if he wanted to hear what we were doing, and he said he would love to, so he lay down on the couch, and we played him Fauré's *Après un rêve* and Satie's *Trois gymnopédies*. He became very peaceful, with a beautiful expression on his face. I think he fell asleep." A few days later, Bill was found slumped over his desk at work, dead of a heart attack at age fifty-nine. Mark came home that afternoon and found the house empty, but there was a note telling him to call his grandmother. He called, and she told him that his father had died. The funeral was three days later. Mark had intended to play the music at the service with Page Smith, but in the end he was too upset and someone else took his place. They played the pieces that had so pleased Bill a few nights before he died, Fauré's *Après un rêve* and Satie's *Trois gymnopédies*.

"The tragedy of my father's dying when Mark was only sixteen," says Maureen, "was that Mark never got to resolve those sixteen-year-old problems that you have with your father. The two of them never got past the rebellion stage." There is a long streak of anger in Morris's work. Asked in a 1988 interview whether he took pleasure in giving pain to bourgeois respectability, Morris answered simply, "Yes." This emotion is inseparable from the qualities that give his work its strength: his idealism, his honesty, his wit, even his way of presenting the body. It has not always served him well—*Dad's Charts* is not a great dance—and it is certainly not restricted to his relationship with his father. But his father, like everyone's, was a force in his mind, and his sense of struggle with the world is probably due in some part to the fact that Bill Morris died before his admiration for Mark could supplant his disapproval, or before Mark was old enough to feel free of that disapproval.

Before his father's death, Mark had made plans with two friends to go to Europe in the fall of 1973 for a long hitchhiking-and-Eurailpass trip. After Bill's death the family's finances were very straitened, but Maxine characteristically urged Mark to go ahead. In June 1973, five months after Bill's funeral, Mark graduated from high school, and in September, the three friends left for Europe. They spent several months in Eastern Europe, traveling and watching dancing. Then, in early 1974, the others went home and Mark settled down in Madrid to study Spanish dance. At this point he was still nursing his childhood ambition to become a Spanish dancer. He took several classes a day in flamenco and jota and toured briefly with the Royal Chamber Ballet of Madrid, a company that performed both ballet and Spanish dance. But he soon became discouraged with the state of Spanish dancing in Spain. The concerts were badly choreographed and badly staged, and the working conditions for flamenco dancers were appalling.

He was also finding it hard to be homosexual in Franco's Spain. In Madrid he had become part of a gay subculture that was very alluring to him but also highly illegal. Gay bars were strictly after-hours affairs, regular clubs that closed at midnight and then reopened an hour later as gay bars. Homosexuals were harassed by the police. Finally, a friend of his was arrested for public effeminacy—an episode that both disgusted and scared him. He wasn't going to try to pass as a heterosexual. Indeed, he was just coming out. He had written to his family from Madrid to say that he was homosexual and got a letter back saying, as he summarizes it, "We love you—it's no problem." Maxine Morris was not surprised by his announcement, though she was sad, she says, "because it meant that he would have a harder time, that he would suffer." He didn't intend to suffer in a Spanish jail, however. His return ticket to Seattle, which he still had, was about to expire. In May 1974, after five months in Madrid, he went home, abandoning his hope of becoming a Spanish dancer.

From then on, his way was clear. In addition to flamenco dancing, many other things were now behind him. His father was dead, and soon after Mark came home from Spain, Grandpa Bill, that ancestral example of dance and fantasy, also died. Koleda had disbanded. Many of his friends were gone. His childhood, in large measure a happy one, was over.

His plan was to go to New York and become a choreographer. Before choreographing, though, he wanted to dance, and therefore his sole effort now was to cram enough ballet training into himself so that he could get a job with a New York ballet company. For a year and a half he took class every day with Perry Brunson, a respected teacher, formerly of the Joffrey. He also performed, made dances, and taught. Finally, in January 1976, he decided it was time to go. Maxine and Maureen drove him to the airport, Maureen weeping all the way, and he boarded the plane for New York. He was nineteen.

A COMPANY

When Mark Morris arrived in New York in 1976, he walked into the last act of the so-called dance boom of the 1960s and 1970s. For fifteen years American ballet had been flourishing. At New York City Ballet George Balanchine was producing the final works of his sixty-year oeuvre. Other ballet choreographers, such as Jerome Robbins, Eliot Feld, and Robert Joffrey, were creating "younger," more naturalistic ballets—ballets with ponytails, ballets without ballerinas—an informalizing trend that in the seventies would culminate in the birth of "crossover ballet" (classical ballet by modern-dance choreographers), full of low-down steps and hybrid vigor.

Much of this activity took place in New York, but there was a surge in dance throughout the country. The number of regional ballet companies in America more than doubled between 1960 and 1975, and the technical skill of American dancers seemed to increase daily. With the help of a scholarship program funded by the Ford Foundation, children flowed out of small-town dance studios into the larger schools attached to New York City Ballet and San Francisco Ballet, where they were trained well and early, to become the homegrown virtuosos—Suzanne Farrell, Cynthia Gregory—who so excited audiences in the late sixties and the seventies. Other excitement was provided by the Soviet defectors: Rudolf Nureyev, Natalia Makarova, Mikhail Baryshnikov. In 1976, PBS launched its Dance in America and Live from Lincoln Center series, whetting the public's interest in an art form that fifty years earlier had barely existed in this country.

All this growth was fed by new funding. Between 1959 and 1983 the Ford Foundation put $43 million into American dance. The government followed suit. In 1965 the National Endowment for the Arts was established, and its dance budget grew year by year. In 1967 the Endowment initiated what was to be called the Dance Touring Program, aimed at getting dance troupes on the road, so that they could be seen by people outside the big cities. In the end, this program not only brought dance companies to the smaller cities; it enabled dance companies to *establish* themselves in small cities, because they could make enough money from touring to offset a low box office at home. Dance spread out across the country.

While the most dramatic growth was in ballet, modern dance too was full of activity. Martha Graham was well past her prime, but she was still a formidable presence, and much of the new work of the period could still be seen, if not as a continuation of her romantic mid-century style, then as a reaction to it. The two most respected middle-aged choreographers were Merce Cunningham and Paul Taylor, both of whom had danced for Graham before going off to found their own companies and create their own more modernist styles. In the younger generation there was a conservative middle ground—people who were trained in a Graham-style modern dance and who then adapted it to their own interests—together with an obstreperous left wing based in Greenwich Village and grounded in the anti-establishment politics and aesthetics of the sixties. This latter group, known by the names of the collectives they formed—they were Judson Dance Theater in the sixties, Grand Union in the seventies—were given the umbrella designation "postmodern dance" by one of their leaders, Yvonne Rainer. Rainer chose this term to signify the group's break with traditional modern dance: Graham and her generation. The exact nature of that break was different for each of them, but this was the period of conceptualism in the art world, and many of the Judson choreographers were also conceptualists, interested not in story or symbol, let alone the sensuous pleasure of dancing to music, but in breaking down and analyzing the components of movement. To study gravity and perspective, they walked on walls. To study context, they moved out of the theater and danced on sidewalks. To isolate movement from its theatrical trappings, they made dances without music, dances without professional dancers, dances without dance steps—just ordinary actions such as sitting, stooping, and walking.

By the late seventies, however, most of the Judson choreographers were turning out a much more theatrical kind of dance. They did not yet go in for the emotionalism that was to resurface in the eighties. Rather, what they produced was something in between emotionalism and conceptualism. Much of the new dance was set to minimalist music and exercised the same appeal. In the work of Laura Dean, Lucinda Childs, and Andy deGroat, lines of dancers skipped or danced or spun endlessly in clean geometrical patterns. Other choreographers, such as Trisha Brown and Twyla Tharp, had a warmer, more disorderly look. Tharp was the choreographer of the moment. Her company looked like teenagers, dancing in the gym, yet in a flash their loose assemblies would snap into a hidden order, their loose bodies into breathtaking feats. They had the power and polish that people sought in the seventies, without renouncing the surly charms that people missed from the sixties.

In January 1976, the same month in which Mark Morris landed in New York, Tharp premiered *Push Comes to Shove* at American Ballet Theatre. Combining Haydn with ragtime, popular dance with ballet, and starring Baryshnikov in velvet trousers rolled up like blue jeans, *Push Comes to Shove* was the quintessential crossover ballet, and one of the most original and popular ballets of the late twentieth century. The following year saw the release of Herbert Ross's *Turning Point*, a film—again starring Baryshnikov—that was to ballet fever of the seventies what *The Red Shoes* had been to the postwar period. Also in 1977 Balanchine created his last big hit, *Vienna Waltzes*, and Dance in America launched its *Choreography by Balanchine* series, in which the great old man adapted many of his finest works for the camera and recorded them at last. In fiscal 1978, the NEA Dance Program dispensed $7 million, its highest budget to date. It was an exciting time for a young person to be starting a dancing career, and in New York, which by then was the dance capital not just of the United States but of the Western world.

Soon, however, the party would be over. Within a few years Balanchine would be dead, and Tharp's company disbanded. In fiscal 1979, the NEA's dance budget peaked; from then on, in terms of buying power, it began shrinking. In the eighties the new ballet companies that had sprung up in the sixties and seventies would be hard put to find ballet choreographers to make dances for them, while the new generation of modern dance choreographers would turn away from dancing to politics.

And Mark Morris's career would seem all the more remarkable for the dearth of dance invention around him.

———

Soon after his arrival, Morris got his wish—he was hired by a New York ballet company, the Eliot Feld Ballet. For the next seven years he performed in other people's troupes: with Feld for a year (1976–77), then with the Lar Lubovitch Dance Company for a year and a half (1977–78), then with Hannah Kahn off and on for three years (1979–82), during which he also put in close to two years with Laura Dean's company (1981–82), followed by another stint with Lubovitch (1983). For about a month in 1979 he worked for Twyla Tharp when she needed some extra people. He would have loved to join Tharp's troupe. He auditioned for her several times, and each time he got to the last cut, but in the end she always took the other person. In 1979 he also auditioned for Paul Taylor, working for him on trial for two weeks, but Taylor too decided not to hire him.

Of the choreographers he worked for, the one who left the deepest mark on him was the least known and in certain respects the most conservative, Hannah Kahn. Kahn had been trained in the dance department of New York's Juilliard School, where the choreography course stressed clear structure, grounded in musical principles: statement-and-development, theme-and-variation, A-B-A. Kahn, who had an analytic mind, absorbed these lessons thoroughly. Her dances tended to be busy, but they were rigorously structured, in a manner parallel to, and clearly mirroring, the music. Morris danced with Kahn over a longer period than with anyone else, and she became his close friend. She was one of the few people with whom he could actually discuss choreography—what made a given piece interesting or not interesting. From those conversations, together with the experience of dancing in Kahn's work, he learned more than from any other choreographer he worked with, and what he learned above all were those principles of composition that she held dear: how to limit material and then develop it—in short, how to *craft* a dance —in keeping with the music. Kahn also taught him how to perform in a certain businesslike, almost deadpan way: "how to flatten and clarify gesture, to perform without projecting . . . Just to dance it purely and well," as he told *The New York Times* in a conversation about Kahn in 1982.

Even with Kahn, however, he didn't remain long. His average stay with a choreographer was about a year and a half. He learned what the person wanted; he did it, he liked it, and he tired of it—a natural enough

The Hannah Kahn
Dance Company in
Kahn's *Resonance*,
1982. Left to right:
Ruth Davidson, Morris,
Carolyn Miner,
Michael McNeill, Teri
Weksler, Keith Sabado
(*Lois Greenfield*)

process for one who intends to do his own choreography. Furthermore, because he meant to do his own choreography, he resented contributing to that of others. On many occasions he saw steps that he had come up with incorporated into his bosses' dances. This is a natural and common occurrence, but it frustrated him to see his ideas used by others. It also frustrated him not to see his ideas used by others: "I found myself coming up with so many alternative solutions to the problems they had. I would solve the problem. I was impatient." Meanwhile, it no doubt tried the patience of his bosses to have him always dancing around on the sidelines, coming up with ideas. Most choreographers (including Morris), when they are trying to solve a problem, want the dancers just to stand still and wait. They may welcome small, pointed suggestions. What they do not welcome is someone jumping around, distracting them. Morris knew this but couldn't, or didn't, stop himself. As he was beginning to realize, he was not good at fitting into another artist's program.

As a performer too, he didn't quite fit in. Morris by this time was an extraordinary dancer. He was physically impressive—handsome and large (5'11")—and possessed of a brilliant technique. He could balance, he could jump, he could turn forever and end in the position he wanted. Above all, as Verla Flowers had noted, he was a musical dancer. He *played* within the beat, prolonging a balance, then rushing the jumps to catch up, smoothing out one thing, roughing up another. Like a pianist, he organized the music, made a story of it: a skill that depends on technique—one must be a good balancer in order to prolong a balance—but then takes it to a new level.

At the same time, he was a highly unusual dancer in that his dancing was both very big—juicy, wild—and at the same time very fine-cut. In the middle of a phrase he would be painting with a mop; by the end of the phrase, he was working with a three-hair brush, producing, at exactly this moment and no other, exactly this shape, perfectly etched, down to the tilt of the fingers, the angle of the jaw. (His timing was miraculous. This is one of the things that made him a great comic.) So he was Verla Flowers's pupil: a ballet dancer and a cowboy dancer, elegant and truculent. The effect was riveting. You couldn't take your eyes off him, whether you liked him or not. And he did nothing to counteract this. "He was big and he breathed hard and sweated and made a lot of noise," Hannah Kahn says. "Most people loved that, but in a small theater it could be a little overwhelming." It was also overwhelming to the other performers. He needed to be a soloist, just as he needed to be his own choreographer, and by the time he had finished dancing for other choreographers he was already both. The Mark Morris Dance Group gave its first performance in 1980.

The critical fact about the founding of the company is that it began as a group of friends. Shortly after arriving in New York, Morris set up house with Penny Hutchinson, his companion from Seattle, who had also come to New York to be a dancer. Hutchinson had found an apartment for $150 a month, a sixth-floor walk-up on Second Avenue and Second Street in the East Village. He took the living room, she took the bedroom, and every day when they came home, they would run up the six flights of stairs, put on the record player, and improvise dances for hours. Gregarious as always, Morris soon made friends in the Feld company, and people were around all the time. "Mark would make dinner," Hutchinson says. "He'd make soufflés, or he'd roast a chicken and make a pâté out of the liver." He was full of ideas, full of fun, unthinkingly generous, unthinkingly overbearing. "You did what Mark wanted," Hutchinson says, "because he wanted to share it with you." Peter Wing Healey, a friend of his from the Hannah Kahn and Laura Dean troupes, remembers the same thing: "It didn't matter what you were doing. You'd have to stop and listen to the Inkspots."

In 1978 Hutchinson and Morris met a young painter who lived next door, Steve Yadeskie, handsome, brooding, and introverted. Hutchinson became Yadeskie's girlfriend for a while, and then Morris became his boyfriend, and together the three of them decided they were sick of the East Village. They wanted to move across the river to Hoboken, New Jersey, which at that time was a working-class town popular with artists because of its large, low-rent living spaces. Through an ad in *The Village Voice* they found an apartment in Hoboken, or half an apartment: a loft space occupied by a painter, Robert Bordo, who couldn't afford his rent and therefore wanted to put up a wall, splitting the loft in half, and sublet the other half. They took it. Hutchinson pulled out at the last minute. ("I decided I'd had enough of boys," she says.) So the new household was to be just Morris and Yadeskie—the first time Morris ever lived with anyone as a couple.

While Morris was away on tour with the Lubovitch troupe, Yadeskie moved in. Then Morris came home. Bordo remembers his arrival:

All of a sudden there was this huge, loud presence in the building. It sounded like elephants. This was a quiet building, with painters. The people downstairs immediately freaked out over Mark's music—and his voice and his jokes and his laugh and his TV. He'd come home from rehearsal or class, and he had this huge fan club of young girls who came too. I'd go over, and Mark would entertain us. He would play all this great music, and he would make up little dances. Then he would turn on the TV and mimic all the stuff on the TV. This would go on for hours, into the night. Then in the morning he'd wake up and turn on I Love Lucy, and it would start all over again. At nine in the morning you'd hear gales of laughter and Lucy imitations.

These revels did not sit that well with Yadeskie. He was a quiet, conservative man. "He tried to suppress Mark," Bordo says. "He hated all the parties. He hated Mark's flamboyance. He hated being gay, and he wanted Mark to be a regular guy, like him." They had fights, and in 1980 Yadeskie moved to Santa Fe, leaving Morris alone in the loft. Not too alone, however. Morris had a close friend in Bordo and another in Donald

Mouton, a dancer from Louisiana whom he had introduced to Bordo, with the result, soon after, that Mouton moved in with Bordo. Two others were already part of Morris's circle: Tina Fehlandt, a dancer who had lived in the same building as Hutchinson and Morris in the East Village, and her boyfriend, Barry Alterman, an acting student. Fehlandt and Alterman had also moved to Hoboken, where they occupied a moldering basement apartment a few blocks from Morris.

Soon another person was added to the group: Erin Matthiessen, one of Laura Dean's dancers, whom Morris met and fell in love with when he joined the Dean company. Matthiessen moved in with him in June of 1981. Like Yadeskie, Matthiessen was as quiet as Morris was loud, but his was a more tranquil quiet. He was a Roman Catholic convert, very devout, and a teacher of Transcendental Meditation. He taught TM to Morris, and they practiced it together. For several years they had a happy, peaceful relationship, with Matthiessen as the steady, responsible partner

Erin Matthiessen and Morris in their Hoboken apartment, 1981 (Donald Mouton)

and Morris as the more childlike and obstreperous one. "When it was my birthday, I had to make him go buy me a present," Matthiessen says. "But we had no arguments. He never said anything harsh to me, ever. He was very loving, very sweet. And he was a wonderful cook."

Matthiessen was more amenable than Yadeskie had been to having people around constantly, and for the two and a half years that he and Morris lived in Hoboken, they staged a continual open house. Alterman and Fehlandt were there almost every night. Morris would cook dinner—"usually a faux-Indonesian variation on rice and beans," says Alterman—and they would eat in front of the quartz heater. Then they would play Scrabble or Trivial Pursuit or watch *Dynasty*. Bordo and Mouton often came over, and there were others too, Morris's friends from the Lubovitch and Kahn companies. "It was like a family," says Hannah Kahn. They gave large, noisy parties, with forty or fifty people, and Morris would choreograph the party, teaching the others a dance, often a folk dance, and then leading off the dancing, just like his grandfather.

"Mark learns by picking things up," says Bordo. "He just grabs things that he finds interesting. Out of them he creates a world, and then he peoples it with people he likes, people who will have fun with him. At that time it was just fun, not company or career. It was just this world of people who all had great times together, and Mark was the center."

But when it came time for company and career, Morris held on to that world, and turned it into a dance troupe. Until 1988 all the sets created for his company were by Robert Bordo. Erin Matthiessen, Donald Mouton, and Tina Fehlandt became members of the company, as did Penny Hutchinson, and Barry Alterman became its general manager. The dancers Morris used for his first concert—Mouton, Fehlandt, Hutchinson, Ruth Davidson, Nora Reynolds, Harry Laird, Elvira Psinas, Teri Weksler—were all friends, several of them from the Lar Lubovitch and Hannah Kahn troupes. (He also used Hannah Kahn in this concert.) Another, Jennifer Thienes, he knew from his childhood dance camp. This was the Koleda principle—the dancing ensemble as a group of friends, dance as an expression of friendship—and he applied it consciously. Speaking to *The New York Times* in 1982 about Koleda's communal ideal, he said, "When I came to New York to dance, I was still trying to make that sense of community happen." When he founded the company, it happened.

Apart from a single work, *Brummagem*, made for Pacific Northwest Ballet in 1978, Morris choreographed nothing from the time he arrived in New York in 1976 until 1980. Finally, in November 1980 he rented the

Merce Cunningham company's studio for two nights and with ten other dancers put on the first concert of what he now called the Mark Morris Dance Group—a concert that included his teenage pieces *Barstow* and *Ženska* together with *Brummagem* and two new dances: *Castor and Pollux*, to his beloved Harry Partch, and *Dad's Charts*, the solo about his father.

The ball began rolling. The following year, 1981, he was given two nights at Dance Theater Workshop, one of New York's foremost presenters of "downtown" dance—a concert important for the fact that it included Morris's first large-scale music-visualization piece, with steps directly imitating the structure of the music. This was *Gloria*, to Vivaldi's Gloria in D. *Gloria* was also his most ambitious work to date. It used a cast of ten, it was "dancier" than anything he had made before, and it took on a large, solemn subject, the emotions of the Roman Catholic Mass, in a manner that was direct and earnest. The year after that, 1982, the group returned to Dance Theater Workshop with another ambitious, dancey work for ten people, *New Love Song Waltzes*, to Brahms's *Neue Liebeslieder*. *New Love Song Waltzes* was to love what *Gloria* was to religion. It took an old sentiment, expressed in beautiful old vocal music, and set to it a modern-looking action. Together, the two works announced Morris's humanistic strain, his effort to reclaim the "great themes," and the great music that went with them, for modern bodies and souls.

Every year, his concerts got bigger. In 1983 the company had two consecutive weekends at DTW, this time with two different programs—ten works in all. (Morris made nine dances in 1983, ten in 1984. He was becoming extremely prolific.) Then in 1984 the group was asked to appear at the Next Wave Festival of the Brooklyn Academy of Music. The Next Wave Festival, at that time still devoted primarily to dance, does not actually present the next wave; it presents the new wave, or even the last wave—artists who have made it on the downtown scene and who therefore, in BAM's estimation, are ready to be shown to a wider, middle-class audience. To appear in the festival is thus a mark of "arrived" status. And to secure the arrival, BAM's president, Harvey Lichtenstein, made a practice in the eighties of encouraging choreographers to team up with currently fashionable composers and visual artists in large-scale collaborative works, so that the show could draw the art crowd and the music crowd as well as the dance audience. This strategy resulted in some very splashy productions in the early eighties—elaborate dance/theater/music/art shows involving such people as Robert Wilson, Meredith Monk, JoAnne

Akalaitis, Lucinda Childs, Trisha Brown, David Gordon, Sol LeWitt, Donald Judd, Robert Rauschenberg, Laurie Anderson, Anthony Davis, and Philip Glass. To play at BAM was thus a big deal for Morris, both a seal of approval and also a test.

He passed it well. The concert opened with a revised version of *Gloria*, then moved on to a rather startling number, *O Rangasayee*, a 23-minute solo for Morris to an Indian raga by Sri Tyagaraja. After the uplift of *Gloria*, *O Rangasayee* looked like the dark side of the moon. In the black cave of BAM's upstairs theater, Morris, dressed only in a loincloth, traveled up and down, up and down, on the diagonal, repeating a sequence of steps, but with each repeat varying the steps—shifting the accent, shortening or lengthening a phrase, just as the music did—and each time descending farther and farther into some consuming inner state, both grotesque and ecstatic. *O Rangasayee* seemed to take the element of blackness in Morris's work—the interest in the lonely, the ugly, the shocking—and bind it to some nobler force, so that it became a motor of transcendence. This burning transaction was then followed by *Championship Wrestling After Roland Barthes*, a brilliant pop study of the teeth-gnashing, floor-pummeling, Kabuki-like histrionics of TV wrestlers.

Not only was each of these pieces very good, but together they sig-

nified an enormous range, something one didn't expect from so young a choreographer. In *Gloria* Morris could be pure-hearted and exalted, like the modern dance of the thirties; in *Championship Wrestling* he could be acidic and pop, like the art of the eighties; and in *O Rangasayee* he could be some dark and private thing, lost in dance, that was wholly his own but nevertheless based on Indian kathak dance, which he had seen while touring with Laura Dean, and on the pseudo-Indian solos that Ruth St. Denis and her husband, Ted Shawn, had done in the early part of the century. (He had performed a reconstruction of Shawn's *Mevlevi Dervish* two years before.) He drew on an immense variety of sources—Baroque music, India, semiotics, TV, life in the city—but above all, he drew on the history of modern dance.

This last element was extremely important. Dance, unlike music, has no score, no text. Therefore it dies continually. If a dance ceases to be performed, it vanishes. (Perhaps 95 percent of what we assume to be the important dance works of the past no longer exist.) If a dance continues to be performed, it changes with each performance, as new performers adapt it to their own bodies, their own times. With very few exceptions, the oldest ballets in the world are less than two hundred years old—the oldest modern-dance works less than a hundred years old—and they have

Morris in *O Ranga-sayee,* 1984 *(Beatriz Schiller [first three photos], Lois Greenfield, Tom Brazil, Beatriz Schiller)*

53

now been revised to the point where their creators would hardly recognize them. They are not the past; they are the present.

This is a state of affairs wholly unlike that of any other major art form of our time, and because of it, the imaginative life of choreographers differs from that of all other artists. Choreographers have no canon—no library, no museum—that will hold the history of their art in suspension, ready for their consultation. All they have is their present tradition. They must create out of that or nothing. Hence originality in dance is both far more conservative and far more radical than in the other arts: conservative because it has only the immediate past to draw on, radical because, given that limitation, a far greater act of reimagination is required in order to make something new.

This unbreakable principle helps to explain a certain poverty in the new dance of the late seventies and early eighties. The Judson choreographers had repudiated their immediate tradition, the tradition of early and middle modern dance: Isadora Duncan, Ruth St. Denis, Martha Graham, Doris Humphrey, José Limón. Where they got their ideas, however, was not primarily from any other dance tradition but from the art world and the intellectual world. Out of these sources they made some interesting work, which, however, had very little dancing in it. At Judson, as Twyla Tharp has written, "you could only walk or run—if you danced, you had sold out." Even once they started dancing again, it is amazing to consider how much activity these choreographers generated out of how small a germ of dance thought—thought about the human body's capacity to create form out of motion. Of the generation that started out in the sixties and came of age in the seventies, the only real choreographic genius was Tharp, who, while she too backed away from mainstream modern dance, turned instead not to the art world or the intellectual world but to an alternative *dance* tradition, popular dance—the jitterbug, the twist, the bugaloo.

But nothing much was coming out of the old concert dance—"middle modern"—or nothing that Merce Cunningham and Paul Taylor hadn't already made in the sixties. In terms of innovation, the line seemed to have dead-ended with them. Then came Mark Morris's 1984 BAM season, and the great surprise of that season: the renewal of traditional modern dance. Morris's dances had none of the sleek containment, the minimalist cool, of the post-Judson choreographers. They were heroic, like José Limón. They were exalted, like Doris Humphrey. Like Martha Graham, they portrayed lonely inner states. Like Ruth St. Denis and Ted Shawn, they drew on "exotic" styles to give beauty and strangeness to the inner voyage. So there it was again, the old, corny subject matter—the human soul questioning itself, seeking its true nature—placed before us with the old, corny forthrightness. And by virtue of new steps, new relations of steps to music and of narrative to dance, it all looked new.

Prior to that season, Morris had had decent press coverage. *Dance Magazine* had been reviewing him since 1980, *The New York Times* and *The Village Voice* since 1982. And after his 1983 concert Arlene Croce of *The New Yorker* had devoted her whole column to Morris. This essay was entitled "Mark Morris Comes to Town," and in Croce's view the arrival was auspicious, for on the evidence of the DTW concert, Morris seemed to have two rare and crucial choreographic virtues. First, he was musical: he drew his dance out of the music. Second, he was able to communicate symbolic meaning (knowledge, emotion) through pure form:

This mastery of mimetic implication in the logic of forms is a mark of wisdom as rare in choreography as musical mastery. No other choreographer under thirty has it; the few of those over thirty who have it have been great. Like musicality, it is a gift, and it appears right away.

What these two abilities amounted to was "the raw gift of choreography," which, Croce wrote,

may be the most individualizing of all gifts to experience. Those who possess it are enclosed in a kind of sanctuary. No word or sound contaminates the freshness of their language, and dance language as we have known it—old academic or anti-academic usage—falls from their bodies like rags. In its place are new sights, which we perceive with a thrill of recognition.

Croce did not use the word "classical," but the virtues she located in Morris are among the defining characteristics of a classical choreographer, and the perception of Morris as a classicist rather than (or as well as) an appealing hooligan dates from this review. It was a prophetic essay— he was soon to become more classical—and it probably got a lot of people sufficiently interested in Morris to book tickets for his next concert, which was the splendid 1984 BAM concert. That show also received a rave review from Jennifer Dunning of *The New York Times*; the next day Dunning followed up her review with a profile of Morris. The tickets were gone in a flash, and when the BAM season was over, Mark Morris was the most talked-about young choreographer in the United States.

For the critics, the reason for the excitement was the one stated above: Morris had renewed modern dance. As Dunning put it, he was "the most solidly promising heir to the mantle of the modern dance greats," a sentiment seconded by Deborah Jowitt of *The Village Voice*: "Had Doris Humphrey been as long-lived as her contemporary, Martha Graham, she might have been pleased to have him as a protégé." The piece that most of the reviewers fastened on was *O Rangasayee*, partly because it was so remarkable, but also because, in its reiteration of the St. Denis/Shawn "Oriental solo" formula, it most clearly demonstrated the birth of new life out of old forms. "What might have been the merest kitsch, or even camp, was in fact a serious act of aesthetic assimilation," wrote Dale Harris in *The Wall Street Journal*. In her review of the 1984 concert Croce too concentrated on *O Rangasayee*, concluding that Morris was "the clearest illustration we have, at the moment, of the principle of succession and how it works in dance: each new master assimilates the past in all its variety and becomes our guide to the future." As these reviews suggest, Morris in the BAM concert had not just revived old modern dance forms; he had revived the old modern dance faith in originality—the idea that each generation will create dance anew, as new geniuses spring up, each with a wholly individual style. (Ballet is less romantic on the subject of originality.) "Pessimists who announced that the line of great modern-dance choreographers had ended with Paul Taylor have been shown up . . . by the work of Mark Morris," wrote Tobi Tobias in *New York* magazine. The prevailing note was one of gratitude, as if Morris had placed a dinner in front of a very hungry group of people.

They had reason to be hungry. By the early eighties, as noted, the dance boom was on its way out. Balanchine died in 1983, a natural enough occurrence—he was seventy-nine—but, with no successors in sight, a terrible blow. As for modern dance, a kind of pall had fallen over the generation of the seventies. Some came to the end of their ideas; others, of their finances. As for the next generation, the rising tide of political anger—gay, feminist, racial—convinced many young choreographers that times were too hard for people to "just dance." Instead, they began producing a kind of political theater, which, good or bad, was nevertheless theater, not dance.

It was within the context of this choreographic recession that Morris gave his first New York concerts. Consequently, for those who cared about dance, this young man who was so thoroughly a *choreographer*—who thought in dance terms, who wanted only to set people dancing—seemed a godsend, the more so in that, while affirming this old value, he was not at all old-fashioned. On the contrary, he was a bona fide angry young man. He looked like a punk rocker and he had come to save dance. In 1984 nothing could have been more welcome. Feature articles on him rolled off the presses. *Time* magazine began reviewing his work. In 1986, less than two years after the BAM concert, he won a Guggenheim Fellowship, two major ballet companies premiered ballets by him, and PBS made him the subject of an hour-long television special—extraordinary attention for an artist who was just turning thirty.

Even as all this was happening, however, there was still no actual Mark Morris company, only a group of friends, dedicated to Morris and his work, who made themselves available to him when he needed them and who spent the rest of the year working as receptionists, waitresses, carpenters—any job they could leave easily when the call came. This is the fate of almost all dancers who perform with small modern dance troupes, but the Morris troupe was not so small any more, or not in reputation. Yet in 1985 Morris could give his dancers only about five months' work, and for much of that time, they were essentially donating their services. For the company's 1985 Seattle/Portland engagement, the dancers flew out to Seattle, slept on friends' floors, spent a month rehearsing and two weeks performing, and flew back to New York—an excursion that cost each of them perhaps $1,000 and for which they were paid $250. This while national magazines were writing stories about them and PBS was gearing up for an hour-long program on them.

Part of the reason for this is that in the performing arts engagements lag far behind reputations. Most dance presenters and most choreographers have their schedules made up a year or two in advance. They are doing today what seemed right to them (and at a fee that seemed right to them) two years ago. But another reason for the slow congealing of the company was that Morris wasn't sure he wanted a company. He never had any question about being a choreographer. From about 1982 on, it was all he wanted to do. What he had difficulty with was the idea of running an organization. As a child of the sixties, he was anti-organization, and the thought of having a dozen or so people to look after frightened him. This was the reason he had called the troupe the Mark Morris Dance Group. It wasn't a company; it was just a group.

He also recoiled from the idea of a career. He never disliked fame.

What he disliked was the amount of self-marketing that goes into staying famous: the grant applications, the publicity seeking, the saying the right thing to producers, board members, journalists. When he came to New York, what he intended to do was *freelance* choreography, the same thing he had done as a teenager. He would make the dances; someone else would make the payroll. And in the mid-eighties he did do a great deal of freelance choreography. But as he was discovering, being a freelance choreographer holds terrors far worse than running your own company: the fight for adequate rehearsal time, the difficulty of getting the dancers you want, the problem of teaching them your own style, the agony, once you finish the piece and leave, of seeing the company the following year readapt it, performing it in the manner of *Swan Lake* or Glen Tetley. The only way choreographers can ensure that their work is done properly is to run, or at least be on staff with, the company that is doing it.

Morris had a company gathering around him, an eager one. The dancers were excited by the success of their recent concerts. They wanted to seek more engagements, bigger engagements—get the troupe off the ground. "But Mark freaked out," says Donald Mouton. "He couldn't talk to us, he didn't know." Indeed, he fled. In early 1984, just as he was beginning to receive wide attention, he did the one thing that an ambitious artist would be least likely to do in that circumstance: he went home. He and Matthiessen hated New York. They longed for Seattle—the blue sky, the ocean, houses with back yards. (Matthiessen was also from Washington.) And so they moved there, effectively removing Morris from the dance world's center of operations.

Very gradually, however, he came around to the idea of a company, with the help of Barry Alterman. By 1984 Alterman was no longer an acting student. He did various jobs from time to time; otherwise he read and hung out with his friends. His only connection with Morris was as his friend and the husband of one of his sometime dancers, Tina Fehlandt. Then, in March 1984, Alterman and Fehlandt went up to Montreal to see Morris perform a new solo in a group concert there. The solo was *O Rangasayee*—Morris had just created it—and when Alterman saw it, he changed his mind about Morris: "Up till then I had thought of him as an artist with potential. But now I looked at this, and potential had nothing to do with it. It was the real thing, major league, right now. I was stunned. I felt as though I had found out that my friend Joey wrote *Moby Dick*." And Alterman began to think that Morris's work was something he would like to foster.

So far, Morris had done all the company's administrative work himself. He wrote the programs; he cut the deals, not always wisely. Various professional managers were offering him their services, but this only made him more nervous. Finally, in late 1984, when he came to New York to rehearse for the BAM concert, he and Alterman had a talk about management. "I don't remember who said it first," says Alterman. "Either I said, 'Hey, I'll do it' or he said, 'Why don't you do it?' I remember that I said to him, 'I don't know what to do. What do you do?' And he said, 'You don't do anything. You just send out a press kit every now and then.' So that was it. I took over the checkbook and paid myself ninety dollars a week. I became the manager of the nonexistent Mark Morris Dance Group."

Alterman's goal was to make the company exist. He was as opposed as Morris to the kind of careerism in which art becomes secondary to the career. To him the ideal of what a company should be was represented by two groups that he had been a fan of for years, Jerzy Grotowski's Polish Laboratory Theater and the famous San Francisco rock group the Grateful Dead. The Grateful Dead he admired because they operated like a family, producing whatever they could in-house, making as few concessions as they could to music-industry expectations, and basically doing what they wanted. The Polish Laboratory Theater he admired for the modesty with which they had presented themselves, shunning publicity, performing in ordinary rooms, seeking to create a "poor theater": no scenery, no makeup, no preview articles. It was with these two sixties-type organizations in mind that Alterman evolved the company's management practices. He got Morris to come to a formal business lunch—just the two of them—in February of 1985. "I said to him, 'Fuck the career,' " Alterman remembers. They would not set up a board of directors, not try to make the right friends. Morris would not move back to New York if he didn't want to. Alterman would not woo the press. He and Morris worked out a press policy whereby, first, they would never send out the standard kind of press release, describing the dances and quoting favorable reviews. Second, they would never seek interview coverage for Morris. Third, any journalist seeking an interview would have open access to Morris, and straight answers to his or her questions. (They have been largely faithful to these rules. Morris now has a few useful friends, but he has paid no artistic price for this. Over the years, Alterman *has* had to muster advance publicity, but the company still has no press representative, which is highly unusual for a troupe its size.)

So salesmanship was what they wouldn't do, but what they would do—this was Alterman's objective—was plan Morris's work life with the company in mind. Up to this point the company had had basically two seasons a year, one in Seattle, one in New York. The rest of his time Morris spent doing other things: teaching, giving workshops, setting works on other companies. If he had engagements to fulfill with his own dancers, often the contract provided for him to bring only four or five dancers, with the result that they could not perform big ensemble works such as *Gloria* or *New Love Song Waltzes*. In other words, these engagements did not really represent the company. That was what was going to change. Though Morris would go on doing some independent projects, the emphasis would now be on company works, company engagements.

But however strong their organizational goals, their anti-organizational instincts were also strong. They had no office, no letterhead. Morris was seldom home to receive calls, or even messages. In 1985 the way you reached the Mark Morris Dance Group was to call Barry Alterman's home number in Seattle—he had moved there too—if by chance you knew that number. And if he picked up, you would be lucky. Alterman's life at this moment was in considerable disarray. His marriage was breaking up and he had hepatitis B. He lived in an unfurnished apartment, where he slept on a futon on the floor for much of the day. If the phone rang, he sometimes answered it, and when he did, his manner was extremely casual. This was natural to him, but it was also a deliberate choice. Both he and Morris were determined that they were not going to act differently just because they were running a company. "They talked to you like working-class drinking companions," says David White of Dance Theater Workshop. As a result, Alterman felt for years that when the company arrived for engagements, the producers were surprised that they had actually shown up.

Nevertheless, the company came together. In 1985 they returned to DTW for three sold-out weeks. In 1986 and 1988 they returned to BAM, this time in the big theater, the Opera House. Also in 1986 they presented a full-evening program, *Mythologies*, in Boston, a town where they were aggressively supported by the local experimental-dance presenter, Dance Umbrella; in 1987 they brought *Mythologies* to New York. In 1986 and 1987 they had summer seasons at Jacob's Pillow Dance Festival in Massachusetts. In 1986, for the first time, the whole troupe went to Europe, and performed in Vienna. They also began extensive touring at home. In 1985, they gave thirty-two out-of-town performances; in 1987, forty-six.

Most of the group hated touring, with its scanty rehearsals and one-night stands. "You come in like a commando, shoot them, and then run away," as Alterman said in a 1988 interview. "This is not artistically satisfying." But touring is the only way that most modern dance companies can make money. They have a product to sell—that year's new dances—and within about two weeks they have sold it to whoever is going to buy it in their hometown. In order to sell it to others, they have to go elsewhere.

This was a period of dizzying change. A group that in 1984 had still been fundamentally a gang of friends had by 1986 become a company that was playing opera houses, going to Europe, making a national television show. The task of administering all this began to weigh on Alterman. He was an idea man. His gifts were for imagining, planning—

deciding what the company should do and then setting up the deal. As for booking hotel rooms and setting up schedules, he had been doing this for two years, but he had no taste for it. "I'm really one side of a brain," he says. He needed the other side, a partner. At that point, the company was using Pentacle DanceWorks, a non-profit management organization, to perform certain tasks for them—grant writing, bookkeeping—and the person Alterman had his eye on was Nancy Umanoff, the extremely efficient Pentacle representative who handled the troupe's account. "Barry took me to lunch at a coffee shop on Chambers Street," says Umanoff.

He said, "Come and work with us. It would be fun." I said, "How much are you going to pay me?" and he said, "I don't know. You do the books. How much can we pay you?" So I went home and drew up this big proposal—what my responsibilities would be, what my fund-raising goals were, what my commission would be, on and on. I gave it to Barry, and he glanced at it and said, "Fine, whatever you want." So that's how I was hired. I stayed at Pentacle, but now I rented the desk space from them. I had a phone installed in the company name. I took an old piece of advertising copy, cut out the company name, pasted it on a piece of paper, and Xeroxed it, so now we had letterhead. No envelopes yet, but letterhead. We were official.

That was in 1986. By the end of that year the dancers started receiving regular pay. In 1987 they exceeded forty weeks of employment. Some of them actually started receiving credit cards in the mail.

Meanwhile, Morris was still doing a great deal of work outside the company. In 1985 he created a Bach piece, *Marble Halls*, for Batsheva Dance Company in Israel. From 1986 to 1988 he did several assignments for Seattle Opera, creating a "Dance of the Seven Veils" for their *Salome* (he managed to persuade the soprano Josephine Barstow to unveil down to a G-string) and a series of dances for their *Orpheus and Eurydice*. He also directed Seattle's new *Fledermaus*—this was his debut as a stage director—and began collaborating with Peter Sellars, the much-discussed experimental opera director. He choreographed ballets for Boston Ballet, the Joffrey Ballet, and American Ballet Theatre.

As he became busier and better-known, his relationship with Matthiessen began to come apart. "It was a bit like *A Star Is Born*," says Matthiessen. Morris traveled continually, and Matthiessen was relegated to the position of stay-at-home mate:

I held down the fort in our little house in Seattle. I would take care of things for him. I would make sure that things were done for his family. I would have dinner with Maxine and Mo [Maureen] once or twice a week. If people wanted to leave messages for him, they called me. I became the way you contacted Mark. He was never at home, or if he was home, it was to answer the phone and get interviewed by somebody in New York. We no longer had a life together.

This was doubly hard for Matthiessen in that he too was starting a career, teaching dance at the University of Washington. But all the household's energy went into Morris's career. Then each of them became interested in others. In the summer of 1984 they went for several weeks to the American Dance Festival in Durham, North Carolina, where Morris was to make a new work. While they were there, Matthiessen fell in love with one of the student dancers; Morris, meanwhile, was in love with someone else; Penny Hutchinson, who was with them, was also in love—all these loves hopeless in one way or another. No one could sleep. Everyone was in agony. "We called that the summer of love," says Matthiessen. "It was horrific." Finally, a year later, Morris moved in with a friend, and he has never again lived as part of a couple.

Everyone who knew Morris in his twenties stresses how sweet he was then—"young and soft," says Robert Bordo. Though he could bully, it was not out of meanness. It was the fullness of his nature overflowing, making you listen to the record he liked, play the game he enjoyed, listen to the joke he thought was funny. He did not enjoy bossing for the sake of bossing. Indeed, he ran the company so democratically that it was only by dint of the dancers' professionalism that the shows got onstage. He hated rehearsing old works. For these, the dancers rehearsed themselves; Morris came in at the end, for fine-tuning. He never made a rehearsal schedule. The dancers decided when they would meet and who would be in charge of the rehearsal. He even let certain dancers help with casting—a policy that was not popular with the others.

But as he became better known, with more and more demands on him, Morris became less sweet. Or rather, all his mental energies became focused simply on making his dances. A telling episode occurred during the final dress rehearsal for the 1984 BAM concert. This was a tense rehearsal. *Championship Wrestling* was barely finished; the show was to go on that night; everyone was nervous. Suddenly Tina Fehlandt fell off another dancer's shoulders and landed on the floor with a terrible thud.

Morris was sitting at some distance from the stage. He did not get up. "Are you injured," he called out to Fehlandt, "or are you just in pain?" "Just in pain," she managed to say. "Then roll over to the side so we can keep going," Morris said. She rolled over, and they kept going. Short of an injury, nothing could break his concentration or induce him to break the dancers' concentration. In the years to follow, his absorption in his work became more and more absolute. This is an old story with artists, and he is no exception. His single-mindedness has helped him immensely—he can go on working even under the most harrowing conditions—but it has also made him harder.

———

Nineteen eighty-six was a year of crisis for Morris. He did a huge amount of work that year, creating *Mythologies* and mounting his first two ballets, as well as working for Seattle Opera and filming the PBS program. At the end of the year, he premiered his *Stabat Mater*, a hard, dry, relentless work about religious anguish—a piece that was not destined to please those who loved him for his wacky humor and sixties uplift. Anguish is not foreign to his work, but *Stabat Mater* was a truly oppressive piece, a reflection not just of whatever he saw as the harsh principles of life but also of his mood at the moment, darkened, probably, by loneliness (he and Matthiessen had separated only the year before) and also by a sense of being swallowed alive by a career. His anxiety on the latter score was not allayed by BAM's Next Wave Festival, of which *Stabat Mater* was part. As usual with the Next Wave Festival, the events were surrounded by a good deal of stylish publicity: opening-night parties with Bianca Jagger and Andy Warhol, expensive program booklets full of ads in which everyone wore a fashionably distressed hairdo and perverse affect. "Mark didn't want to be part of some phony avant-garde art scene," says Robert Bordo, who designed *Stabat Mater*. "He kept saying he was not an avant-garde choreographer—he was just a serious traditional choreographer. He believed that." But by taking advantage of BAM's up-to-date publicity machine, he became, willy-nilly, part of the machine, and this was a philosophical hardship.

Worse troubles followed. Two weeks after the opening of *Stabat Mater*, while warming up for a show in Ottawa, he broke his foot, and for five months he couldn't perform. "You couldn't go near him," says Tina Fehlandt. "He was like a badger caught in a trap, snapping at people as they went by." Even before the injury, his choreographic career had taken a toll on his dancing. Now, between inactivity and beer, he put on weight. He slimmed down when he started dancing again, and in the late eighties he remained (as he remains in the nineties) one of the most enthralling dancers on the American stage, but after about 1986 he never again commanded the sheer *technical* arsenal that he had possessed in the early eighties.

At this point he also began to receive some bad press, which invariably comes after a wave of good press. Some reviewers claimed that his choreography was too simple, above all, too simple musically—that it just copied the music step-for-note. Another complaint, though it was often implied rather than openly stated, had to do with a kind of double-sidedness that is absolutely fundamental to his vision, an ability to see and express two opposing aspects of an experience simultaneously. Often those two aspects are the solemn and the ridiculous, but they may also be the beautiful and the affected, the grotesque and the comic, the exalted and the brutal. (*Stabat Mater* was an example of the last.) And as a kind of overarching opposition, Morris has always been in the habit of using fine old classical music, which tends to put audiences in a worshipful mood, and then setting to it steps that have a blunt, vernacular look, which disturbs that worshipful mood and leaves spectators wondering, "Is he making a joke?"

This marshaling of contraries confused and annoyed some people, including some reviewers, whose task of explaining the work was not made easier by its double-sidedness. (Nor do reviewers like to feel that jokes are being made that they don't get.) The problem was compounded by Morris's habit, in interviews, of insisting on his utter simplicity. "Often my things look clichéd," he said in a 1986 interview.

But clichés were all true at one point. I did a piece once called Ten Suggestions *to Alexander Tcherepnine's Piano Bagatelles—and I just wanted it to be music visualization—that was the goal. It was, "This sounds like this—so why not just do that?" I mean, look at Balanchine's* Liebeslieder Walzer. *They're love waltzes. That's what they are. So why move chairs around in black and white leotards to that sort of music? What you do with Brahms waltzes is wear gloves and kiss hands. It doesn't mean it's corny. It means it's true. So that's what I do, too. What I'm saying is, what do you do with a hoop? You jump through it. What do you do with a ribbon? You swirl it. What do you do with a chair? You sit on it.*

So I go for a certain reality.

But as it happens, Morris's dances almost never look clichéd, in large part because of their double-sided character. A perfect example is the dance he refers to here, *Ten Suggestions*, a solo that he made for himself in 1981. *Ten Suggestions* is, as he claims, a music visualization, based on the little music-visualization dances created by early modern dancers, often with the help of ribbons, hoops, and other lyrical accessories, to express the feelings aroused in them by music. But this is not all that *Ten Suggestions* is. It is a *study* of the genre, and one of the finest comic dances Morris ever made. In a pair of pink pajamas, he comes charging onstage, and as the music plays, he creates—on the spot, it seems—little dances that mimic the music's moods and gestures. When the melodic line goes up, he climbs up on a chair; when it goes down, he falls to the floor; when it goes fluttery, he flutters a ribbon; when it becomes jaunty and march-like, he puts on a pith helmet and marches. And all the while he uses his big, loose body and his great capacity for awkwardness to offset the poetic nature of those images, so that what we end up seeing is not something naïvely idealistic, like the music visualizations of Ruth St. Denis and Doris Humphrey, but a distanced, critical view of such dances: a portrait of the human soul, on some kind of midnight prowl, imagining a fine destiny for itself in response to music, and *creating* that destiny, by dancing. It's very funny—funny because of the distance between the body and its aspirations—but it is also poignant, full of respect for childhood, when such improvisations normally begin, and for dancers, the people who try to make adult lives out of that childhood romance.

So *Ten Suggestions* is not the simple, true-hearted little thing that he claims. But this does not mean that he is being disingenuous in his interviews. In fact, he is more true-hearted, more idealistic and sentimental, than most other intelligent people his age. He cries at sad movies. He is not above signing "I love you" to the audience in American Sign Language at curtain calls. He likes watching *Mister Rogers' Neighborhood*. And this is the side of him that is speaking when he protests to interviewers that he is just being direct and simple. (In 1982 he told *The New York Times* that he wanted to move back to Seattle because "you can't be corny in New York anymore . . . It's the whole hipster scene.") At the same time he is more critical, more iconoclastic and dark-minded, than most other people, and that is what makes his idealism profound rather than naïve. But the tension between the two is very striking, and in a post-Freudian age, where it is generally assumed that the less generous motivation is the truer motivation, the contrast between idealism and iconoclasm in his work has sometimes been taken to mean simply iconoclasm—or indeed camp. "The use of a genuine talent in the service of camp flamboyance . . . is a side of his personality, both offstage and on, that immediately removes him from the artistic lineage so often claimed for him," as Anna Kisselgoff put it in *The New York Times* in 1990. This was not the first time his work was called camp, and the accusation galled him deeply.

The designation of Morris's work as camp probably had as much to do with his public persona ("a side of his personality, both offstage and on") as with the work. For some, it was hard to take seriously a man who, upon being asked by a journalist why he had his long hair cut off, said that it was getting caught in his lipstick. How much distaste for homosexuality ("camp flamboyance") was involved in this reaction? Probably a little, but only insofar as homosexuality entails effeminacy. Many famous choreographers are homosexual, a fact that is never held against them, indeed never mentioned, by the dance press, because they are not effeminate. Morris, though he does not wear lipstick, is effeminate, or one side of him is. (As noted, the other side is a flannel-shirted truck driver.) And many people dislike effeminacy, particularly on the stage, where it seems to them *de facto* "flaunted." To quote one such reaction, Eva Resnikova in *The New Criterion* described Morris as being "effeminate to a degree difficult to stomach even for a veteran dancegoer largely inured to this *déformation professionelle*." But even more than effeminacy, what gave offense was probably the effrontery that for obvious reasons tends to accompany effeminacy. In his early interviews, as noted, Morris rarely failed to point out that he was gay. For a young homosexual in our time, this is one logical option—to make oneself a nuisance on the subject, to keep bringing it up, until finally it might start to look like part of life—and journalists welcome it, because it is provocative.

Nor was it just his homosexuality that was endlessly bannered, but other unconventional things about him: his long hair, his funny clothes, his smart-aleck remarks, his evil-smelling clove cigarettes. This was the usual personality-profile writing; Babe Ruth's Stutz Bearcat and Jean-Paul Sartre's strabismus got the same treatment. Morris eventually complained about it. "What cigarettes I smoke, and how long my hair is, and if I'm fat or thin, or butch or femme . . . You can write anything you want about it, but it has zero to do with my dances," he told one interviewer. Actually, his personality has a great deal to do with his dances, but in the dances the themes born of his personality are endlessly reimagined, whereas in life they remain the same. Nevertheless, this *was* his personality; he couldn't stop being it. It was not something for which he deserved fame, yet it was easier to write about than the thing for which he did deserve fame—the dances—and it was what many editors and readers wanted to know about anyway. Other people, however, got tired of hearing about it. Why, they asked, did this man get so much publicity for waving a beer bottle around and shooting his mouth off—or, indeed, for being homosexual? There were homosexuals before Mark Morris.

This controversy must be understood in the context of the depressed dance world of the late eighties. Amid those doldrums, the wave of support for Morris set up an imbalance in the politics of the dance world. "Why . . . is there the feeling, however dubious, that there is no one else [besides Morris] out there?" asked Anna Kisselgoff in *The New York Times* in 1990. "Doesn't Paul Taylor do the same thing better? Isn't Ralph Lemon as interesting?" In fact, for many dance fans, and many reviewers, no one else of Morris's generation *was* as interesting, but to other reviewers this seemed undemocratic. Two years before, Kisselgoff had already tried to right the balance by assigning Morris a more modest ranking. "Mark Morris is not a great choreographer but he is a fluent and entertaining one," she wrote in 1988. Likewise Clive Barnes in the *New York Post*: "He is far from being a bad choreographer, but he is also far from being a good choreographer."

The reaction escalated as Morris acquired the support of big-name people outside the dance world. For *Mythologies*, based on the writings of Roland Barthes, Susan Sontag, who had written about and edited Barthes, contributed a note to the program: a mark of high-intelligentsia approval that several dance reviewers commented upon icily. Nor was his popularity with the dance press increased in 1989 when the highly fashionable photographer Annie Leibovitz published in *Vanity Fair* a series of photographs for which Morris had posed in various stages of undress and with his face heavily made up, so that he looked like a beefy drag queen.

By late 1989 the reaction had become more bitter. Of Morris's *Dido and Aeneas*, which in general was rapturously received by the American press, Kisselgoff wrote: "In the end, it's just good old Mark Morris again . . . would-be enfant terrible." Of Morris's *L'Allegro, il Penseroso ed il*

Moderato (1988), which was widely declared a masterpiece, Barnes wrote that it was a "commonplace, and totally irrelevant, staging of Handel's baroque score." (This review was accompanied by a photograph of Morris captioned "Mark Morris, totally irrelevant.") Barnes added that Morris was "the darling of New York's dance avant-garde." Kisselgoff issued a similar warning. "The other day," she wrote, "a Boston newspaper de-

Morris backstage, 1986
(Donald Mouton)

69

scribed him [Morris] as having been 'anointed the successor to Balanchine,' although it is not clear by whom." "Or perhaps it is," she added darkly. Later in the same piece, she wrote: "The idea that some of Mr. Morris's works are codes, accessible to an inner club, is what makes it attractive to that inner club in the audience," thus raising the question of what made Morris's work attractive to the thousands of other people, not members of the putative club, who at this point were buying tickets to see his shows.

The division was not absolute. (A month before her "inner club" article, Kisselgoff gave a very warm review to *L'Allegro*.) Nevertheless, sides were taken. There were two little wars in the New York dance press in the eighties. One was over the question of whether Martha Graham's late work deserved the same praise as her earlier work. The other was over Mark Morris: whether he was actually a major talent. Dance critics split in much the same way over the two issues—in general, a yes on one meant a no on the other—a fact that reflects not just tastes but also the social and political structure of the dance press: who likes whom, who influences whom, who occupies what position in relation to whom.

By the time the press war got going, however, Morris was no longer in the United States, for reasons that have already been described in part. In June of 1987 Gérard Mortier, the director of the Théâtre Royal de la Monnaie, the national opera house of Belgium, found himself in an awkward position. Recently he had been embroiled in financial disputes with the Monnaie's director of dance, Maurice Béjart, whose 60-member Ballet of the 20th Century was the opera house's resident company. Finally, just ten days earlier, Béjart had sent Mortier his resignation. This news was not altogether displeasing to Mortier. He had little liking for Béjart's choreography. But Béjart was immensely popular with the Brussels public, who regarded him as a sort of Belgian national treasure. "This was the most difficult moment of my years in Brussels," Mortier said later. He needed to fill Béjart's place quickly and, if possible, with someone very special. Furthermore, he needed not just a choreographer but a whole company, for Béjart was taking the Ballet of the 20th Century with him.

Casting about for ideas, Mortier called the director Peter Sellars, whose work he admired. (Mortier had just given Sellars his European debut, at the Monnaie, the month before.) Could Sellars recommend someone? Mortier asked. Yes, he could. "I told him that Mark was the most talented choreographer I knew," Sellars remembers, "and also that he was someone who would be right for an opera house—that he could work with orchestras and choruses, that he could appeal to a wide audience, that he could hold an opera house stage." Mortier replied that he had never heard of Morris. "Then come to Stuttgart," said Sellars. That's where Sellars was at that moment, and that's where Morris was too, both of them showing their work at the same festival. Mortier flew to Stuttgart the next day, went to Morris's concert, and afterward invited Morris and Barry Alterman to dinner. Over dinner he described to them the resources available to the dance director of the Monnaie: a year-round contract for all the dancers at an average yearly salary of $33,000 (plus medical coverage), a vast studio complex, an office complex, a fully staffed costume shop, the services of a live orchestra and chorus, the use of a beautiful old 1,100-seat Baroque opera house, the Monnaie—or if they didn't like that, any other theater in Brussels—plus a secretary, a masseuse, and indeed whatever else might be needed in order to put on a dance show. He then asked Morris if he would take the job and bring his company with him.

To understand what this offer meant, one must recall the circumstances of the Mark Morris Dance Group in 1987. In view of the fact that they were only seven years old, they were quite successful. But in terms of resources, this meant little. In Europe the arts are heavily subsidized. (Hence the scale of Mortier's offer, which would not have been unusual for a French or German opera house either.) In the United States, by comparison, the arts receive paltry funding, and dance companies eke out a poor living. In 1987 Mark Morris's dancers worked for him about 40 weeks a year—the rest of the time, they had to find other jobs or go on unemployment—and for this they made an average of $14,000 a year. They had no benefits, no medical coverage, and above all no job security, no guarantee of work. The company's productions were equally squeezed financially. There was a constant hustle to come up with the money for the live music that Morris felt was essential to his work. As for costumes, most of them were bought on Canal Street. Sets were usually out of the question. (Of the forty-eight dances staged live by the company between 1980 and 1987, only one, *Stabat Mater*, had a decor more elaborate than a draped cloth or a few potted plants.) Furthermore, Morris had only twelve dancers. He longed to do larger productions. If he went to the Monnaie, his company would not only have year-round work, decent salaries, sets, costumes, and live music; it could grow.

Still, the drawbacks to the deal were considerable. It meant moving to a city famous for its conservatism, and a city in Europe. Morris's work was very American—American in its imagery and humor, American in its classicism, its emphasis on dance values. There was no reason to believe that the Brussels public would like it. Furthermore, there was the matter of uprooting. More than half the dancers were married or living with someone; they would have to leave their mates (or induce them to come, as several did). Those who were single still had apartments, friends, and lives in New York which they had no wish to give up. For them, and for Morris too, the sheer financial advantages of Mortier's offer—the salaries—would not have offset these disadvantages.

What was irresistible was the physical plant that was offered, and the kind of working conditions this would make possible. The life of the Mark Morris Dance Group, as of all modern dance companies without a home studio (that is, perhaps 90 percent of all small dance companies in America), was a continual act of struggle against disorder and dispersal. Having no studio of its own, the company had to rent rehearsal space, space that was rented by other troupes at other times of the day, so that there was no way to prolong a rehearsal if the rental period ended in mid-inspiration. At the end of the hour, they had to clear out, and even take up the tape that they had laid on the floor to mark the size of the stage the dance was being made for. (This meant re-laying the tape at the beginning of each rehearsal.) They left in sweaty clothes, for there were typically no showers, no dressing rooms, and then they reassembled the next day, possibly in a different studio. Getting the dance produced was the same process. Each concert was a new beginning, with a new presenter, a new financial deal, a new theater. It was an immensely wasteful system.

In Brussels, on the other hand, they would have their own headquarters, with four studios—each a different size, for different needs—plus dressing rooms and showers. Morris would not only be able to rehearse when he wanted, for as long as he wanted; he could also give a daily company class, to train and develop the dancers in his style. And when a piece was finished, he could turn to the Théâtre de la Monnaie to provide the stage, the sets, the costumes, the program booklets, the live orchestra—the chorus, if need be—and put on the show. What Mortier had offered him, in other words, was a completely different way of working, one in which, unhindered by chaos and waste, he could try his skill to the utmost. This was not something he could turn down.

Why Morris accepted is thus no mystery. Why Mortier offered, after seeing only one performance, is a more interesting question. Obviously, he liked the performance. "I was so moved," he told a reporter from *Vanity Fair* in 1989.

Just to see this Gloria was enough to know that this man is special. It's his attitude toward the music. I would say Béjart uses music for his spectacle. Mark Morris serves the music. That's a big difference. Another difference is that Mark has a very subtle sensibility. He's not a man who comes with a big knocking, like this is what I want to show and I want to explain this . . . But I think the biggest difference, and it is really 180 degrees, is the humor. Finally, I find an artist who has humor.

Of these three qualities—musicality, subtlety, and humor—the most important was almost certainly the first. Mortier was a music lover, and this was one of the reasons he did not care for Béjart's work. Béjart was in the habit of splicing together excerpts from different musical compositions—"two measures of Beethoven, one cry of rock singer," as Mortier put it. Furthermore, because of his splicing habits and also because he liked his music loud, he preferred taped accompaniment to live accompaniment, a practice that was hateful to Mortier on aesthetic grounds and which also meant that Béjart's company made no use of the Monnaie orchestra. Morris, on the other hand, *based* his choreography on music and insisted on live accompaniment, pleasing Mortier on both counts.

Morris had other things in his favor. Sellars's recommendation undoubtedly meant a lot to Mortier, and in view of the fact that Sellars had just hired Morris to work on one of his operas, Mortier may have thought that in Morris he would be getting something like Sellars's mix of traditionalism and iconoclasm—exactly what, as a forward-thinking opera house director, he was looking for. Furthermore, Morris was a politically canny choice. Because he was American, neither the Walloon (French-speaking) nor the Flemish (Flemish-speaking) factions of bicultural Belgium's quarrelsome arts community could accuse Mortier of favoritism. Of course, Morris was practically unknown in Europe, but on such short notice it would have been very hard to get someone with a bigger reputation. Furthermore, hiring an unknown could work in Mortier's favor. If this obscure person turned out to be a great find, then Mortier would get the credit for having discovered him. If he turned out not to be a great find, Mortier would still be a bold, risk-taking fellow who had given a young artist a chance.

Finally, Morris was a practical choice. He was not a freelance choreographer who would have to come, hire dancers, and then take years to build a company and a repertory. He had a company and a repertory, a ready-made dance machine that could simply be plugged into the Monnaie. And it was an inexpensive machine. Twenty-odd modern dancers cost far less to keep than sixty ballet dancers, with all those point shoes to buy. And so, while many people were amazed at the news that a long-haired oddball from Seattle had been chosen to be the director of dance at Belgium's royal opera house, Morris in fact was as logical a choice for Mortier as Mortier was for Morris.

For Morris's dancers, however, the move was not necessarily a good choice. Had the dancers voted, the company would probably not have gone. But they did not vote. Morris decided to go, and he asked the dancers to go with him. In a show of loyalty and cohesiveness typical of the company, they all, without exception, went. Indeed, two former members of the company, Erin Matthiessen and Holly Williams, rejoined the troupe for the Belgian excursion. To hire additional dancers—some for a few months, for a special project, others for the permanent company—Morris held auditions in Brussels and New York. It says something about the company's popularity in America at that time (and also, perhaps, about the appeal of the Monnaie salary) that the New York audition drew five hundred dancers, from whom ten were chosen. Three hundred dancers tried out at the Brussels audition, and three were chosen. In one leap, the company grew from twelve to twenty-seven. Between late August and early September 1988, day by day, the dancers flew to Brussels in small groups so that Nancy Umanoff could meet each group at the airport, take them to furnished apartments, give them keys, and tell them where to eat in a city that most of them had never seen before and that would be their home for the next three years.

The story of the company's Belgian adventure will be told in a later chapter. It is time to talk about Morris's dances.

THE BODY

One of the things that has endeared Mark Morris to his audience is the emphatically human look of his company. In the troupe's early days, the women tended to be large—the "girls' basketball team," someone commented at a 1983 concert—and the men small. In other words, they looked more like regular people than like a dance company, where size differences between the sexes are greater than the human norm. But what is most striking about the lineup of dancers who have passed through the Morris company is simply the physical variety within the group. Some of the women *are* large, and have discernibly female bodies. ("Big bottoms, large breasts—okay with me!" Morris said to a journalist in 1992.) Others are tiny. Teri Weksler, who danced with the company for its first nine years and was one of Morris's most prized dancers, seemed almost weightless on stage. "A paper cup," Morris used to call her. One of the men, Guillermo Resto, looks like a wrestler; others are delicately built. One man is gray-haired, another balding. Two have dreadlocks.

Morris's dancers are also older than the average American dancer. For most of the company's existence, the majority of its members have been over thirty. And they are a vivid ethnic assortment. Of the troupe's past and present dancers, one is Puerto Rican, one Vietnamese, two black. One is half Japanese, one half Filipino, one half Indonesian. No one wears glasses onstage, but otherwise they look a lot like the crowd one might meet at the cash machine.

They also move like human beings. On occasion they perform the kind of "ordinary movement"—plain walking, sitting down in a chair— that was introduced into dance in the sixties by the Judson Dance Theater. For the most part, however, what they do is not ordinary movement but a carefully designed choreography that stresses qualities we think of as ordinary, such as weight and effort. Weight above all. "Gravity is our friend," Morris said to an interviewer in 1989. "At least, we modern dancers like it." This love of gravity is one of the things that make people, when they look at his work, think of the early modern dancers, such as Isadora Duncan, who reintroduced weight into concert dancing at the turn of the century. Morris's dancers tend to stand in *demi-plié* (on slightly bent knees), with their bare feet flat on the floor. They look solid; you can feel their weight in your mind. And often, when they jump, they don't cushion the landing by bringing the foot down in stages (ball, then heel). They land with a thud.

Indeed, they are always thudding, falling, smacking the floor. In *Gloria*, the prayer-for-mercy section begins with a man crashing onto the stage from somewhere high in the wings, as if he had been dropped down by a backhoe. In *Dido and Aeneas*, when the wicked Sorceress (played by Morris) comes running onstage along a balustrade, her feet smack the wood loudly with each step. A reviewer once commented that Morris used his feet as if they were webbed, a remark that reportedly annoyed him very much but which had some justice. Flesh against hardness—he loves this sound.

In insisting on the relationship of the body to the floor, Morris is telling not just a hard truth—the earth is beneath us, we're mortal—but a delicate truth, about what the body is. Never has flesh seemed more human than when, in Morris's dances, we hear it come up against the unyielding floor. In *Behemoth* (1990), his most terrifying work, he turns the screw even tighter: a lone dancer, lying on his back, moves slowly upstage by pushing himself with his feet, and the traction of his sweaty back against the floor makes a low moaning sound. We cannot see the man's face; we only hear this moan, the report of what is tender and alive against what is hard and cold.

What Morris is interested in is exposure, and this helps to explain another curiosity of his choreography, his love of the buttocks. "People have always said we have big butts," he commented to Christine Temin

of *The Boston Globe* in 1989. "We *do* have big butts." As it happens, only
a few of the dancers (including Morris) have big butts—that is, normal
butts, not dancer-thin—but what all of them have is choreography that
emphasizes the buttocks. *Demi-plié*, to begin with, tends to push the
buttocks out. (According to company wisdom, Morris's heavy use of *demi-
plié* actually increases the size of the buttocks.) Beyond that, Morris is
constantly showing the buttocks. In the Waltz of the Flowers in *The Hard
Nut*, Morris's 1991 version of *The Nutcracker*, seven dancers lie down on
their backs with their heads to us and execute a half-somersault, so that
we look directly at their back ends—seven of them, all in a row, blandly
greeting the audience: an image all the more remarkable in that these
people are supposed to be flowers. They repeat the maneuver four times,
lest we miss the point.

    The costumes aid in the exposure. In a number of Morris's early

Marble Halls. Left to right: Keith Sabado, Penny Hutchinson, Ruth Davidson, Guillermo Resto, David Landis, Tina Fehlandt (Tom Brazil)

pieces, what the dancers wore was simply underwear: Jockey shorts, boxers, jogging bras. Elsewhere too, the costumes he has favored—smocks that end at the crotch, tights and jumpsuits that end at mid-thigh, like long-line girdles—tend to be revealing. These costuming preferences have occasionally presented problems in Morris's work with ballet companies. Whatever feelings his own troupe may have about letting their bodies be seen, most ballet dancers want to look slim-hipped on stage. Lawrence Rhodes, the artistic director of Les Grands Ballets Canadiens, once recalled with a philosophic smile the day when his female dancers first tried on the costumes—swimsuit-like leotards (designed by Robert Bordo) that ended at mid-thigh, leaving the rest of the leg bare—for a ballet, *Paukenschlag*, that Morris made for them in 1992. "That was a very sticky day," Rhodes said.

"I love to see their butts," says Morris. That love is not erotic, or not mostly. If it were, their butts would look sexier, and presumably the men's buttocks would be more in evidence than the women's, which they are

not. No, what he is after is the thing that is *underneath*, both literally and metaphorically. The buttocks are an innocent, hardworking part of the body—soft and round, the seat of humility, the place that gets kicked. To Morris they seem to represent something modest and tender and unacknowledged, the body's vulnerability. At the same time, what they represent in dance terms is the body's dignity, for they are the motor of action: they contain the pelvis, from which the movement originates. So in both senses the buttocks harbor a fundamental truth, and one that in Morris's eyes is validated by the fact that it requires exposure. For him, truth is always hard to find. Veils have to be dropped. Once, describing to a journalist why he loved conducting choreographic workshops, he said, "It's like we all pull our pants down"—a telling metaphor. In one of his dances, *Striptease* (1986), the performers do pull their pants down.

And it's not just the buttocks he is interested in. He also makes heavy use of the crotch. In his *L'Allegro, il Penseroso ed il Moderato*, when the vocal text speaks of a goddess giving birth, three women lie down on the floor and spread their legs. In his *Lovey* (1985), we see a woman in baby-doll pajamas on all fours, butt out, with her back to us—a startling sight. In *Gloria*, in the middle of a slow, plangent, here-is-my-soul passage, the dancers bend down and, with one arm in front and one behind, clasp their hands at their crotches. The effect is not at all sexy. This is not the crotch grabbing of rock singers ("Look what I have here") or of alley mime ("Screw you"). On the contrary, there is often a note of pain—the dancers in *Gloria* look as though they are hanging on to their crotches for dear life. Elsewhere, the point, again, is simply exposure: something private being revealed, something inside being forced out.

Another way Morris exposes the body is by refusing to refine effort out of his choreography. The reader should try the crotch-grab that the dancers do in *Gloria*: bend down, join the hands, fore and aft, between the legs, and then stand up straight. It is almost impossible to do, and it is certainly impossible to do with grace. Most dance is designed, and cast, in such a way that however difficult the steps, they can be executed with a look of ease. Indeed, this is one of the great pleasures of watching dance: to see something so hard be done, it seems, so effortlessly. Morris's logic is the opposite. He gives the dancers steps that cannot be performed with a look of ease—turns so hard-flung that they can't be finished neatly, steps that must be completed in one count when, to be done without rush, they need two, stretchings and reachings that push the dancers beyond any control over their appearance. "In a lot of the movement," says Donald

Mouton, who danced with the company for nine years, "your job is to push one extremity as far as you possibly can. It's not just step right, step left. You have to bring your left leg all the way around until you can't go any farther, so you have to go to the next place. It's not a decorative thing at all."

On the contrary, it is a struggle. Toward the end of *The Hard Nut* Morris has about half the cast of the ballet come onstage to do *pirouettes à la seconde*. *Pirouette à la seconde* is a virtuoso ballet step in which the dancer—almost always a man (Baryshnikov was famous for this step)— sticks one leg out at a 90-degree angle to the body and then performs a pumping turn in place. The more turns, the more spectacular the step: the dancer looks like a pneumatic drill. But the extended leg must be kept absolutely straight and at 90 degrees, and the dancer's balance must not waver. For this reason, there is usually some allowance in the choreography for the dancer to end the pirouette when he chooses (that is, before he starts to fall over). Furthermore, *pirouette à la seconde* is normally done solo; if two people tried to do it together, they would tend to go out of unison and thus rob the step of its look of focused perfection. Morris, however, has not just one or two people but ten people—none of them professional ballet dancers, many of them struggling to keep the leg from bending and drooping—perform *pirouettes à la seconde* in unison, with no allowance for ending early. The effect, and the goal, is not a look of perfection but one of good-humored effort. It is like watching ten people try to climb a flagpole simultaneously. In other pieces the dancers show a kind of blunt purposefulness that, combined with the kind of steps they do, makes them seem like children in a Christmas pageant. They are trying to do their job, and that's all. No matter how proficient the company has become, they have never lost this look of innocence.

Morris often underlines the quality of effort by casting his dancers against type, against ease. "I remember, when he gave us a step in rehearsal," Mouton says, "and we all did it, if he said to you, 'That's a natural for you,' that meant you weren't going to get to do it." The kind of thing Mouton got to do was, for example, the lark in *L'Allegro*, a role exactly opposed to his four-square, blocklike body type. Similarly, Teri Weksler, the tiny "paper cup," was given the role of the lead sailor in *Dido and Aeneas*, a role full of big, heavy hops and big, squatty *pliés*, a role, in other words, that called for size and weight. Morris doesn't always cast against type. (The dancers who alternated with Mouton and Weksler in these roles—Jon Mensinger and Jean-Guillaume Weis, respectively—

were naturally suited to them. Mensinger is delicately built; Weis is a hulk.) But he does it often, and deliberately, "so they can't do imitations of themselves," as he once explained in an interview.

What he is trying to get at through all this exposure can be seen in his 1982 *New Love Song Waltzes*, a work that became a big audience favorite. Set to Brahms's song cycle *Neue Liebeslieder*, the piece is a love dance, but whereas most love dances are transfiguring, molding the human form into longer lines, sweeter harmonies, as if love naturally made us superhuman, *New Love Song Waltzes* tells the opposite story: love makes the dancers human.

The opening is thrilling. As the lights go up, we see a single woman, Ruth Davidson, crouching at the back of the stage. She runs toward us, jumps into *demi-plié*, leaps upward, executes a full turn in the air, her skirt flying up meanwhile to show her strong thighs, and then lands, bam, in *demi-plié*, facing us straight on. This is an explosive announcement, and what it announces is what the vocal text is telling us at that moment: "Abandon hope of rescue, O heart, / when you venture on the sea of love." It is a declaration, in bodily terms, of the violence of love and the sheer, exposing effort love puts us through: how it turns our heads, lifts our skirts, makes us tear around.

The rest of the piece follows in the same vein. There are fifteen sections—a ring dance, a cascade dance, an exploding-down-the-middle-of-the-stage dance, and so on—each with a lesson about love. But in all of them, the force of love is to make the dancers struggle. They hang by their legs from each other's necks. They haul each other around by the armpits. They fall, and others step over them. At other times they don't so much struggle as simply move with utter bluntness. They take hard little hops; they stoop; they squat; they sit on each other's arms.

In what is always the audience's favorite section, the dancers, in pairs, take to the floor and embrace, but not in a poetic manner. They lie smack on top of each other, tangling their legs together, letting their skirts hike up, showing us the insides of their thighs. Looking at them, we can feel the actual heaviness of another human body, the warmth of the flesh, the burden of it. They feel the burden too, and as the dance proceeds, the dancers get up one by one and move over into other pairs of arms. They are always restive, always searching.

New Love Song Waltzes, like *A Midsummer Night's Dream*, is about love not as something that two people feel for each other and can therefore resolve—this may be the only love dance in the world that contains no partnered duet—but as something that one person, or all humanity, feels: love as a goad, a yearning, changeable in its object but not in its force. This is an extension of Morris's concern with human vulnerability, and the voice of that vulnerability is the body. Somebody trying with all his might to hook himself onto somebody else by a body part that can't hold him, and in the process showing his bulging tendons, his clamped gluteals: that, for Morris, is romantic love, its comedy and its sorrow.

It is no accident that *New Love Song Waltzes* is set to vocal music. Since 1980, half of Morris's entire repertory has been set to vocal music —an extraordinary percentage. There are probably a number of reasons for this, but according to him, the main reason is that singing comes out of the body: "When you have a person reading music and playing the violin, you have the sound of that, but it's one generation removed from the body. Singing is like dancing. It's the body, the body in the world, with nothing in between, no instrument between." The closer something is to the body, the more interesting it is to him. And of course the voice comes from *inside* the body—the lungs, the throat, the mouth—and sounds like it: liquid, fleshly, urgent. It too is a private part.

This intensely visceral idea of dance is something for which there are obvious sources in Morris's early life. Both the main styles of dancing in which he was trained as a boy, flamenco and Balkan folk dance, are stamping styles. They give an oral report of the rhythm, not just a visual report, and it was from them that Morris learned to love the sound of the foot coming down on the floor. The Koleda Folk Ensemble is also the obvious model for effort in dancing, for the image of dance as a bunch of regular people trying to do something together. Indeed, the Morris company in their *pirouettes à la seconde* in *The Hard Nut* look like a Koleda flashback: a big group, a hard step, a good will. Another possible model is Verla Flowers's dance recitals, where every child got a part—got to be a cowboy or a sugar plum—and worked hard at it. As for the love of vocal music, Morris grew up singing. He came by it all naturally.

But for the particular way that the Morris troupe looks—human, un-glamorized, naked almost—there is another source, the troupe itself. As with all dance companies, what they are onstage is something like what they are offstage, and what they are offstage is unusually unassuming and comradely. The troupe began as a group of friends, and though some of those people have since departed and been replaced by people hired from auditions, they are still a group of friends. Of course there is competition within the group, and there are resentments over who gets what role.

Rehearsal is not democratic; Morris says what he wants, and the dancers do it. But there is a spirit of common cause. According to Morris, the reason he chose the dancers he did for his early company was not just that they were friends: "They were learning how to dance at the same time that I was learning how to choreograph. It happened at the same time." That is one of the reasons that over the years the dancers have tended to be older. Simply, they are his age, because they started out with him. In turn, the fact that they are close to him in age makes the troupe more democratic. "Nothing in this company is ever mandatory," says Tina Fehlandt, one of Morris's original dancers, "and when it is, I'm gone." Of course, some things, if not mandatory, are strongly recommended, and the troupe today is not as democratic as when they were starting out. Still, the feeling of fellowship is strong.

Morris has kept the group cohesive by being very loyal—he rarely lets a dancer go—and very nepotistic. More than half the administrative staff were hired from among boyfriends of people already with the company. He also promotes from within. The troupe's performance pianist, Linda Dowdell, began as their rehearsal pianist. "What has happened to me is really strange," Dowdell says. "I am not a world-class musician." And Morris prizes world-class musicians. But instead of hiring someone from the outside to play for his concerts, he pushed Dowdell along—an indication, as she puts it, of his "odd, unusual respect for the collectivity of which he is sort of in charge." Within two salary levels, based on seniority, all the dancers are paid the same, and many of them are to be found at the same bar after the show, with Morris at their center, ordering another round and keeping everybody up too late.

With this sense of equality comes a certain humility. In his troupe, Morris says, "you can't be that selfish, and you can't be that important, because you're just not. Neither am I. I'm just the boss of all these people who aren't really important, and neither am I." Again, his humility is not what it used to be, but it is still a philosophical conviction, and you can see it projected onstage: human bodies toiling, and toiling together.

That humility may have a darker side. Several of the older members of the troupe claim that Morris sees himself as ugly. This is not an uncommon emotion in the dance world. Having to go out night after night and show their bodies to large groups of strangers, many dancers are very sensitive about what they imagine to be their physical imperfections. (Cosmetic surgeons do a good business with ballet dancers.) And what others feel but do not say, Morris does say. He says that he felt ugly as a child. The fact that he has given himself so many grotesque roles suggests that he may also have felt ugly as an adult, a condition that, according to some of his dancers, he generalizes to them. "He wants to show off how odd we are," says Erin Matthiessen. "He sees himself as odd and broken."

But because this matter so closely touches their self-esteem, the dancers probably overstate the case. If Morris wanted to make the dancers look odd, he could do so, whereas they usually look immensely appealing. Matthiessen goes on to describe the situation more precisely:

In his choreography you cannot at all cover yourself up. He says, "Do this." Okay, I do that. And when I do, the whole world is seeing something about me that I don't know what it is, but if I did, I would try to hide it. I want the world to see beautiful lines and all the training I've been through. He doesn't want to see that at all. He wants to see what's uniquely me. So the thing about working with Mark is that you always feel exposed, vulnerable, as if you had said something you shouldn't have. You feel kind of embarrassed afterwards, and not knowing what really happened. People come up to you and say you were fabulous, and you don't know what they're talking about.

What Morris is intent on is not ugliness but, again, exposure and struggle. According to Jon Mensinger, he conducts auditions on the same principle, looking for people who seem somewhat awkward or unconfident: "If there isn't something about them that's a little vulnerable, they don't have a chance." We have seen the same principle in his casting: those for whom the dance being rehearsed is a natural are the ones who won't get to do it.

For Morris, a look of mastery, of taken-for-granted achievement, is the face of false pride. "I hate, more than anything, people dancing *at* me—dancing in my face . . ." he told an interviewer in 1992. "Like, 'Watch me. I can do this and *you* can't.'" Indeed, he associates this look with falseness in general. "What Mark talked about from the very beginning," says Donald Mouton, "was that what he hated in the dance world was that so much of it was fake—fake sentiment, fake sexuality, fake love." And what he talked about in the beginning he is still talking about. "The big thing," he told a critic in 1989, "is not to tell lies . . . I can tell in shows when other choreographers, pieces, dancers, audiences are lying. I can tell it in my own dancers. And in myself." According to Keith Sabado, one of Morris's most frequent corrections in rehearsal is "You're *fa*-king!"

This phobic sensitivity to falseness may have something to do with being homosexual and thus having had to operate in false situations. (Part of the reason he left the Eliot Feld troupe and got out of ballet, he has said, was that he "got tired of pretending to be a straight guy in love with a ballerina.") Presumably, it also has something to do with his family— both with their high moral standards, of which this is a carryover, and with their unremitting kindness, against which this is a reaction. And of course it has to do with the times in which he grew up, the sixties and seventies. Both Morris and his company—or its older members, the ones who started out with him—show many of the incidental manners of the sixties youth culture. They are warm, informal, down-to-earth, anti-genteel. They swim nude. They talk about their bodily functions. They tell you things they shouldn't, or not if you're a journalist.

Morris's own indiscretion with the press is legendary. During his first months in Brussels, when his appointment at the royal theater was already a matter of controversy—in other words, when it would have behooved him to watch himself—the Belgian Queen, as noted, attended one of the company's performances. Morris was invited to meet her after the show. Later he joined his fellow dancers in a bar, and they asked him how his audience with the Queen had gone. "Terrific," he said. "Best blow job I ever had." These words were spoken in front of a reporter, who included them in the article he was writing about Morris. They were promptly removed by his editor, but many other Morris *bons mots* have made it into print. In all the interviews I have had with Morris he has never once told me anything off the record—that is, not to be quoted with his name next to it. On one occasion he declined to answer a question. ("I'm not going to tell you about that, because I don't want my mother to read about it in a book.") Otherwise, he seems to have assumed that if something was true, he could say it. He also assumes that his jokes will be taken in a good spirit—an insistent naïveté reminiscent of the sixties.

But the sixties connection goes only so far. Whatever his horror of falseness, Morris does not base his work on any claim to a restorative "trueness," nor does he offer the kind of woolly naturalism that in the art of the sixties (and later) was so often put forward as the alternative to the fraudulence of bourgeois life. Asked about the effortfulness of his style of dancing, he answers, "It's not effortfulness. It's non-effortlessness . . . I'm not stating the opposite of something else, like, 'Here, check this out, it isn't conventional beauty.' The thing I'm making, I think it's beautiful. I'm not doing an 'anti' anything.''

The exposed look of the body on his stage might look like an ''anti'' something, and in some of the early dances it probably was, at least in part. *Gloria*, which has ten dancers in gray street clothes dragging themselves across the floor on their stomachs to Vivaldi's exalted Gloria in D, has something in common with Jerome Robbins's *Dances at a Gathering* and Paul Taylor's *Esplanade*, those benchmark works of the sixties/seventies youth cult, with their gangs of fresh-faced young folk skipping and running and falling to the accompaniment of sanctified high-art music. Like them, *Gloria* shows a certain Franciscanism, an exaltation of what is plain and openhearted and innocent, as opposed to what is fancy and fake.

But despite this moral balm, most of Morris's work is free of sentimentality and also of naturalism. However natural the dancers' bodies may look, what they are doing is not natural. Leaving aside the extreme complication of the patterns they are making—the structure of the choreography, all of it pinned to the structural complications of the score—the steps themselves, plain though they may look, are highly artificial, ''made up.'' People do not naturally fall onto their stomachs and drag themselves across the floor by their arms, let alone do this in a line of seven, in canon. Weight, exposure, struggle: all of these, in Morris's work, are carried far beyond what is normal. They are artistic strategies. For Morris, they give the dance its vividness and edge, its sheer specificity—this image, no other—and hence its symbolic force.

In 1987 Morris created a piece called *Strict Songs*, to a score by Lou Harrison that involved a large chorus singing adaptations of Hopi chants. *Strict Songs* is a hymn to the holiness of the world—the chorus sings of the deer on the mountains, the fantail goldfish, the falling stars—and it is full of dancers dressed in brown, green, and blue (for earth, plants, and sky) skimming across the stage. At the same time, it is clearly about death, and images of pain and struggle are interspersed among the more ecstatic moves. In the last moment of the piece, those two strands come together in a culminating image. Five couples (the full cast) are onstage. In each couple, one person lies down on the floor on his back, and the other person, placing the first person's feet against his stomach, launches himself into the air, where he levitates, balanced atop the first person's legs, as the curtain comes down.

This is a hellishly difficult maneuver. For the second person—the "flier"—not to fall, the feet must be placed exactly right on the abdomen, and the takeoff into the air must be done with exactly the right thrust. We watch the dancers going through all this with immense care and deliberation. But then, once fliers are launched, we are shown an amazing sight: five people floating in the air. They have died and gone to heaven. At the same time, in the effort they have gone through—some of them are still trembling as they float there—we see how hard it is to die, how hard to get to heaven. Or rather, we feel it, in the body, because it is the body's struggle that we have witnessed.

This is merely an extreme case of what goes on in all of Morris's choreography. The quality of the body's effort has changed as the work has developed. In the early dances there is more fumbling, more awkwardness, and also more sweeping, more emotionalism. In the later dances, the body is neater, more exact in its action. But in all of them the facts of the body are made very clear. This is partly because Morris loves those facts and partly because they accord with his idea of truth. But above all it is because he needs the full force of the body in order to show the force of the soul. Only in the body's resistance to its intention—the fact that the thighbone can only rotate so far in the hip socket, the fact that it is almost impossible to balance a 130-pound body horizontally in the air on somebody's feet, the fact that whatever you are trying to do up or out, your body is at the same time pulling you in and down—can he outline starkly enough that intention: somebody trying to *do* something.

Insofar as he is interested in ugliness and toil, it is for the same reason.

What he is really after is beauty and mastery, but he wants them exactly at the moment when they come into being—when they emerge from what was not beautiful or mastered—so that we can see them clearly. There are many, many ways for a dancer to get into the air, and most of them are designed to look easy. By making the dancers of *Strict Songs* struggle to get in the air, Morris catches that action in the moment of its birth; we see something appear that wasn't there a moment ago. The sheer unexpectedness of that event gives it a miraculous character or, rather, reveals its miraculous character. The dance is launched into metaphor, and what were dancers become angels.

LOVE AND SEX

If Morris in his early years was often described as provocative—the bad boy of modern dance—one of the main reasons was his violation of common notions of masculine and feminine: to begin with, his violation of the rule that a couple must be a man and a woman. Choreographers before Morris had shown us female-female partnering—it was a staple of French nineteenth-century ballet—and also male-male partnering, which is considered far more daring. But Morris in his early dances carried this sort of thing much further, made it a sort of program. In the opening section of his 1984 *My Party* four couples dance side by side—one FF, one MM, one FM, one MF—and that is the message: no rules, free choice. In *New Love Song Waltzes* the thing that made the partner-swapping scene so surprising and funny to the audience was not just that the dancers crawled in and out of various pairs of arms but that they did so without regard to the sex of the other person. A woman disentangled herself from the embrace of a man and fell into the arms of a woman, et cetera. No problem.

But the issue was not just what men and women could do in love; it was what they could do in general. Far more meaningful polemically than the partner-swapping scene in *New Love Song Waltzes* is a scene that comes immediately afterward. A woman is carried in, in a lyrical posture. She surrenders her weight completely to the man holding her; she gazes

upward, into the beyond. Typical woman: physically fragile, spiritually powerful. And a few measures later, a man is carried in, in the same posture, also by a man. It is a lesson.

In the two years following *New Love Song Waltzes*, 1983 and 1984, Morris reiterated the lesson again and again. In *Dogtown* (1983) it was the women's turn to act like men: to be doggy and rough. At one point in this dance, a woman casually picked up a man and tossed him to the floor, where he landed with a crunch. In *Championship Wrestling*, made the following year, there was a hilariously ferocious slow-motion punch-out in which the combatants were two women, the two daintiest women in the troupe. As has been pointed out, however, the women in the early troupe were not notably dainty, and part of the reason for this, and for the smallness of the men, was so that Morris could do gender-bending maneuvers: place the men in lifts, have the women throw the men. "My guys are articulate," he said later, "and my gals are brutish. And they're both both. They can all do everything."

New Love Song
Waltzes Left to right:
Jean-Guillaume Weis,
Megan Williams, Alyce
Bochette
(Klaus Lefebvre)

91

What he wanted was to extend the range of expressiveness for both sexes. In the traditional way of dancing, as he described it in a 1987 interview with Tobias Schneebaum, "the bassoon and the French horns and the timpani come on and the men run around and pretend they are fighting one another. Then the flutes and the oboes and violins come on, and the women cooperate perfectly . . . That's the choreographic way." The men's range, in particular, seemed to him narrow: "In rehearsal I say to women, 'Act like a sixty-five-year-old man.' And they can. I tell straight men, 'Now dance like a thirteen-year-old girl.' They're embarrassed." "Women have a richer and more varied emotional life than men," he has said elsewhere. He wanted to see if men couldn't have it too.

Above all, he wanted it for himself. Morris has repeatedly made solos for himself that border on or invade female territory. *Ten Suggestions*, the 1981 solo in the pink pajamas, was an appropriation of a female privilege. It was women—Isadora Duncan, Doris Humphrey—who, in the early days of modern dance, had done the sort of tender, introspective, my-soul-responds-to-music solos that inspired *Ten Suggestions*. The year after *Ten Suggestions* Morris made *jr high*, the dance in which he looked for breasts on his big chest and inspected his fingernails as if checking a manicure. This was a piece about growing up homosexual. *Ten Suggestions* was about growing up to be a dancer, including the female half (or, in the last two centuries, the female nine-tenths) of that realm: discovering emotions in oneself, treating them with respect, responding to pretty things—a ribbon, a hoop, music—and relating them to one's inner life.

But by 1983, reflections on growing up had been burned away, and in *Deck of Cards* he gave himself a forthrightly androgynous role. To a country-western song, "Say It's Not You," the lament of a man whose girlfriend is cheating on him, Morris comes out in an orange dress and pumps and does a dance full of swirling, sweeping moves—female

Morris in *Deck of Cards* (Tom Brazil)

moves—at the same time that, with his hands, he is miming the *man's* feelings, the words of the man's song. In other words, he is both the man and the woman, and not just in his dance but in his body too: again and again, as he turns, the dress unfurls to show us Morris's big hairy legs, a man's legs.

This is not a drag act. Most drag acts, by dint of their energetic but always imperfect imitation of one sex by the other, reaffirm the separation between the sexes. The point of a drag act is that you can still tell the difference: gender is permanent, immovable. Morris, however, is not trying to conceal the difference. He is saying that the two can exist in one body. (Remember *Dad's Charts*, where father and son coexisted in one body.) At the end, just before he exits, he covers his face: the man's grief, the woman's shame. Choreographically, it's a simple solo—sketchy, even—but it is the most aggressive statement Morris has made about sexual difference. It's also more profound than that. It seems to point to the instability, the doubleness, of all things: how minds can possess each other, how the betrayed can secretly sympathize with the betrayer. It is a frightening little dance, partly because it takes on such a large subject in such simple terms.

Since he has so little faith in conventional notions of masculine and feminine, it is not surprising that Morris shows little romanticism on the subject of sex. Here is Schneebaum questioning him:

What do you think is the essence of sexual feeling? What is it that you seek in sex?

I don't have a lot of sex. [Sex is] hormones, probably like rutting . . . It's like a mandrill's genitals turning red. People go into heat, and that's wonderful, but it's not love.

And since it's not love, he shows it to us with no mists, no veils. When there is a sex scene in one of his dances, usually what happens is that two people frankly take to the floor, one on top of the other. To complete the demystification, this is usually done in groups, to the music, like any other step. Cruder sex is treated in the same way, just more crudely. In *Dogtown* the dancers move along on all fours, strictly to the beat, and when they bump into somebody else's behind, they mount and dismount, also to the beat. In *Lovey* the dancers perform a whole inventory of proscribed sexual acts, but they do it with plastic baby dolls and in unison,

or sometimes in canon. This does not leave much to inflame the mind.

Probably the furthest Morris ever went in the demystification of sex was his 1986 *Striptease*, based on Roland Barthes's 1955 essay of the same name. The point of Barthes's essay is that stripping de-eroticizes—that it is a form of bourgeois self-deception. The point of Morris's dance is also that stripping de-eroticizes, but his focus is less on social hypocrisy than on human vulnerability. The piece has a cast of eight, all stripper types —the bride, the cowboy, the construction worker, the girl in leather. First they process one by one down the middle of the stage, trying to pique our interest with their "theme" accessories. The construction worker unscrolls his tape measure at his crotch. The leather girl gives her motorcycle helmet a lusty slap. The cowboy sucks his gun. But somehow these allurements are a little off. Indeed, they are very funny. Furthermore, once they are over with, the strippers have little to do except strip, and as usual

Rob Besserer in *Striptease*. In background, left to right: Donald Mouton, Tina Fehlandt, Ruth Davidson, Morris (Tom Brazil)

in such routines, the flow of fantasy is repeatedly disrupted by the mechanics of clothes removal. One man, trying to get his trousers off, stumbles over his pants legs. A woman hobbles around with one shoe off and one shoe on.

Eventually, however, they manage to get their clothes off, and now the dance resolves itself into a group walkaround. The dancers traipse around the stage in a circle, adding whatever little bumps and grinds they can in order to keep up the spirit now that, with their clothes, their alluring identities have been shed. (The nadir is reached when one man—it is Morris—launches into the twist, so that his penis flops back and forth forlornly.) But of course, to have them walk around like this—naked, in a circle, like a livestock sale—is very nerve-racking. "That dance is extremely uncomfortable, to do and to watch," says Teri Weksler (the bride in later performances). Once it is finished, their act is over, but not the piece. In a final stroke of reality, the dancers go around the stage, stark naked, and pick up their discarded clothes. Then they leave, their belts and veils dragging behind them. As they do this, they look sort of sweet; they have the natural chastity of nakedness, the thing Barthes stressed in his essay. But they also look like plucked chickens. You want to lend them your jacket.

Striptease, then, is about the gap between fantasy and reality in erotic life: the hugeness and extravagance of our imaginings, the smallness and innocence of the vessel into which we pour them—the body. But the critical point of Morris's dance (unlike Barthes's essay) is that the fantasy is the *strippers'*. They believe in their acts, dress them in the best outfit they have, perform them with enthusiasm. And the acts don't work. Indeed, they are hopeless. The closer the strippers bring us to the imagined prize, the more it is not that prize but just a little naked body. The effect is comic, but it is also tender, and embarrassing too. The same is true of the sex scenes in Morris's other dances. They don't look lurid. On the contrary, what impresses you is simply the fact of exposure: the fleshy insides of the women's legs, their colored panties. It's like watching children play doctor.

So the attitude toward sex, though demystifying, is not necessarily reductive. It is just not romantic. The place of romance is taken by other emotions. Tenderness is one; tragic feeling is another. Of all Morris's works, the one that is most blunt sexually is his *Dido and Aeneas*, set to Purcell's 1689 opera, which in turn was based on Virgil's famous tale of Aeneas' dalliance with the Queen of Carthage on his way to Italy. (In

*Opposite:
Dido (Morris) "press'd
with torment," Dido
and Aeneas
(Tom Brazil)*

Morris's version of the opera, the singers are placed in the pit or to the side of the stage. The stage is given over to the dancing.) Purcell's libretto, written by the poet Nahum Tate, is notably chaste, for the opera was written to be performed by a girls' school. Dido's passion for Aeneas, which even the pure-minded Virgil described in terms of fire and arrows, is spoken of merely as pity for his hardships. As for the consummation of that passion, it is not only never seen; it is barely referred to.

Morris reverses this trend, creating a profoundly sexual dance. Since Dido is a queen, Morris's choreography for her and her court is very stylized—angular, hieratic, as if it were taken from some ancient court tradition—yet even these emphatically noble dances are forthright about sex. When Purcell's Dido, in her first aria, sings of being "press'd with torment," Morris's Dido places one hand on her breast and one on her abdomen, both pointing downward, and slowly opens her legs. She tells us where it hurts—not just in the heart. Later in Act I, when she accepts Aeneas' love suit, she again opens her legs. We know what is coming.

And in Morris's version it comes. At the opening of Act II, scene 2, when the court has gone to the woods to hunt, Dido and Aeneas stand alone at the back of the darkened stage. Aeneas is gazing out at the Mediterranean. (The sea is painted on Robert Bordo's beautiful backdrop.) Dido lies down on the floor and pulls him toward her. He lies down on top of her, has one brief spasm, and then gets up again and resumes gazing at the sea. There it is, in miniature—the whole story: her love, his destiny, her abandonment. And there is the consummation, at the exact center of the opera.

Soon after the consummation, Aeneas sings, tellingly, of his success in the hunt: "Behold, upon my bending spear / A monster's head stands bleeding." These are the most sexually frank lines in Tate's libretto—a clear announcement, albeit cloaked in metaphor, of Dido's coming death and of the cause (Aeneas' "spear"). But Morris goes further, dropping the metaphor. In the dance Aeneas, instead of holding up a spear, holds open his tunic. The gesture is not indecent. His back is to us, and the courtiers avert their eyes. The only one who sees what Aeneas is showing is Dido. She stares at it with stony dignity, as if she were gazing at her death, which she is. The weaving of forthright sexual meaning into dancing of monumental gravity continues to the very end of the piece. In the final scene, when Purcell's Dido sings that she is forsaken, Morris's Dido slaps the insides of her thighs—an unequivocal gesture. Even in the moment of death, we are not allowed to forget that sex was the cause.

Dido is not the only heroine of this opera. Playing opposite her is the
Sorceress, who hates the Queen and engineers her ruin. (She appears to
Aeneas in the guise of Mercury and tells him that, by Jove's command,
he must leave for Italy. Once he leaves, Dido dies.) The Sorceress is an
anti-Dido—as much as Dido is simply good and noble, so much is the
Sorceress simply evil and base—and she has an anti-court, her coven of
witches. The parallel is clear enough in Purcell's opera, but in the dance
Morris makes it clearer by having the same dancer, in the same costume,
play both Dido and the Sorceress, and by using the same ensemble (again
in the same costumes) for both the courtiers and the witches.

The dancing at the two courts could not be more different, however.
If the courtiers' dances look like a moving hieroglyph, the witches' dances
look like a fight in a bar. The treatment of sex differs accordingly. Where
the courtiers give us noble and contained expressions of sexual feeling,
the witches are exuberantly, hilariously obscene. In the famous "Ho, ho"
chorus, where they celebrate Dido's coming death, the singers sing:

> *Destruction's our delight,*
> *Delight our greatest sorrow!*
> *Elissa [Dido] dies tonight,*
> *And Carthage flames tomorrow. Ho, ho!*

Miming the words "Elissa dies tonight," the Sorceress pulls an invisible sword straight up from her crotch to her gullet. In one stroke she goes from sex to death. She follows this with a kind of flip of the hand at her abdomen, like guts falling out. It could not be more coarse. Then, as the other witches imitate her, she lies down at the front of the stage to watch them, and, while watching, she quite noticeably masturbates, to orgasm. (To my knowledge, the U.S. premiere of *Dido*, in 1989, was the first time female masturbation was openly portrayed in mainstream American dance.) When she is finished, she wipes her finger on her skirt. It is a startling moment, and not just because somebody is masturbating onstage but because it shows, with no mitigation, the connection between sex and death that is at the heart of Dido's story. This is the same crotch Dido was pointing to in Act I. This is what she was talking about: sexual passion. And the point the witches are making here in their dirty little mime-dance—the point of most seventeenth-century tragic drama, that passion can lead to death—is borne home in reality in the very next scene, when Aeneas leaves and Dido dies.

The two scenes, in fact, are the same scene—they tell the same story, first comically, then tragically—just as Dido and the Sorceress are the same woman, the noble and ignoble sides of the human mind. This connection is what Morris stresses by stressing the story's sexual meaning. By adding obscenity to the witches' violence and thus linking their violence to Dido's passion, he gives tragic force to evil, shows that it is not something outside us but something within us. And by bringing out the sexual side of Dido's struggle, he makes that struggle more wrenching. There is no image in the dance more poignant than Dido's "press'd with torment" gesture, at once so sexual and so regal, so composed, so handsomely designed. To be a queen is one thing; to remain a queen in such circumstances is another. Conversely, Dido's queenliness dignifies sex. Seeing it in her, we see that it is not just the black joke the witches make of it (though it is that too) but a monumental human fact, a crucible of the soul. This meaning is not there on the surface of Tate's script—as befits a girls' school play, the libretto is more assured on the subject of how unmarried women should treat men's advances—but it is there in the music, and it is the reason this opera has lasted. Morris has simply underlined the meaning, creating what is essentially a tragedy of sex, akin to *Othello* or *Phèdre*.

Dido is a recent work. It was made in Brussels, in 1989, and it signals a change in Morris's treatment of sex. Where before his attitude was anti-romantic, ironic, now it is more respectful. The iconoclastic impulse, the need to show us the distance between the fantasy and the reality, is gone. The view is tragic.

There has been a corresponding change in his handling of masculinity and femininity. Since 1984, there have been fewer lessons in how women can act like men and men like women. Or rather, the lesson has been absorbed into a larger impulse. The prime example is *Dido and Aeneas*. It was Morris who played Dido and the Sorceress: the largest and greatest role of his career. In it he does not show himself to us as a double exposure of male and female, as he did in *Deck of Cards*. Instead, he is unequivocally a man—he wears no dress, just a black tunic like everyone else in the cast—playing what is unequivocally a woman. In part, his masculinity serves the portrait of femininity. To Dido his big male body gives the quality of monumentality that is so essential to her pathos. As for the Sorceress, here he uses his masculine qualities—his size and his truculence—to make her truly bawd-like: coarse, violent, hilarious. Still, we never forget that this is a man, and the fact is critical. The violation of sexual identity depersonalizes the portrait, just as masks presumably did in Attic tragedy. This, and not just Morris's size, is what gives Dido her grand, marmoreal character. Raised above the wall of gender, she becomes almost abstract. In the words of a Belgian critic, Thierry Lassence, "What is put before us is not so much the image of Dido as the idea of love itself . . . Love [in *Dido*] is neither feminine nor masculine. It simply is." Nevertheless, it is still *strange* to see a man play a woman, and therefore this love comes before us with a new strangeness: a pungency, a pointedness, something that makes us hold our breath. So what was once, in Morris's work, a question—can a person be both a man and a woman?—becomes in *Dido* a poetic strategy. Psychology and politics have become art.

This can be seen in other recent work as well. Morris's attitude toward love and sex is simply more relaxed. For instance, he has finally created drag acts. *The Hard Nut*, his *Nutcracker*, contains several superb travesty roles. But like most modern travesty roles, they are based on an acceptance of the difference between male and female, and they are played for comic and virtuoso effects. In other recent pieces, he shows more directly an acceptance of differences between masculine and feminine. In his full-evening dance *L'Allegro, il Penseroso ed il Moderato*, which he made immediately before *Dido*, there is a flat-out boys-will-be-boys number, in which the twelve men of *L'Allegro*'s cast do a circle dance that is repeatedly interrupted by their socking each other in the face. The dance is a satire—it is known within the company as the "stupid men's dance"—but it is not on the warpath. It is funny and forgiving. Furthermore, it is followed by a matching number, a circle dance for *L'Allegro*'s twelve women, that is one of the loveliest things in *L'Allegro*, and central to the work's meaning, but based on a wholly traditional view of femininity. The women, in chiffon gowns, move slowly in a ring, as if around an altar. They are nymphs, priestesses. In any case, they are the eternal feminine, and the feminine as we know it from the dances of Isadora Duncan, Ruth St. Denis, and Doris Humphrey—the soulful sisterhood of early modern dance.

L'Allegro's two circle dances are in fact an exact embodiment of what Morris, in that 1987 interview, told Tobias Schneebaum was the "choreographic way," where the men run around and fight and then the women come out and cooperate. (Ironically, he may have already had the two dances in mind when he made this remark. *L'Allegro* was not premiered until late 1988, but he began planning it long before.) In keeping with this traditionalism, same-sex couples are rare in *L'Allegro*. This does not mean that Morris has abandoned his effort to broaden the expressive range of men and women. You can see it in *L'Allegro* in the picky delicacy with which a man portrays a lark and in the iron-thighed vigor of the female nymphs and goddesses—a sort of second-stage feminism. Nevertheless, his attitude is newly open, magnanimous.

There is a limit to his openness, though, and beyond that limit lies the *pas de deux*. In Western theatrical dance of the last two centuries, the male-female duet has been the fundamental unit of dance structure and meaning. The moment when the man and the woman dance together: this is what all the other parts of the dance lead up to or away from, and it is the idea on which ballet technique has built itself. (The development of point work was dependent on the assumption that a man would be there to support the woman as she stood on her unstable points.) When modern dance arose at the turn of the century, it was far less duet-oriented. Isadora Duncan and Ruth St. Denis were basically soloists; Martha Graham didn't have a man in her company until it was ten years old. But eventually modern dance too became increasingly organized around the *pas de deux*. For years, this has been the traditional center of concert dance, as of social dance, and Morris is not particularly interested in it.

Since the founding of his company in 1980, he has put more than eighty dances before the public. Of these, only two, *One Charming Night* (1985) and *Beautiful Day* (1992), are *pas de deux* in the strict sense: a man and a woman doing a dance that involves partnering. This is a remarkable fact, but less important than the status of the *pas de deux* in his group works, for that is how most choreographers feature the *pas de deux*—not in dances with a cast of two, but in larger dances of which the *pas de deux* is the hub. In Morris's group works the *pas de deux* is not only not the hub; it seems to be the last thing he considers. In most of his group works, it is absent altogether, a fact all the more striking when, as in *New Love Song Waltzes* and *Love Song Waltzes*, romantic love is the *subject* of the dance, or at least the subject of the song the dance is being done to, a matter that Morris almost never ignores. (The lack of partnered duets in *New Love Song Waltzes* and *Love Song Waltzes* is all the more noticeable by comparison with Balanchine's famous *Liebeslieder Walzer*, which is set to the same music and is practically all *pas de deux*, including some of Balanchine's most rapt and profound essays in that genre. Morris had not seen *Liebeslieder Walzer* when he choreographed *New Love Song Waltzes* in 1982, but he saw it before he made *Love Song Waltzes* in 1989.) Elsewhere, he will introduce couple dancing but then shift the focus. Either he will have more than one couple doing the duet simultaneously, thus blocking our romantic identification, or the duet will break off into another form.

The most memorable example is the *grand pas de deux* in *The Hard Nut*. *The Hard Nut* is, at least in part, a classical ballet, and it is a story of love—two reasons to expect a *pas de deux*. Furthermore, the *pas de deux* is written into Tchaikovsky's score, in its classical Russian form: an introduction, an adagio, two variations, and a coda—a formula specifically designed by the Russian ballet masters to give us an anatomy of love. (Adagio, with partnering: man and woman need each other. Solo variations: man and woman are two different things. Coda, with partnering again: all the more reason they need each other.) Finally, this is one of the most famous *pas de deux* numbers in ballet history. Everyone knows the music and knows that it is supposed to be a *pas de deux*. In sum, Morris could hardly have avoided giving us a *pas de deux* at this point, and he did give us one, but with a difference.

First of all, the adagio is performed by the couple *with* the ensemble, as a sort of collective duenna. There are lifts, the way there are supposed to be in an adagio, but the man does not lift the woman; they are *both* lifted, by the ensemble. For the variations, the ensemble finally goes away, and the man and the woman do their separate solos. But then, when it is time for them to dance together again in the coda, they don't. They exit, and the ensemble performs the coda, not forgetting, however, to do the virtuoso steps that are normally given to the man and the woman in the coda. (This is where we get the mass *pirouettes à la seconde*.) On the last stroke of the music comes the last stroke of irony. The coda of a *grand pas de deux* often ends in a spectacular display step, two of the most common being the shoulder sit (the woman jumps up and sits on the man's shoulder) and the "fish" (the woman dives to the floor in an arc, like a fish, and the man catches her and holds her in the air). Morris, to conclude his *grand pas de deux*, gives us *both* the shoulder sit and the fish. Six couples from the ensemble do shoulder sits, and in front of them, six other couples from the ensemble do the fish. Meanwhile, the lead couple, the people who should have been doing these steps, are nowhere in sight. As Erin Matthiessen commented, the dance is "a *pas de deux*, all right—a *pas de deux* for twenty-four people."

––––––

In seeking reasons for Morris's special treatment of sex and sexuality, it is tempting to point immediately to the fact that he is homosexual, and many writers have pointed to it, as sufficient cause, or at least have concentrated heavily on the supposed "androgyny" of his work. Actually, there are other important reasons—for one thing, his unusual dance training. While the *pas de deux* may be central to most Western traditions of theatrical dance, it is not central to the two traditions in which he was most intensively trained, flamenco and Balkan folk dance. Flamenco is fundamentally a solo form, Balkan dance a group form, and Morris's work, which stresses solo and especially group work, can be seen as an overlay of the two—forget homosexuality.

A second important factor is his age. In his generation, not just homosexual choreographers but many heterosexual choreographers have gone in for gender-testing dances, with men being lifted by women and people of the same sex partnering each other, and also for unisex dances, with no differentiation between men and women. And in this they were preceded by the generation before them, by choreographers like Laura Dean and Lucinda Childs, whose unisex group works Morris admired greatly as a young man. Indeed, this was a trend from the sixties, but by the seventies and the eighties, with the women's movement and the gay-rights movement, it was not just a trend; it was almost a habit. While the *pas de deux* may be the traditional center of Western concert dance, that tradition has been almost wholly breached in recent experimental dance. What Morris has done in this regard is by no means unique.

Still, he has gone further. Nobody else has had his dancers mount each other like dogs. Nobody else has choreographed a slugfest for women. And while others may have eliminated the *pas de deux*, no one else has created an ironic reversal on the scale of the *Hard Nut grand pas de deux*. Morris's questioning of traditional images of sex and love has been extraordinarily stubborn, extreme, sustained. For this, homosexuality was certainly a cause, but it was only an early cause, the cause of other causes, which, by a circuitous route that can only partly be mapped, resulted in *his* specific work.

To begin with, his homosexuality presumably won him to the idea of range. Having discovered masculine and feminine aspects of himself, he must have imagined that everyone had more aspects than gender could explain. That, after all, is the message of his gender-breaching: not that everybody should be homosexual, but that most people have larger inner lives than sexual definitions will allow them to draw upon. Likewise, the experience of avowing homosexuality was no doubt an important source of his devotion to truth-telling, but the truths he ended up telling—that there is a doggy side to love, that there is a big difference between sexual fantasy and sex—are certainly not confined to homosexual feeling.

His avoidance of the romantic *pas de deux* follows the same pattern: simple cause, complicated result. It is not as though, having no interest in male-female romance, he also avoided male-male romance in order not to offend bourgeois audiences and thereby left his work with a gaping hole where this essential interest should be. To begin with, he has no problem about offending bourgeois audiences. Considering that he has shown us a witch masturbating, it is unlikely that he is suppressing a wish to create male love duets. No, if homosexuality was the cause, what it turned him away from was not just the heterosexual duet but the romantic duet, and the whole romantic formula: the idea that the coming together of two individuals is a crucial symbol of life's meaning.

It is safe to say that in his youth Morris dreamed of falling in love with one person and living happily ever after. It would be hard to grow up in our culture without entertaining this dream, and it is likely that when he found Erin Matthiessen he thought he had achieved it. But his idea of love was stamped, very early on, by his experience in Koleda, and that experience was not about couples living happily ever after. Remember his words: "I fell in love with the group. I fell in love with several individuals in sequence, and they fell in love with each other." And that is exactly the situation that is portrayed in the first dance he made about love, *New Love Song Waltzes* (created, incidentally, while he was living with Matthiessen and long before their breakup). All the while that the songs are proclaiming the singer's passion for the one true love, the dance is proclaiming that there is no one true love. It is not for nothing that the audience laughs in the partner-swapping scene. While the singer is singing of the soft grasses where one can lie down with one's sweetheart, each of the dancers is lying down with nine sweethearts. The view of love is already distanced, skeptical, and full of tragic potential.

Morris's later treatments of love and sex constitute a kind of arc in the fulfillment of that potential. *Dogtown*, made the year after *New Love Song Waltzes*, is a sort of flip side of *New Love Song Waltzes*—the same truth, minus the sweetness. Here we are shown that dogs do the same thing: go from one to the next, mount and dismount. Though *Dogtown* is brutal, it is still cheerful. But soon after, in 1985, when he and Matthiessen separated, comes a year of wrath. In 1985 Morris made *Jealousy, Lovey*, and *One Charming Night*. *Jealousy* is a virtuoso solo for Morris, a monumental and poisonous dance in which he wrenches himself into tortured shapes while his arms twist around his body like snakes—a flat-out portrait of erotic jealousy. (The music is the "Jealousy" chorus from Handel's opera *Hercules*.) *Lovey* goes further. A suite of five dances to songs by the Violent Femmes, it is Morris's most notorious, most scabrous work. The song for the central section, "Country Death Song," tells the story of a man who takes his young daughter out to the mountain, throws her down a well, and then hangs himself. The Violent Femmes are a postpunk rock group, and their tale is unalleviated by liberal feeling. (We do not hear that the man's unemployment insurance had run out.) It chugs along like a regular ballad, but instead of being about a man wrecking his pickup or cheating on his wife, it is about a man murdering his child. The dance, likewise, does nothing to cushion the shock. It bluntly acts out the events—indeed, makes them blunter by using comedy, or at least stereotype. The father wears boxer shorts; the mother crosses herself; all the characters perform broad, simple, exaggerated gestures that look like something out of a TV cartoon: infanticide *à la Batman*. And the conjunction of these two elements—the cartoonish and the unspeakable—makes for a kind of blank, staring evil that is really unique. Furthermore, this central dance is flanked by dances in which the characters from

Lovey. The father
(Keith Sabado) throws
his daughter (Tina Feh-
landt) down the well
(Jennifer Thienes)
(Tom Brazil)

"Country Death Song" manipulate little plastic baby dolls in ways that
are thoroughly obscene—all orifices, all ways. Everything is fevered,
squalid, cruddy. This is sin utterly devoid of glamour.

Morris got the idea for *Lovey* from watching his niece Amanda, Marianne's daughter, play with her doll—kiss it, feed it, love it, yell at it, hit
it, kiss it, feed it. From watching Amanda and Lovey (for that was the
doll's name), it was not a long jump to imagining how far love could go,
in how many directions of rage and desire, when turned on an object that
could not protest, or when it had no object at all, when the person was
utterly bereft. (These are dolls, after all, not human beings.) Often, when
Lovey is performed, you can hear labored breathing in the audience during
pauses in the music. It is a truly shocking dance. I have heard it condemned
as a social menace—the use of the dolls, wrote a Seattle critic, "should
set the anti-child-porn movement back 10 years"—and I have heard it

defended as a protest against social ills. It is neither. It is a portrait of complete erotic despair. In its firm knowledge of how love can be turned to evil and in its sheer, unshaded grasp of evil, it is like an Old Testament story, or some medieval church portal showing souls being snatched down to hell by grinning devils.

One Charming Night, the third love dance that Morris made in 1985, is less terrible but more insidious. It shows a young girl—Morris has said that he imagines her as being eight years old—in a room. She is obviously waiting for someone to arrive. He arrives: Mark Morris, in a dark suit and red eye shadow and doing a very strange dance—elegant, too elegant, its big, sweeping, flying moves punctuated with tiny, fastidious hops and with *gargouillades*, a very special ballet step in which the dancer leaps into the air, pulls up both legs, and then shakes them out in a delicate little flickety-flack before landing. *Gargouillades* are usually done by a woman; to see them done, perfectly, by a large man in a business suit is odd. The girl is fascinated, but the minute she shows interest, the man seems to have a qualm. He starts to leave. She detains him. Finally, conquering his scruple, he sits down next to her, and as the singer launches into a praise of God—the dance is set to various Purcell songs—the man takes the girl in his arms, pulls her to him, and begins sucking her neck: a long, passionate suck. (We see him from behind, his back heaving with ardor.) Sated, he then rips open his cuff button, bites his own wrist to draw blood, and offers it to the girl to suck. She accepts. After this consummation, she pushes him away, has regrets, gets hysterical. He quiets her, whispers something in her ear, and hoists her gently on his back. She spreads her arms like wings, and together they fly away.

Here, at last, is a thoroughly romantic dance, with all the romantic conventions in place: the man's dangerous aspect, the woman's fear and attraction, his scruple, her conquering of his scruple, the consummation, her regret, his conquering of her regret, their elopement. It is the only full-fledged portrait of male-female passion that Morris has made, and it is about a vampire seducing a little girl.

After this exorcism, Morris did not make any important works about love for three years. Then in early 1989 he created *Dido and Aeneas*, in which all the poisons that had percolated in his mind in relation to love—demons and snakes, obscenity, cruelty, hilarity—were still there, but occupying only half of *Dido*'s world, the witches' half. The other half was Dido, his first genuinely noble portrait of a soul in love and his first tragic portrait of love's failure, and all of this created on his own body.

Opposite:
One Charming Night.
The girl (Teri Weksler)
sucks the blood of the
vampire (Morris)
(Beatriz Schiller)

If *Dido* shows that he had solved a problem about masculinity and femininity, it also shows that he had solved a problem about love. Four years had passed since his separation from Matthiessen. Presumably he was over it. He was over something else too. The role of Aeneas in *Dido* was danced by Guillermo Resto, the person Morris fell in love with in 1984, thus precipitating his breakup with Matthiessen. The passionate friendship between Morris and Resto had no easy resolution—Resto is heterosexual—but it lasted for a long time. Eventually it settled down into what was simply a close friendship. (The two men lived together during the three years in Brussels.) In 1987 Resto sustained a severe knee injury—he was hit by a bicyclist—and while recuperating, he was separated from the company for a year. When he rejoined them, in Brussels, Morris gave him the role of Aeneas as a welcome-back present. Presumably, that sorrow too had been laid to rest. These facts do not explain the creation of a work such as *Dido*, but they may help to account for its suremindedness, its tragic calm.

Since *Dido*, Morris has made several works about love, and they are calmer still. The most sublime of these is *Beautiful Day*. When it was premiered in 1992, *Beautiful Day* was Morris's first male-female *pas de deux* in seven years, since *One Charming Night*, but it has none of the romance or perversity of that piece. To the so-called Bell Cantata, "Schlage doch, gewünschte Stunde," traditionally attributed to J. S. Bach but probably by Georg-Melchior Hoffmann, the man and the woman do a quiet, almost businesslike dance, much of it on the floor. There are big moves, "emotional" moves—stretches, lifts—but they are executed in a plain, precise way. The woman will embrace the man's neck, or he will embrace her foot, and then, when the bell chimes in the orchestra—it sounds repeatedly (hence "Bell Cantata")—they will pull back their hands to echo the chime, but again with a kind of precision that forestalls any emotional climax. Were it not for the dance's intimate character, you would never guess it was a love duet. Whatever the two dancers are telling each other, they both already understand it, have for years.

The text of the Bell Cantata has to do not with romantic love but with divine love. *Schlage doch, gewünschte Stunde* means "Strike at last, you longed-for hour." (That is why the bell is chiming; it is striking the hour.) And the longed-for hour is the hour of death, when the singer will see God in the face. In the final moment of the dance, the man lifts the woman into the air—it is a low lift: again, no dramatics—and she lies back in peace, facing heaven. She is looking at God, and her friend has helped her.

None of Morris's other recent love dances is as exalted as this, but in all of them romantic love has resolved itself into something less romantic. *The Hard Nut* is of course about love—Marie finds love with her Nutcracker, just as in other *Nutcrackers*—but this is treated as puppy love, and aside from his pleasure in showing the brave Marie's triumph, Morris does not seem deeply engaged with it. As noted, he steals most of the *grand pas de deux* away from the couple and gives it to the ensemble. He allows the couple a long duet immediately afterward, but it is not a very interesting dance, and most of its best steps are openly copied from an earlier and far more moving *pas de deux* in *The Hard Nut*, a duet for the Nutcracker and his uncle, Drosselmeier. This latter dance, Morris's only sustained male-male *pas de deux*, is not a romantic number. Its character is heroic and tender; it is about family love and growing up. In any case, the fact that the most poignant duet in this boy-meets-girl ballet is a duet for the boy and his uncle—and that when the boy and girl are finally allowed to dance together, their steps (and so, by extension, their feelings) are borrowed from that earlier family-love dance—is a sign of something.

One can point to certain works in which Morris's lack of interest in romantic love may actually have been damaging. Of the five classical ballets that he has made for companies other than his own, only one— *Drink to Me Only with Thine Eyes*, from 1988—is on the level of his best modern-dance works. That may be because, uninterested in boy-girl love, he tends not to use partnering, which is one of classical ballet's fundamental modes of expression. To make a classical ballet without male-female partnering is like composing a piano sonata without using the black keys. Modern-dance technique, however, is not built on partnering. (As a form that stresses weight and freedom, modern dance might be said to *resist* partnering.) So by de-emphasizing partnering in his modern-dance works—that is, more than nine out of ten of his works—Morris was not quelling any of the form's built-in potential.

But the far more important point is this: that the absence of romantic love, that expectable and venerable outlet, made way in his imagination for the hatching of other ideas of love. What are these loves that he shows us? Dog love, vampire love, uncle love, angel love, doll love—they have no name, but they are all part of the psychology of love, as we know not just from the police blotter but from our own lives and from literature, and it is very interesting to see them in a dance.

The one love that Morris has concentrated on more than any other does have a name: community. The idea of the group as the fundamental unit of meaning in the dance was there in his work from the beginning. *Gloria*, made in 1981, is the story of a group emotion, the group standing for humankind. But as Morris's idea of love developed through the eighties, his sense of the group became more thought-out, more philosophical. This ensemble emphasis reaches a kind of apotheosis in a work that he made in 1989, immediately after *Dido*: *Love Song Waltzes*. *Love Song Waltzes* is a companion piece to *New Love Song Waltzes*. The two works are set to matching pieces of music, Brahms's *Liebeslieder* and *Neue Liebeslieder* respectively. They are costumed, cast, and structured similarly. Like *New Love Song Waltzes*, *Love Song Waltzes* has no sustained couple dances, but this time you don't miss them, for the tone of the dancing, and consequently the tone of love, is entirely different from that in the earlier work. In *New Love Song Waltzes* the reigning emotions were yearning and turmoil. The dancers reached out to one another in desperation. In *Love Song Waltzes* the dominant moods are tenderness and deliberateness. The dancers again reach out to one another, but in friendship.

The most moving section of *Love Song Waltzes* comes with the song "Nicht wandel." Here are the words:

> *Do not stray, dear love,*
> *In yonder flowery meadow;*
> *It is too wet, too yielding,*
> *For your tender feet.*

> *All flooded are the paths*
> *And tracks there,*
> *So profusely have my eyes*
> *There shed tears.*

On the stage, the dancers form a circle, with one man in the middle. He "strays," as in the song. Something seems to be calling him. He keeps trying to break out of the circle, but the dancers keep catching him and lifting him back into their midst. The tone is protective. "Don't go," they are saying. "Your place is here, with us." All along, for nearly ten years, Morris's dancers had been presented as a group. But in this piece they *mean* to be a group, and their interests are those of the group: kindness and work. They have a dance to do, and everybody belongs in it. In such a situation, the interests of the couple have no place. Nor is there any surviving fuss over masculine and feminine. There is same-sex partnering in *Love Song Waltzes*, but no attention is called to it.

One non-group concern does survive: the situation of the individual. At the end of *Love Song Waltzes* one man waltzes each of the other eleven dancers off the stage, one by one, until finally he is alone. He pauses, and then, as the lights go out, he walks offstage by himself. For a dance that has taken the group as its subject, this is a stark ending, an admission that, the group notwithstanding, we are also alone, and we die alone. (The ending looks like a death.) But this does not undo the meaning of what has come before. Insofar as we transcend aloneness, we do so in the group. And what the group does is dance. It is significant that when the man is left alone on the stage, he stops dancing. He doesn't waltz out; he walks out. When the others are gone, the dance is over, literally and figuratively. Dance and the group are the image of life as against death.

It hardly needs to be said that this idea has a personal meaning for Morris. His life is his group and the business of making them dance. This has been the case for years, but when the company moved to Brussels in 1988, the group took on a new meaning. Stuck in a foreign city, far away from their friends and their interests at home, the dancers drew closer together. At the same time, company unity was endangered. With the move to Belgium, Morris had doubled the size of the troupe. A dozen new people arrived, people who were not only strangers, but, for the most part, considerably younger than the "old company," and all of them strong, eager to work, and happy, when called upon, to take over the roles of the "old company." The threat that this posed was soon fulfilled. In July of 1989, for various reasons (not just the dilution of the company), four of Morris's most senior dancers—Susan Hadley, David Landis, Donald Mouton, and Teri Weksler—resigned and went back home. That fall, in the months that followed their departure, Morris made *Love Song Waltzes*. The message *Nicht wandel*—don't go—undoubtedly had a personal meaning.

It was more personal still. Another thing that happened in the summer of 1989 was that Jon Mensinger, one of the members of the "old company" and for several years a very close friend of Morris's, found out that he was HIV-positive. Mensinger is the man who keeps escaping and being pulled back in "Nicht wandel." The plea is quite direct. To Morris, to have his company threatened by dancers quitting might have seemed a symbolic death, but Mensinger's peril was not symbolic.

Nor was this the only time that Morris had come up against AIDS in his personal world. Like most dancers, he knew a number of people who had died of the disease. Many of the men in his company were nervously getting blood tests. He had reason to fear for himself too. In 1987 Steve Yadeskie, the man he had lived with in the late seventies, died at the age of thirty-three from a bacterial infection. In a 1989 interview, when queried about the prospect of old age, Morris said, "I won't live that long." Why? the interviewer asked. "AIDS," Morris replied. "I wasn't celibate all the time I lived in New York."

Morris is not much of a sexual adventurer. His pattern has been to fall in love and remain faithful or, when not in love, to go home and listen to records. Furthermore, since his separation from Erin Matthiessen, his most involving relationships have always been with heterosexual men. Since late 1989 the whole of his love life has been taken up with a platonic but nevertheless intense relationship with a German dancer, Hans-Georg Lenhart—ten years younger than he and heterosexual—who began dancing with the company in Brussels. (When the company returned to the United States, Lenhart went to dance at the opera house in Ulm, in southern Germany, but he and Morris travel to see each other.) Still, as Morris said, he hadn't been celibate all those years in New York. Between that fact and Yadeskie's death, he had reason to worry, and plenty of reason to worry for his company, the majority of whose men have always been homosexual.

The effect of AIDS on American society in the eighties was to put an end to the happy aggressiveness that marked the sexual revolution of the sixties and the gay-rights movement of the seventies. What had begun in pleasure and provocation ended in sobriety and sorrow. Whatever remained of the utopian spirit of those earlier decades resolved itself into a generalized emotion of charity. That emotion is very much present in *Love Song Waltzes*. Indeed, it is present in many of Morris's works of the past few years, including much happier ones, such as *The Hard Nut*. (It is worth noting that Jon Mensinger was one of the two men originally slated to dance the role of the Nutcracker. He pulled out because he was too ill to rehearse. He finally resigned from the troupe at the end of 1991.) But AIDS was only one factor among many. A spirit of charity, of transcendence, is where Morris was headed anyway. He *always* had a melancholy view of love. It is there as much in *New Love Song Waltzes* as in *Love Song Waltzes*. What is new in the latter dance is not sadness but soberness, and the positing of the group not just as a condition of existence but as the answer to existence.

That too, the idea of group love, is where he was headed all along. It had to happen eventually that he would find a philosophical meaning in the way he had always liked to dance and to see dance: in a group. And of course that experience of dancing in a group goes back to his youth, to Koleda, where it coincided with his first experience of love. This equation—dance, love, group—and its connection with Koleda are very clear in his mind, as he indicated in an interview during his time in Brussels:

People often complain that my dances look as though they could be done by anyone at all. They can't. They're hard to do. But it is true that I want it to look as though these are people who are dancing, as in folk dance or ethnic dance, where people are answering the call, "Come on, let's dance!" That's probably the first thing that human beings did when they stopped throwing rocks at each other, and the history of dance begins with them, the first people who joined hands to dance together.

That, and not romantic love, is the symbol of life's meaning. Hence Morris's decision to give the *grand pas de deux* in *The Hard Nut* to the ensemble. This big number, he said, this triumph-of-love dance—how could he give it just to Marie and the Nutcracker, when their love was not something that they alone achieved but something contributed to by everyone in the ballet: the parents, the party guests, the snowflakes, even the rats? Everybody had to be in the big dance, he said: "They all helped."

HEAVEN AND HELL

After love, the most important subject of Morris's choreography has been the life of the spirit. Viewed historically, this is no surprise. Modern dance began, in large measure, as a spiritual movement, a response to the decline-of-the-West pessimism of the turn of the century. It was a common belief among intellectuals of that period that modern civilization, through the combined force of science and industrialization, had sundered the body from the spirit. Cut off from religion and from the land, Western people now inhabited some airless region between heaven and earth, where they wasted their minds on vain researches, wasted their bodies on empty sensualities. "Primitive" peoples, people who still tilled their fields and fired their altars—they still had "wholeness," and they would inherit the earth. As for Western civilization, its hour was up.

Many different movements arose to combat this perceived decadence. The turn of the century swarmed with health reformers, theosophists, utopians, nature-hike clubs, all intent on reforging the primal link between body and soul. Modern dance arose in the midst of these reforms. Indeed, it was one of them: the dance wing of the anti-decadence movement. As the early modern dancers saw it, dance, the art that was made with the body, was in a unique position to restore body to soul. Yet ballet—which at that time was almost the sole form of Western concert dance—had not only failed to address decadence; it was decadence itself, "an expression of degeneration," as Isadora Duncan put it. Lashed into their corsets and point shoes, and performing their arcane, unnatural steps, ballet dancers were the very symbol of the body's alienation from the spirit. To rediscover a soulful way of moving, Western dancers would have to throw off their point shoes, throw off their contortionist technique, and relocate their spiritual center, from which a new, true dance would then naturally flow. In her "Dance of the Future," written around 1902, Duncan laid out the program:

Man, arrived at the end of civilization, will have to return to nakedness, not to the unconscious nakedness of the savage, but to the conscious and acknowledged nakedness of mature Man, whose body will then be the harmonious expression of his spiritual being.

Other early-twentieth-century founders of modern dance stressed different aspects of reform, but all of them believed that they were restoring to dance its spiritual foundation. "I demand of the dance . . . that it reveal the God in man," wrote Ruth St. Denis, whose Orientalist dances—fusions of sensuality and spiritual uplift (her version of the reunification of body and soul)—were as influential as Duncan's work in the founding of American modern dance. In Germany, the other birthplace of modern dance, the movement was led by the Hungarian Rudolf von Laban, who, as he wrote, dedicated his dance reforms to "the great goal of healing . . . our race and finally humankind."

This spiritual rescue mission was carried forward by the succeeding generations of modern dancers. Martha Graham, Doris Humphrey, Helen Tamiris, Katherine Dunham, José Limón, Anna Sokolow, Alvin Ailey— all drew on religious traditions, religious symbolism. When they were not dancing about their souls, the modern dancers of the thirties through the fifties were often dancing about social injustice, a subject that also lent itself to a certain religiosity, a "religion of man." And regardless of the subject, it was taken for granted that the technique of modern dance, by virtue of its naturalness—its emphasis on weight, its use of bare feet, its fidelity to such functions as breathing and falling—fostered, even guaranteed, profundity. In the famous words of Martha Graham, "Movement does not lie," or at least modern-dance movement didn't.

Thus, as the critic John Martin put it, "The modern dance is not a system; it is a point of view"—and often a rather churchy one. (This is one of the reasons the general public has always preferred ballet to modern dance. Ballet is willing to let you have a good time.) The war between ballet and modern dance is said to have ended in the sixties or seventies, but scratch a real modern-dance choreographer and you will still, in many cases, find a modern-dance partisan, with plenty to say on the subject of ballet's spiritual vacuity. In a 1992 interview Mark Morris used a telling metaphor. There were many ballets that he loved, he said, but in his view the institution of ballet was

like organized religion, where everybody means the best, everybody means to love one another and everything, and everyone thinks they've found the true God. Except that by empty ceremony and ridiculous rules, the God part goes away . . . I think that people are drawn to ballet . . . because of the physical artifice and that it has nothing to do anymore with people communicating things to other people . . . I would rather see something that is legitimate instead of pretty. Pretty isn't pretty to me.

Ballet, then, is the Church of Rome, dazzling and corrupt. Modern dance is Protestantism—pure in heart, vernacular in tongue—seeking to restore the spiritual values that the Church has forsaken.

The overt spiritual aspirations of modern dance held for a very long time. They were dampened somewhat by the conceptualism of the sixties, but in the seventies, particularly with the advent of the new, Indian- and African-inspired "trance music" of Steve Reich and Philip Glass, spiritual transports resurfaced. Laura Dean's dancers, spinning endlessly in one spot, looked like dervishes. Lucinda Childs's dancers—light-footed, impassive, dressed all in white—looked like new-wave angels, moving to some unheard planetary song. The dancer-as-celebrant was back.

With all this history behind him, Morris's interest in spiritual matters would seem unremarkable. After all, he danced for Laura Dean and loved her work, as he did Lucinda Childs's. But he is of a different generation. If the conceptualism of the sixties put a dent in modern-dance spirituality, the political troubles of the eighties more or less collapsed it. To the young choreographers of that decade—that is, Morris's generation—the dancer-as-celebrant was an anachronism, for in a society riven by racism, sexism, and homophobia, there was little to celebrate. Above all, in the face of the AIDS epidemic, a note of celebration would be impudence. To the generation of the eighties, AIDS was not just a disease. In its preferential attack on despised groups (homosexuals, blacks, Latinos) and in the resistance of powerful groups to research funding, to prevention programs, and eventually to the flood of sexual material that, in protest against these facts, washed through the art of the eighties, the AIDS crisis seemed to symbolize all the ills of the society. And in the dance and performance art of the decade it became a banner, bloody and immediate, under which artists paraded those ills before the audience. This was their solemnity, their rapture—political rage. As for religious feeling, that was the property of the "religious right," and therefore no friend. Even a more generalized spirituality, anything that suggested the universal or the eternal, was out of place. The griefs these artists were concerned with were not universal. And they were not eternal; they were of today, and had to be stamped out tomorrow.

So for Mark Morris, in the eighties, to make dances about the soul, about griefs that were suffered by all humankind and that had no earthly remedy, was to take a decidedly traditional position. Actually, even in relation to modern-dance history—to the seven decades of spiritual-minded dancing that preceded the eighties—Morris's religious works had a traditional look, for most of them were set to old Christian music, music that was part of the Roman Catholic and Lutheran services and that dealt, accordingly, with orthodox matters: prayer, penitence, the Virgin Mary. The religiosity of modern dance, however ecstatic, was generally non-denominational. Insofar as it traded in orthodoxy, this was usually not mainstream Christian orthodoxy but rather Hinduism, Sufism, Greek mythology, New Mexican Pueblo cults—something remote enough from the audience so that they could feel its spiritual glamour without having to worry about its sectarian concerns. And more often than not, the spiritual center of the dance was simply a nonspecific rapture, Platonic or pantheistic or humanitarian. Most of the makers of America's early and middle modern dance were leftists, and they thought what leftists generally think about organized religion. "From my earliest childhood I have always felt a great antipathy for anything connected with churches or Church dogma," wrote Isadora Duncan, and most of her sisterhood agreed with her.

Actually, the first of Morris's religious dances, Gloria, made in 1981 and revised to its present form in 1984, does slip under the wire of secular religiosity. Though it is set to a grand old piece of church music, with soloists, chorus, and orchestra, and though its text is addressed to an old-fashioned God, a God who can damn as well as save, Gloria is a friendly piece of work. In the "Laudamus te" ("We worship thee") section, the dancers click their heels for joy and do a little step that looks like the Suzie-Q. In the "Quoniam tu solus Sanctus" ("For thou alone art holy"), they do an old jazz step. There are parts of *Gloria* that look like children's games; other parts tell little jokes and stories. In one section a crippled woman is healed. Elsewhere this same woman does a step where she rotates her arms like propellers and takes off backward into the wings. She looks like a child pretending to be an airplane.

Gloria also has a strong, comforting feeling of community. The dancers seem to be *people*—they wear little dresses, Bermuda shorts—and whatever they suffer, they suffer it together. They are Common Humanity, sorry for their sins, grateful for God's blessings. They support each other, and the earth supports them. At the end of the dance, they form a big X across the stage, and two by two, they twirl and fall to the ground. The iconography is orthodox. (The X means Christ.) So is the text; it is the "Amen." But in this ecstatic fall to the earth, the dancers show us a picture of the natural unity of body and spirit that would have gladdened the anti-orthodox heart of Isadora Duncan. These are not shivering souls, seeking the answer. They have the answer.

It is simplicity. In *Gloria* we see the emotional eloquence of Morris's simple style—his vulnerable bodies, his blunt steps. At the opening of the "Laudamus te," a man runs onstage, clicks his heels, then launches himself into a dance of praise that Morris seems purposely to have made a little bit awkward. The dancer goes into arabesque, but stiffly. He turns, but with one foot nailed, as it were, to the floor, while the other foot pushes. Again and again, as his body pulls him down, he tilts his face upward. Here Morris seems to be showing us what the sense of the divine is really like for human souls. If he had given the dancer smooth, streamlined steps—high jumps, long stretches—the effect would have been entirely different. The *dancer* would have been divine. Instead, we get a Brueghelesque image: weight, bulk, mass, something distant from the divine and therefore, in its reach for the divine, truly moving.

Beyond the choreography, there is the austerity of the production: no set, no fancy costumes. In contrast with the pomp of the music—the chorus, the trumpets—the dancers look extremely plain: ten little people in gray street clothes. One part of Morris's brain belongs, or belonged, to the holistic wing of the sixties counterculture, with its belief that a return to good values could be effected by a return to simplicity, to yogurt and sandals and communal farming. Commenting once on a series of photographs of his company by Philip Trager—photographs taken outdoors, with the dancers in the nude—Morris wrote:

I love seeing people naked, and it feels good to be naked outside. I love seeing these people planted in the ground, sturdy as hydrants. It helped me remember the child's belief that if you run naked with your eyes closed no one can see you.

Earlier, when his company had to set up a non-profit foundation to accept contributions, he called the foundation Discalced. Why? asked an interviewer. "You know, barefoot," he answered, "like the Carmelite nuns."

Nakedness, barefootedness, the wisdom of the child—the whole equation of simplicity with spiritual worth—these values are part of the primitivism of the sixties, which in turn was a revival of the turn-of-the-century primitivism that gave birth to modern dance. (It is not just the use of weight that makes people think of Isadora Duncan when they see the work of Mark Morris.) This tie with the sixties is probably an important factor in Morris's popularity: many people in his audience came of age in the sixties, and even for those who didn't, the belief that truth lies in plainness is still a beloved idea, an American idea, the idea behind Shaker chairs and the Gettysburg Address. In any case, the sixties connection is certainly an important factor in *Gloria*'s popularity. This piece is to the Mark Morris Dance Group what Alvin Ailey's 1960 *Revelations*, set to Negro spirituals, is to the Ailey company—the audience's favorite work, the troupe's signature work—and that is because, though it was made in the eighties, *Gloria*, like *Revelations*, is in some measure a liturgical dance out of the sixties.

But only in some measure. In *Gloria* there are already signs that salvation may not be so easy, even for the barefooted. The clearest indication is the opening. The music begins on a joyful note, but what we see before us is not joyful. A small light at the back of the stage reveals two figures, a man and a woman, moving toward us side by side. The woman walks with a hobbled, wrenching gait, as if she were in leg irons. The man crawls on his stomach, with only his arms to pull him forward, as if his legs were paralyzed. Finally, they make it to the front of the stage. The man struggles to his feet, opens his arms, and gazes upward. But whatever he sees is too much. He crumples to the ground again, the lights go out, and the chorus now enters the musical line, singing "Gloria!

Gloria!'' at the top of their lungs. When the revised *Gloria* was premiered in 1984, it was danced in the Brooklyn Academy of Music's upstairs theater, the Lepercq Space, a huge black cavern with a 40-foot ceiling. To see these two lonely, crippled figures inch their way forward, as if crawling out of a hole, and then—when it seemed as though they had escaped and the man rose—to have him fall again, and the theater plunged into total darkness, and what seemed like a thousand voices boom out "Gloria! Gloria!" from the speakers mounted overhead, was to feel something that had nothing to do with the optimism of the sixties. If this was the glory of God, it was a distant thing, and the audience was given a minute and a half to sit in the dark and think about that while the voices went on singing.

The sense of sin and remorse that is the subject of this opening section is healed in the course of the dance, but Morris doesn't let us forget it. The leg-irons walk reappears later, and the stomach crawl is done again

Gloria. The ensemble doing the stomach crawl, Ruth Davidson standing *(Klaus Lefebvre)*

and again, by the whole cast. In the middle of the piece comes a section, the prayer-for-mercy section ("Domine Deus, Agnus Dei"), that is an expansion of the man's struggle at the opening, and it is performed by the same man. It is a lonely, anguished dance, with no resolution. At the end of *Gloria* there is a resolution, the falling X formation, but this fall is exactly the same, special fall (one hand reaches over the head; both arms open; the body twirls and collapses) that the man did at the opening. Though the sin has been forgiven, it was a real sin, cause for real humility. *Gloria* may be full of humanism, but this is not secular humanism. On the evidence of his work, Morris does believe in states of suffering and illumination that go beyond human understanding. He does think that people have souls and, as in *Lovey*, that they can lose them.

This became very obvious when, two years after the revised *Gloria*, he premiered another religious dance, *Stabat Mater*, the most grief-stricken work he has made. The music is Pergolesi's *Stabat Mater*, again a work written for the Roman Catholic Mass. The text concerns the sufferings of the Virgin Mary as she watched Christ die on the Cross. The singers describe her grief and ask that they may share it, and also share Christ's torment—feel his wounds, hang on his Cross—so that when they die they can go to heaven. The scale of Pergolesi's composition is modest, just two voices (no chorus) plus strings and continuo—a much smaller affair than the Vivaldi Gloria. And its tone is one of sweet pathos. But as in parts of *Gloria*, Morris hears in the tone an undertone, the tale of agony—the weeping, the blows, the nails driven through the hands—that Pergolesi wreathed in his tender song. That brutal emotion becomes the subject of the dance.

The steps in *Stabat Mater* have none of the ingratiating quality of *Gloria*: no heel-clicking, no toy airplanes. The dancers grip their stomachs, kick their own legs, drop each other. When the word "hang" comes up in the text, for Christ's hanging on the Cross, the dancers, with their backs to us, hang their hands down between their legs—a crude gesture that becomes even cruder when it is later repeated for the word "mother." (We are presumably being reminded that Mary gave birth to Christ, that he came out from between her legs.) When the singers sing of Mary's grief, three dancers lift another dancer and turn her, full circle, in the air— Mary overturned by sorrow. As she is turned, the dancer remains stiff as a board. This is not the Mary we are used to, the beautiful Virgin of the Renaissance, melting into the arms of the Evangelist. This is an early Christian Virgin, or a peasant-art Virgin: a block, a stick, the grief that

turns one to stone. In all these actions the humility conveyed is not a choice, a moral position, but a fact, the fact that life humbles us whether we want to be humble or not. Throughout *Stabat Mater*, the dancers gaze upward, but with stiff necks, tight chests, as if they were afraid of what they were going to see.

The sense of suffering is made worse by the dancers' spatial imprisonment. *Stabat Mater* is in three parts, each backed by a different drop curtain. In the first part, the drop leaves the dancers only the front third of the stage; in the second part, the front two-thirds. Only in the last section do they have the whole stage to dance upon. Furthermore, those drop curtains are painted with crosses, the first a huge black cross that seems to be in flames ("For that one," Robert Bordo, the designer, recalls, "Mark wanted a *wall* of Catholicism, something oppressive"); the second a medium-sized brown cross ("For that one," Bordo says, "Mark brought me a little wooden cross that he had bought on the street—very crude,

East Village handmade"); the third a small cross, gleaming white (Bordo: "I copied it from Giotto"). So the dance is confined in orthodoxy as well. Unlike *Gloria, Stabat Mater* gives the audience no leeway to imagine that this is not really religion, that it's some sort of secular faith. This is really religion. (As Morris said in an interview, the dance, like the text, is about "a personal identification with Jesus' wounds.") Nor is there any comforting image of community or "humanity." The dancers are in leotards, not Bermudas. They are not people; they are a dance.

Stabat Mater is unrelenting, above all, in its structure. It is put together like an algebra problem. There are twelve dancers, divided into three troops, and twelve dances, divided into three parts, with the three different drop curtains. In each part, only a prescribed number of dancers can be onstage—four in the first part, eight in the second, twelve in the third. "I wanted it to be as rigorous as Lucinda Childs," Morris has said. The effect of that rigor is to deny the dance's emotion any relief. As one of its dancers, Rob Besserer, put it, "It was a tight, airless dance. All the steps turned the wrong way. It was completely unsatisfying to dance." And in some ways it is unsatisfying to watch. It is like a paradox: so bloody a tale, contained in so impassive an image. "It's as dry as toast," as Morris put it.

Of course, the dance builds. The number of dancers increases, the stage opens, the crosses go from black to white. And in the final section of the "Amen," Morris allows this fanatically tight dance one burst of freedom. The singer has just prayed that when his body dies his soul may go to heaven. Now, in the "Amen," we see it go. The company lines up, double file, facing the audience. In each line, the dancer at the rear takes off and slaloms down the line, until he reaches the front, whereupon the next dancer at the back does the same thing, and the next and the next. In its circularity, this is an image of eternity, and it starts out in an orderly manner. But eventually it explodes. The dancers no longer wait their turn; they are all running. Then, suddenly, they remember themselves. The running stops, and each of the dancers freezes in one of the key motifs of the dance—the gripping of the gut, the backward leap, the woman overturned. At the very last second, one man runs offstage. He has died, apparently, and his soul is running off to find out if it has earned a place in heaven. The rest of us are left to contemplate again the dire story of the dance, all its themes now laid out for us side by side, as on the panels of an altarpiece.

Where did Morris get his religious sense? He had a conventional religious education. Bill Morris insisted that the family attend church. Mark went to Sunday school, where he remembers "coloring the Moses and cutting him out," and thence to regular services with his family—he also sang in the boys' choir—until, in the usual pattern, he reached adolescence and began resisting having to go to church. Maureen by this time was protesting too. (Indeed, she developed an allergy to the church. It made her sneeze. Maxine Morris, ever generous, believes that this may have been due to the furniture polish used on the pews.) So Bill relented. He and Maxine went on attending church, but the children didn't have to go if they didn't want to.

Except for sporadic capitulations, that was the end of Mark's participation in the activities of the Mt. Baker First Presbyterian Church, and to this day he is quick to disassociate himself from any conventional religious practice. "I'm not part of any club," he told David Vaughan of *Ballet Review*. Like so many others of his generation, he associates churchgoing with narrowness. Indeed, he associates it with his father and with his father's conventional-minded family. On the other hand, his mother's family—Grandpa Bill with his tap dancing, Grandma Mabel with her ragtime playing, Uncle Jim with his moviemaking, Aunt Audrey with the pink hair, and above all Maxine—this fun-loving bunch he associates with a truer, non-denominational faith. "My mother's family were not church types at all," he told an interviewer. "But very full of love. My father's family was a little more staunch, more rightist. They were Presbyterians by guilt and not by love."

So he turned away from orthodoxy, but not from religious feeling, and there was plenty around him to support that feeling. The West Coast, particularly the Northwest, with its astonishing natural beauty, tends to breed a sort of pantheistic religiosity. Morris felt this tug, and it later found expression in *Strict Songs*, the dance that has the angels flying at the end. With its score by the California modernist Lou Harrison—the musicians bang on bowls of water—and with its text based on Hopi chants and its dancers dressed in the colors of earth, water, and sky, *Strict Songs* is a "dance doxology" of the kind that Ted Shawn used to do, except that the religion is not Christianity but West Coast pantheism.

Another influence, though later, was Erin Matthiessen. Matthiessen had converted to Catholicism at age twenty, and during the time that he lived with Morris he was still deeply involved in religious matters. "He had little Jesus cards all over the place," says Robert Bordo. (Matthiessen is now a monk. He entered a Benedictine monastery in 1992.) Matthiessen's devoutness did not rub off on Morris—"Mark is a modern spiritualist," Matthiessen says, "and very worldly about it." But Morris was a "seeker" at this time of his life. (Once, in his early twenties, he even put in a weekend with Werner Erhard's self-actualization seminar, est, which must have been interesting for those present.) He joined Matthiessen in certain of his religious pursuits. When they were in India, they went together to see Mother Teresa. (They weren't able to speak to her, but they watched her participate in the Mass.) On Christmas Eve, Morris attended midnight services with Matthiessen. They meditated together.

Probably the most important spur to Morris's religious feelings, however, was simply his emotional life. Morris is the child of his mother's family: he loves fun, and he creates fun around him. "You feel that if you're not where he is, you're not having the optimum good time you could have," says Rob Besserer. And like certain other fun-loving people, he has an enormous capacity for desolation. For a young man, he has made a lot of pieces about death, but what is striking in his work is not so much death as a kind of death-in-life, a vision of horror and grief that is unequaled in the work of any other contemporary American choreographer except Paul Taylor (by whose example Morris may have been emboldened to deal in these matters) and that is made all the more terrible by the fact that it is placed before us with no lament, no complaint, even. On the contrary, the tone is often dry or cold or even humorous, with the result that the birth of this horror has the same kind of unsentimental reality such things have in life. I have already described two works of this kind, *Lovey* and *Stabat Mater*. *Dido and Aeneas* is another. Though Dido's death is noble, the progress of the piece, jumping back and forth between Dido's world and the witches' den, is such as to tell us that, for everything in the world that is noble, there is something set to kill it—and something we like. We learn this lesson from ourselves when, immediately before Dido's death, Morris makes us laugh at that death in the hilarious "Destruction's our delight" chorus. Destruction becomes our delight too. Then, one scene later, we see the destruction happen. Watching *Dido* is like being swallowed by a snake.

Dido is typical of Morris's "black" works in that, when the force of blackness is to be embodied in a single role, he himself takes that role. Choreographers who dance in their own works often cast themselves consistently from piece to piece; they fit into their own vision in a certain way. Antony Tudor, in his many passion-versus-respectability ballets, typically cast himself as a figure of respectability. Martha Graham, in most of her works, played the role of a woman called to a high, daunting mission. And Morris often casts himself as an image of the demonic: a goblin, a witch, a vampire, a fury. He has a gift for these roles, a gift for the grotesque, and he may be loath to impose them on others. He may also feel a need to take personal responsibility for so personal a vision of life's built-in terror.

As is often the case with artists' emotions, the clearest example is an early one, before the emotion became too complicated by wisdom or by art. *The Vacant Chair*, created in 1984, is a solo set to three old parlor songs of the utmost genteel sweetness, "The Vacant Chair," "Trees," and "A Perfect Day." As the piece begins, most of the stage is dark. But in a small circle of light at the front of the stage, we see a music stand and, on it, a little drawing of a chair. All the suggestions are of domesticity: a parlor, a singer, a point of light in the darkness. Then, out of the darkness, like a monster out of a bog, crawls Mark Morris (or, in an alternate cast, Rob Besserer), dressed only in his Jockey shorts and with a brown paper bag over his head.

The first song, "The Vacant Chair," written during the Civil War, is about a young man who has died in battle. The singer hymns the boy's courage, his innocence, his mild blue eyes, and with each refrain he tells how, when the boy's family now gather for their evening prayers, there will be one vacant chair. While this song is going on, what Morris does, basically, is fall, again and again. During the verses describing the boy's heroism, he succeeds in getting up and does a sort of marching step, but the image of heroism is undercut, needless to say, by the fact that he has a grocery bag over his head. And soon he is down again, landing with a smack on the floor. So while the song is telling one story about death—how you pray and carry on—the dance is telling another story, far more brutal: the blindness of death, the helplessness, the blue-eyed boy a mess on the floor. The song is consolation; the dance is inconsolability.

The same logic governs the next two songs. "Trees" is a musical setting of Joyce Kilmer's well-known inspirational poem ("I think that I shall never see / A poem lovely as a tree"). It describes how a tree, as it grows, rises toward God and "lifts [its] leafy arms to pray." But while the song rises, the dance collapses. At the beginning, Morris oozes up slowly from behind the music stand, and when the singer speaks of the leafy arms, he sticks his arms out. But the arms are gnarled and spastic, and the leaves already sere. (He has taken the paper bag off his head and torn it in two. These become the brown leaves.) And from then on, his body

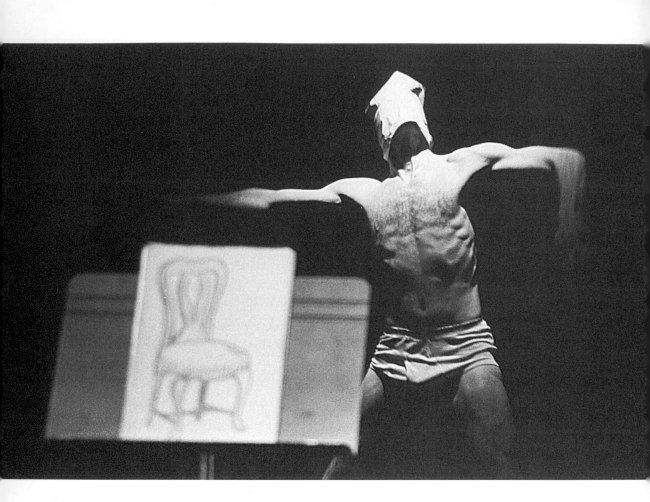

descends again, as slowly and gruesomely as it rose; the tree has died. In "A Perfect Day," while the singer describes the sweet melancholy of parting from a friend, Morris alternates between striking noble poses—the singer's noble thoughts—and careening violently across the dark stage, like someone reeling from a blow. At the end of "Perfect Day" he goes over to the music stand, knocks it down, and walks offstage.

Audiences often laughed at *The Vacant Chair*, the joke, presumably, being the subversion of a corny old gentility by an honest, up-to-date brutality. Morris says he found this laughter incomprehensible:

That dance is not funny. It's humiliating. I did it in my underpants, with a paper bag over my head. And the first movement is done blind. You don't know which way you're facing or where you're traveling or anything. This is it, and it's not pretty. It was a dance about people going away from each other. That's the text of all those songs as I could see it. I wasn't doing a joke in any way.

But there *is* humor in *The Vacant Chair*, black humor. The joke is defeat, and not just defeat by life—war, death, people going away from each other—but also the defeat, or partial defeat, of our attempts at transcendence by the black truth of our loss. So *The Vacant Chair* has the same layered logic as *Dido*, and is about the same thing. There we got Dido and the Sorceress; one noble, one ignoble, version of the same truth. Here we get the songs, with their God and their sunsets, and we get the dance, with its monstrous figure of grief. As I said earlier, Morris habitually tells two sides of the same story at once. This doubleness sometimes makes audiences nervous, and that is one of the reasons they laugh. The other reason is that the contrast between high and low is indeed comical, however terrible its meaning.

Apart from its boldness and economy, what is remarkable about *The Vacant Chair*, and about Morris's work in general, is the sheer extremeness of its emotion—the absolute vision of grief, grief as an utter loss of meaning, the loss of God. (In this sense *The Vacant Chair* is as much a religious work as *Gloria* or *Stabat Mater*. So is *Lovey*.) On the surface, Morris's life would seem to have little basis for such a vision. It is possible that *The Vacant Chair* is a memory of a period in his teenage years when, it seemed, everyone died on him at once. First his father went, in 1973. Then, one by one, his mother's family, the happy Crittendens, began dying. Aunt Louise, who had taught Maxine to tango, also died in 1973. The following year, the beloved Uncle Jim died; then, the year after that, Grandpa Bill; then, two years after that, Grandma Mabel, whose favorite song was "A Perfect Day." (It was she who taught it to Mark.) In seven years, Mark lost five close family members. "It got to the point," Penny Hutchinson remembers, "where the phone would ring, and he would start shaking."

These shocks had been preceded by others. One night in 1971 Bill Morris left a light burning next to some papers in the downstairs den, and by the next day a fire started. No one was home, but the house was gutted, and everything the family owned was gone. Mark's piano, Maxine recalls, was "a hunk of charred black, with a big white melted streak where the keys were." All his sheet music and records were also destroyed, and with the expense of rebuilding the house, the family was in no position to replace them. A few months later, just after the family had moved back into the house, their car was rear-ended on a highway while all of them were in it. They managed to struggle out of the car before it blew up in flames before their eyes. Mark was fourteen at the time. Two years later, Bill died, and the run of deaths began.

Worse things have happened to people, but one does not need to be a war orphan to develop a tragic sense of life. All one needs is a normal portion of sorrow, which his life provided, and the ability to think in universal terms—to take one's emotions seriously and relate them to human life in general—an ability I believe Morris learned from music. This is something that all people, in some measure, learn from music. That is why they cry when they hear a sad song. Their own sadness, inchoate before, becomes clarified by identification with the song. That identification means, furthermore, that they aren't the only ones who are sad. Life is sad, and they are part of the sadness of life. The emotion is thus eased out of privacy and vagueness. It is further eased by the fact that the song dignifies the emotion, says that it has some meaning and moreover —by virtue of music's abstraction—some ideal character. So the emotion is released, we cry, and for that moment we feel the tragic sense of life.

But Morris didn't just hear a song. He spent his teenage years (and has spent his adulthood) completely absorbed in music. In the process he learned that Bach and Vivaldi had emotions similar to his, and so he began to think of his experience in general terms: not his burned piano, but loss; not Puget Sound, but the beauty of the world. And from there it is not a long leap—no leap at all, actually, since much of Bach's and Vivaldi's music was religious music—to thinking in religious terms: not Puget Sound, but grace; not the loss of the piano or the grandmother, but the loss of one's soul.

In Morris's early work, such matters are addressed from a certain distance. In *Gloria* it is humankind we see, not this or that human being. In *The Vacant Chair* we don't even see something human. Morris's face is hidden from us for most of the dance. These very generalized images were probably his way of getting accustomed to such extreme ideas of grace and loss—edging up to them, as it were, and overcoming embarrassment about their religious character. It may also have been his way of preserving their extremeness, preventing them from petering out into the personal or the psychological.

But as I said earlier, Morris's work in recent years has undergone a kind of relaxation. The disaster of love no longer takes the form of vampires. It wears a human face, Dido's face. And after the abstraction of religious feeling in *Gloria*, *Stabat Mater*, and *Strict Songs*, Morris in 1992 made *Beautiful Day*, the dance in which, to the chiming of the Bell Cantata, two people work to get one of them to heaven. This piece is wholly different from Morris's other religious dances. It is intimate—a transaction between two people—and as a result it is more complicated emotionally. It takes place at the intersection of personal love and divine love, and all the energy of the piece goes into the hard job of realizing in dance terms what the resultant mix of feelings might be: what it would be like to love someone and also to leave him, and want to leave him.

It is not easy, these days, to sell religion to the theatergoing public. Indeed, it wasn't easy for Morris to sell it to himself. To start with the obvious, it was politically uncomfortable. However sustaining and taken-for-granted religion may have been for Bach or Vivaldi, for artists today it often represents the forces that are against art. The early modern dancers were not the only ones who had to turn their backs on the principles of their upbringing in order to become artists. So did Morris. In his high school, and with his father and his uncles, for a boy to choose to become a dancer (and a forthright homosexual) was to swerve from a certain orthodoxy, and religion is allied with that orthodoxy.

To overcome such a problem, it would seem, only a small act of imagination was required: one merely launched oneself into the meta-religion, the unorthodox, holiness-of-the-world religion, of the sixties, and this is what Morris did as a teenager. But even in that religion there is still the danger of a bland, smiling piety, of a vague, furry-brained mysticism. As I said, Morris has a kind of mania about honesty, and his religious works are full of self-testing, full of reminders—to himself as much as to anyone else—that the leap of faith can be too fast, too easy.

The primary test is the dance style itself, Morris's refusal to let the body go beautiful, go significant, without a struggle. In *Gloria* the sliding-on-the-stomach maneuver is not just an expression of humility. In its real, grunting awkwardness, its slight edge of comedy, it is a criticism of any too self-forgiving notion of humility. In *Gloria*, though, humility is rewarded. The dance ends in ecstasy. In the later religious works, that reward is withheld, or held out only briefly. In *Stabat Mater*, it comes in one burst of freedom, which no sooner bursts than it is reined in again. And in *Stabat Mater*, paradoxically, the very orthodoxy of the piece—its flaming crosses, its cruelty, its bloody and Baroque religiosity—is like a test. It erects a wall between us and the dance, and asks us if we can cross it. Many reviewers couldn't. There is probably no work of Morris's that has so mystified the press as *Stabat Mater*. Was he *serious*? they seemed to ask.

He may have asked this too. At the premiere, when he took his bows, he was wearing a big pink plastic crucifix around his neck. His explanation of this is that someone gave him the crucifix shortly before the premiere, so he decided to wear it. But to the audience it looked like a joke, a little repudiation—"Don't get me wrong, I haven't converted"—and it may have served that purpose for him as well. On the other hand, the crucifix may not have looked funny to him, or not too funny. (Remember that he spent four years living with Matthiessen's Jesus cards.) Religious expression is not necessarily in good taste, and Morris isn't keen on good taste anyway. When things start to look too tasteful, he will fix them. *Strict Songs*, that clean, whole-grain, redwood-loving, California dance—a dance that could have been commissioned by the Sierra Club—was dedicated to Liberace, who died shortly before its premiere. Liberace was a Californian too, a very representative one, and for many people he was as inspirational as the redwoods.

The same logic seems to be operating in the credit line that Morris puts in all his programs, to the effect that the Mark Morris Dance Group thanks "Maxine Morris and god." On the one hand, God is being thanked. On the other hand, it is hard to miss the fact that he has been restyled as god, and takes second billing to Mrs. Morris. Likewise, for years Morris has been in the habit, at curtain calls, of dropping into an extravagantly humble bow, with praying hands, as a gesture of thanks to his dancers. The thanks are undoubtedly sincere, but the bow is a little too much, as if Morris could not show humility without at the same time commenting on shows of humility. This is the kind of thing that drives some people crazy about Morris, but it is completely natural to him. Once, when he was asked why, in the angel-launch at the end of *Strict Songs*, he made the maneuver so complicated that it could not be done in a smooth, lyrical way, he said, "It's because I'm embarrassed enough about my religious feelings. And also, I like to see a bigger spectrum of action." His angels are not going to be launched without difficulty, and his faith is not going to be launched without Liberace.

Actually, if piety is what he is worried about, his work is already shielded from that by its fundamentally symbolic character. Though Morris feels free to refer to real life whenever this suits him, his primary mode of expression is not mimetic. Instead, he works within the logic of the body to create dance movements that correspond to the feelings created in him by the music. Dance and music are fundamentally non-representational. To paint a picture or tell a story, they have to be added to somehow—given a costume, a libretto. Left to their own devices, what they create are open symbols: a falling cadence, a hobbled walk, things that we understand with some part of the intelligence different from what we bring to representational arts.

It is in these open symbols that Morris works. In *Gloria* there are no praying hands. Humility is not on its knees; it is on its stomach. And it is humility only by inference. Likewise, the angels at the end of *Strict Songs* are not necessarily angels. What they are are bodies being lifted into the air on the soles of somebody else's feet, together with certain connotations of that act: that this is something we never do, that it is very hard to do, that it is dangerous and the dancers know it, that it looks amazing. Those are the thoughts that rise in our minds as we watch this action, and it is to them that our emotion attaches, not to the idea that these are angels, which is a thought that comes only later, or may not come at all. Morris is willing to discuss these figures as angels, but they could be something else—stars, for example. (That is what the chorus has just been singing about: "the galaxy, and the turquoise cloudless heaven.") The first time I saw them, I thought how some American Indian tribes used to lash their dead to the branches of trees, so that conceivably you could come upon a place and look up and see dead people in the sky. In any case, all we know while watching this moment of the dance is what the logic of the body tells us: that this is something both difficult and sublime.

Knowing that, we know the dance. Morris's religious works do not require a religious audience. Even his *Jesu, Meine Freude*, the only one of his religious works that actually does look pious, was loudly applauded—by what looked like average, secular-minded audiences—when it was premiered in Boston in 1993. In the case of some of Morris's religious dances, many spectators probably don't know that the subject is religion. This fact is hard to ignore in *Gloria* and *Stabat Mater*, but you could miss it in *Beautiful Day*, where there are no crosses and the text is in German. Indeed, "miss" is the wrong word. The text, with its prayer for death and salvation, was part of Morris's inspiration in making the piece, but what is important to the dance is, again, what the body tells us—here, that something is happening that is both very grave and very intimate. In a sense, one no more needs the text to understand *Beautiful Day* than one needs to know humoral psychology in order to understand Balanchine's *Four Temperaments*. It helps, or it makes one's understanding different. But everyone knows the truth that humoral theory tried to explain—that the human personality has many sides to it—and most people know the intersection of the grave and the intimate.

Not only do they know these things; they want art to address them. So does Morris. He is as sensitive as anyone else to the risk of sentimentality in such matters. Hence his self-criticism, his naysaying—his willingness to portray child murder as a cartoon, to give a vampire seduction a happy ending. But his skepticism, instead of quelling his sense of the ideal, has simply kept it honest. Meanwhile, what has kept his work honest is the symbolic character of his dance imagination, which is entirely natural to him (not a form of self-criticism). As long as the power of an angel image depends not on a white robe or a seraphic smile but on sheer physical facts, which the spectators must feel physically before they can understand them emotionally, the image either works or it doesn't, but it cannot pretend, because it is not claiming any significance that it cannot communicate physically. (In this sense Martha Graham was right. Movement does not lie. It doesn't have the power to.) And so Morris has been able to make dances about the life of the spirit. His doing so might have been expected to narrow his public. Instead, it has enlarged it. He gets tired of *Gloria*—next to *Ten Suggestions*, it is the oldest dance in his current repertory—but the company is still performing it, because it is so popular with audiences.

THE STORY

orris is in many ways an old-fashioned moralist—one of the few ways in which he resembles the other choreographers of his generation. He believes that art has discussable content, and he will happily explain the content of his dances, even if you haven't asked. Queried about some detail, he will say, "That's because that piece is about death" or "That's because they're in love." And if the dance is about something terrible, he believes it can be justified by redeeming social value. "I think the most important thing in a work of theater is that it be presented with a good spirit, humanely," he said once in a television interview. "Art can certainly be very ugly"—he was introducing *Dogtown* here—"if the point is the opposite of that." If the point is not the opposite of that, the work is objectionable. Once, in 1984, at a performance of Twyla Tharp's *Nine Sinatra Songs*—a piece that in its final section shows a woman being yanked around by a man—he stood up in the audience, yelled "No more rape!" and walked out of the theater. "I can defend every single measure of my choreography . . ." he once said to Alan Kriegsman of *The Washington Post*. "I can hold it up in a court of art."

In keeping with this moral emphasis, Morris's dances tell stories. Actually, it is hard to know which came first, the stories or the moral emphasis, for he is a born storyteller. Give him the smallest, most abstract piece of music and he will find in it some dramatic situation. Elsewhere, as in *Dido and Aeneas* and *The Hard Nut*, he has undertaken long, detailed narratives. And again and again over the years he has set his dances to songs. To take only the works discussed so far, *New Love Song Waltzes*, *Love Song Waltzes*, *Deck of Cards*, *Dogtown*, *Lovey*, *O Rangasayee*, *The Vacant Chair*, *Strict Songs*, and *One Charming Night* are all set to songs, and they are about what the song is about.

Actually, a good indicator of Morris's devotion to narrative is his devotion to vocal music. As noted, half his works—41 out of the 84 dances he has made since 1980—have been set to vocal music. In the modern history of Western theatrical dance (that is, since the Renaissance), no other choreographer has shown this measure of interest in song. And the cost of singers being what it is, no choreographer who cared about live accompaniment *would* show this measure of interest in song without a good reason. One reason is Morris's background. Again, much of his training was not in theatrical dance but in ethnic dance, Spanish and Balkan, both of which normally involve singing. Another reason I have already discussed: his love of the fleshly sound of the voice, which seems to him the musical counterpart of the dancing body. But to judge from his work, there is another, less subtle reason for his love of vocal music: he is interested in what the singer is saying. He likes the stories.

Since about 1983 no Mark Morris dance to vocal music has ever ignored the text, and some of these dances illustrate the text to an extent that is probably undreamed of by most of the audience. A good example is *New Love Song Waltzes*, with its Brahms songs set to a series of love lyrics by Georg Friedrich Daumer, a minor nineteenth-century German poet, plus one poem by Goethe. In this piece, when the singers sing of shadows, the dancers shadow each other. When a singer speaks of rings on her fingers, the dancers join hands and form a ring; when she says she gave her rings away to a worthless lover, the dancers step out of the ring. One song speaks of a house of cards falling, and the dancers collapse forward. In another song we get fire imagery:

Opposite top: "How my eye burns." Bottom: "Your hut will catch fire." Ruth Davidson (light dress), Susan Hadley (dark dress), and Jon Mensinger in New Love Song Waltzes (Beatriz Schiller)

> *Neighbor, guard,*
> *Guard your son from harm . . .*
> *O how my eye burns*
> *to inflame him!*
> *If his soul is not kindled*
> *Your hut will catch fire.*

On "how my eye burns" the dancers cover and uncover their eyes. On "Your hut will catch fire" two women form a block with their bodies, and a man jumps over them, like a man jumping out of a burning house. Two songs later, the image is rain—"From the mountains, wave upon wave, / come torrents of rain"—and the dancers wash over the stage in overlapping waves. The next song is about lying down on the soft grass with one's beloved, and the dancers, in pairs, lie down on the floor. (This is the partner-swapping dance.) Three songs later, the metaphor is wind, and the dancers fly across the stage like the wind. "Before you stands the one thing you value," says the following song, and the dancers dance in couples; "forever forbidden is a happy union," runs the next line, and the couples break apart. The next verse is:

> *No, beloved, do not sit*
> *so close to me! . . .*
> *Even though they burn in your bosom,*
> *subdue your longings,*
> *so that the world shall not see*
> *how dear we are to each other.*

Here Morris outdoes himself in text illustration. Again we have couples embracing on the floor. In each couple, the two pairs of arms go on embracing, so that the burning bosoms are joined, while the two pairs of legs walk away from each other, obeying the command, "do not sit / so close to me." In the final song, the singers sing to the Muses—art alone, they say, allows one to transcend the pain of love—and the dancers file onstage in a spiraling chain with the lead dancer pointing to heaven, to the Muses. This long list probably covers about half the instances of word-painting in *New Love Song Waltzes.*

Most spectators probably have no idea that this is going on. The songs are in German, and about half the vocal texts Morris has used have been in foreign languages. But even when the text is in English, most of the audience will not pick up the word-painting. The words are not clear enough, and the dance goes by too fast. In a recent review Eva-Elisabeth Fischer, a very observant critic, wrote of *New Love Song Waltzes* that Morris "hardly gives a thought to the texts." Fischer is German, as is the text.

What, then, is the artistic value of the word-painting? Well, the audience gets some of it, even without the words. No one needs to be told what it means when two people lie down on the floor together. Furthermore, these actions match the music. In *New Love Song Waltzes* Morris is not the only one imitating the text—Brahms is too—and the choreography is imitating both the words *and* the music. When the lovers lie down on the floor, the music is soft, lullaby-like. When the dancers race across the stage like the wind, the music is racing. The spectators don't have to hear the words; they hear the music.

Prior to all this, however, the words have served a more important purpose: they have given Morris movement ideas. Unlike ballet, with its rich lexicon of steps built up over the last four centuries, modern dance does not have an established academic vocabulary. It is too young—only a hundred years old. Furthermore, part of the tradition of modern dance is that each choreographer is allowed, indeed bidden, to make up his or her own *new* vocabulary. Morris, in his choreography, draws on a number of established styles—Spanish, Balkan, other ethnic forms, various modern dance techniques, ballet—but he too is creating his own vocabulary, and like all choreographers, he is to some extent creating a new vocabulary for each dance. Vocal music helps him do this. The Daumer poems that make up the text of *New Love Song Waltzes* contain a whole world of image and reference—rain, wind, fire, house, gate, grass, eyes, heart, tears—the iconographic world of the nineteenth-century love lyric. Out of these, Morris spins his movement images—shadowing, showering, flying, bursting, lying down, embracing, separating, carrying, dancing in rings—and that becomes his iconography, the world of the dance.

The two worlds are only loosely connected, because language and movement are only loosely connected. What can language say about a storm? That it comes from the mountains, that it falls in wave upon wave, that it involves rain. What can movement say about this? Only that it falls in wave upon wave—no rain, no mountain—but it can say other things that language can't: about the excitement of falling, about the giddiness and terror of having something happen to you in wave upon wave. Similarly, poetry, in telling us about the Muses, can say that they are kind, that they bring relief from the pain of love, that they are the only thing that does. Movement can show us only a woman pointing upward; it can't say to what. (God? A star?) But in the kinds of things this pointing can do—show us something going upward at the end of a dance where everything has gone downward; tell us, with the tension in the shoulder joint, how pointing means yearning; make the pointing dancer trail a whole chain of dancers behind her, so that they seem to be spiraling into the sky—it can say much that language can't about transcendence. And that, after all, is what the Muses are, transcendence, just as the storm is not a storm; it is passion. So the two languages, words and movement, rise from the same base, human consciousness, and tell different versions of the same story, the one more specific, the other more general, a matter of suggestion rather than signification.

The literalness of the translation varies from dance to dance in Morris's repertory. In some dances, like *New Love Song Waltzes*, he is doing rough imitations of the lyrics. Elsewhere, the imitation is more exact. Certain of the dances in *L'Allegro* are straight out of grade-school Creative Dramatics. (And Morris made them up based on Creative Dramatics.) In other dances the narrative method is very close to that of "I'm a Little Teapot" or, in its more detailed moments, to French mime. (When, in the 1982 *Songs That Tell a Story*, the singer speaks of a door, a dancer draws a door in the air and then opens it.) Some dances use already established gestural languages—*Ten Suggestions* draws on the lyrical language of early modern dance (roll a hoop, fly around like a fairy), the 1988 *Fugue and Fantasy* on the dark expressionism of middle modern dance (stare at something scary in the wings, move toward it haltingly), the 1989 *Wonderland* on the language of film noir (hide something in your pocket, scream, fall dead)—so that the gestures invoke not just the situations they are referring to but the whole atmosphere of the art form they are borrowed from. Some of the dances employ actual sign languages. Many of the steps in *Strict Songs* are simply elaborations of the American Sign Language gestures for the words the singers are singing at that moment—"leaf," "tree," "moon," and so on. (When *Strict Songs* was premiered in Seattle, there was an ASL signer at the side of the stage performing these gestures while the dancers were dancing them. Then Morris found out that Lar Lubovitch had just used an ASL signer in a dance, so he dropped the signer from *Strict Songs*.) The immensely rich gestural repertory of *Dido and Aeneas* draws on almost all these sources, together with the beautiful hand-languages of Indian and Indonesian dance.

But no matter how imitative the gesture, it expands on its own, physical terms. This is the key to Morris's narrative: it is only half narrative. It indicates things from the world we know, and we are grateful for that, but then it goes on to live a life of its own, the life of suggestion that is appropriate to movement. Many of the gestures are imitative *only* by suggestion. In *Dido*, for example, there is a fixed gesture for "fate," and it is performed every time the word "fate" is sung. The dancer stretches

Morris performing the
"fate" gesture, *Dido
and Aeneas*
(The Independent/
Geraint Lewis)

his arms out sideways and up, twists his wrists, and splays his fingers. Since the word "fate" comes up seventeen times in the opera, always accompanied by this gesture—indeed, sometimes accompanied by a whole stageful of dancers doing this gesture—the audience may get the connection. But in the meantime, the gesture has so much fateful poetry of its own—the long, outward stretch of the arms (fate controls the whole world), the raising of the arms (fate is directed by heaven), the muscular tension in the shoulders (fate is powerful), the spidery splay of the fingers (fate is terrible, or will be for Dido)—that the body can carry the weight of that meaning without our having to hear the word. In the process, the piece becomes a dance. When a gesture does not enlarge in this way, cutting loose from its word, throwing out new filaments of meaning, the piece is that much less a dance. Either it turns into mime comedy, which may be very good, as in *Songs That Tell a Story*, or it turns into a failure. What it never turns into is naturalistic drama. In most of Morris's work the face is deadpan and the movement is either very blunt or very stylized. He may miss his mark through dancing, but he never tries for it through acting. "He always hates it when you start to *portray* something . . . God forbid you should act!" says Mikhail Baryshnikov, who has created a number of roles in Morris's work and who loves to act.

The semi-gestural movements that Morris uses supply not only much of the poetry of his dances; they give each dance its shape and character. Of all the fundamental traits of Morris's style, there is hardly one that is not intimately tied to a working method that he developed at the beginning of his career and has been faithful to ever since. For every dance he works out a series of key movements—perhaps five or seven for a short dance, twenty or thirty for a long dance—and then he creates the dance by cycling and developing these movements: pulling them apart, elaborating them into something else, passing them from dancer to dancer, soloist to ensemble, changing their "pitch," their rhythm, their duration, combining them with other, non-key movements, forgetting them for a while and going on to something else, then bringing them back and reminding us of them again. There is no mystery as to where he got this method. It is the method of music. And this is what makes his dances *half* narrative. Many of his movement motifs seem to be parts of a story. However, they are developed not like a story, in a discursive, "horizontal" way, but like music, in a "vertical" way—through harmony and counterpoint, through repeating the motif in new contexts. "The architecture of music has educated me," he told an interviewer in 1984. "I've learned a lot about choreographing from people like Handel." Indeed, he learned his modus operandi.

For certain dances, such as *Stabat Mater* and *Gloria*, I have already given a partial list of the movement motifs. Here, for *Gloria*, is a fuller inventory:

1. The leg-irons walk
2. The stomach crawl
3. The twisting fall
4. The "little airplane" takeoff
5. The heel-clicking
6. The Suzie-Q
7. The crotch grip
8. The "devil leap": a leap done with the torso bent forward, so that the body has a spasmodic look
9. The "faith healer": one person places his hand on another person's forehead and knocks that person over backward. (Morris saw a faith healer, Katherine Kuhlman, do this when he was a teenager in Seattle.)
10. The skating walk: the dancer walks not by lifting his feet but by sliding them in arcs along the floor

11. The "announcement": the dancer places one hand on his waist and crooks the other arm upward in front of him, like a medieval page making a happy announcement.

These movements, together with a number of others that, while interesting to look at, would be boring to read about, are Morris's cards in *Gloria*. He plays them again and again, and he does the same, with different cards, in every dance. Sometimes—partly for a dramatic purpose but also, perhaps, to help us—he lays all the cards out in a row. At the end of the "crippled woman" dance in *Gloria*, the crippled woman, now healed, does a good half of *Gloria*'s key movements all in a row, in one long, ecstatic phrase. It's as if she were saying, "Now that I can walk, I can do everything." In *Stabat Mater*, as we saw, Morris reiterates all the key motifs simultaneously in the last moment of the dance. Here the message seems to be "This is the story of the Passion—don't forget it." But even when

The "faith healer" Joe Bowie (left) and Jean-Guillaume Weis (right) with the ensemble in *Gloria* (Tom Brazil)

the motifs are not actually listed, they are very easy to see, and this gives Morris's work an extraordinary clarity. His dances are like those clocks that have a piece of glass for a face. When you look at them, you don't just find out what time it is; you see the machinery—the springs, the gears—by which that conclusion was arrived at.

With his materials so fixed and clear, Morris can make very powerful points in his manipulation of them. In *Gloria* the fact that the fall the group does at the end is the same one the man did at the beginning is not lost on us, or not on the inner mind. And so, when we get to the end, what we see is not just an ecstatic group fall; it is an ecstatic group fall that was once a painful solitary fall. Hence the meaning of *Gloria*: that humility, starting in pain, ends in grace, and that part of that grace is fellowship.

The same kind of progress can be traced in *The Hard Nut*, in Morris's cycling of a hand-to-heart gesture. This motif comes up for the first time in the first tender moment of the ballet: the duet danced by Drosselmeier and his nephew, the Nutcracker, after the Nutcracker's victorious battle with the rats. In the dance, Drosselmeier leads the boy, lifts him, points his way ("You are a man now—go forth into life"). He also repeatedly places his hand on the boy's heart ("Part of being a man is to know that you have a heart, that you can love"), and the boy in turn places his hand on Drosselmeier's heart ("I have a heart? Like you?"). Now, we know that Marie is waiting in the wings. Indeed, it was to save her that the Nutcracker battled the rats. So we wait for him to find his heart's home in Marie.

But then we get a surprise: the next time the hand-to-heart appears, in the coda of the *grand pas de deux*, it is done not by the Nutcracker or Marie but by the ensemble, which at that moment includes a cross section of the entire cast—the rats, the flowers, the snowflakes, Marie's family, the people from the Russian dance, the French dance. So love is not just a thing between two people; it is something shared by the whole world. Having understood that (for they have watched the ensemble do this), Marie and the Nutcracker finally have their love duet, and they place their hands over each other's hearts. They have found love in each other, but it is a love that was taught to them by the world and that now joins them to the world. As I have said, Morris's fundamental idea of love is community. If he is going to make a ballet about the love between two people—which is what, in making a *Nutcracker*, he has undertaken to do—then they are going to learn that love from others.

On paper, with this connect-the-dots technique, Morris's way of developing a motif might seem pat. On stage, it is the opposite. If there is any danger, it is not that the progress of the motif will seem too obvious but that it might get lost amid the many other things going on at the same time, some of them echoing the development of that motif, some of them modifying or complicating it. The fact that the love between Marie and the Nutcracker is given to them by the world is communicated to us not just by the hand-to-heart motif but by other circumstances as well. When the two lovers come together, the Waltz of the Flowers immediately occurs. (Nature blesses their union.) When the couple are supposed to have their *grand pas de deux*, it is invaded by all the other characters in the ballet. ("They all helped.") When Marie dances her solo in the *grand pas*, it is a copy of a solo performed earlier by her mother. (She has learned to love just by growing up, by becoming a woman, like her mother.) When Marie and the Nutcracker finally get to dance a duet, many of their steps—not just the hand-to-heart—are copied from the duet between the Nutcracker and Drosselmeier. (Their man/woman love is an extension of uncle/ nephew love.) So the establishing of this macro-micro love is a compli- cated business, and its meaning becomes complicated in the process. For Marie to become a woman like her mother, or for her to inspire in her young man the very same feelings he had for his uncle, is not everything we might have wished. Morris does not shy away from these implications. When, at the end of the ballet, Marie and the Nutcracker walk off into the horizon, a nice, fat remote-control rat scuttles along after them. If your love has been given to you by the world, a corollary of that is that your love may be no better than the world. Your cellar will have rats, like everyone else's.

In a few of Morris's dances the development of a motif is so methodical and profound that the whole dance rides on it. This is the case with what must be called the guts motif in *Dido and Aeneas*. The motif is introduced in Dido's very first dance phrase, in the "press'd with torment" gesture. As we saw, Dido places one hand on her chest and one on her abdomen, both pointing downward, and opens her legs. The meaning is clear—she is in love—and it is disastrous. She has a kingdom to worry about. She can't afford this passion.

The courtiers allay her misgivings. Don't fret, they say, you can run the kingdom *and* have love. She gives in. But the next time we see the guts motif, we realize she was right to worry. During the hunt scene, the so-called Second Woman, a lady-in-waiting, performs a dance to entertain the hunting party. The subject of the dance is the story of Diana and

Actaeon: how Actaeon, while out hunting, spied the goddess at her bath and how she, in revenge, turned him into a stag, whereupon his hounds turned on him and ate him alive. So this is a story of death met through sexual temptation, and to lock in the connection with Dido, Morris reiterates the guts motif. When the words "mortal wounds" come up in the Diana and Actaeon song, the Second Woman digs her hands into her abdomen and pulls them apart. It is a horrible gesture. The Second Woman is moved by her own story and is telling it as vividly as she can. She doesn't realize the connection with Dido, who is sitting in front of her with Aeneas, watching the dance.

At this point we may not see the connection either. But then, immediately after the Second Woman's dance, another gut is revealed. Aeneas-the-singer boasts of his success in the hunt—"Behold upon my bending spear / A monster's head lies bleeding"—and Aeneas-the-dancer, as we saw, holds open his tunic. If the terrible truth was not made clear by the Second Woman's hunt story, it is now unavoidable, and it is immediately reflected in the music: a storm begins. Dido-the-singer sings, "The skies are clouded, hark! how thunder / Rends the mountain oaks asunder," and on "asunder" Dido-the-dancer performs, against her own gut, the same disembowelment gesture that the Second Woman just performed. The storm is love, and Dido is going to be torn apart.

Soon afterward, we get the witches' "Destruction's our delight" chorus, with the Sorceress drawing the invisible sword up from crotch to gullet and then flipping her hand open at the gut, like entrails falling out. The other witches repeat her gut joke. This whole scene, with the witches hunkering down and sticking imaginary daggers into each other, is basically a gut dance. Indeed, all of *Dido* is basically a gut dance. Not just the witches but also the courtiers, Aeneas' sailors, and Dido herself are continually dropping into huge *pliés*. This low, squatty stance gives them a look of great solidity but also a look of mortality. We see the body giving in to the pull of gravity: dust proclaiming its origin, and destiny, in dust. Life is heavy. Dido will soon gladly lay it down.

Before she does, the guts motif is repeated one more time. In her lament, when the singer sings, "May my wrongs create / No trouble in thy breast," Dido, standing behind her sister, Belinda, presses her hand down on Belinda's chest, and Belinda opens her legs. This action, accompanying Dido's last words, is a reiteration of the "press'd with torment" gesture that accompanied her first words. So we are brought full circle. We have found out everything there is to know about guts: that they are sloppy and obscene (they flop out when you get disemboweled), that they are the seat of courage (Dido has "guts"), that they are the seat of life and of new life (the womb, which in Dido's case never bears the fruit of her love), that they are the seat of passion and also of nobility (it is through her passion that Dido becomes noble). It was all foreseen in that first gesture, and now it is completed with the repetition of that gesture. The guts motif does not carry the whole weight of *Dido*. There are fixed gestures for perhaps thirty words in the libretto: "fate" (which we saw), "empire," "storm," "fire," "beauty," "death," and on and on. But the guts motif is the soul of the dance. It has the same importance in *Dido* that key motifs have in Wagner's operas, and is developed in the same way, always weaving, changing, gathering in new meanings, always there in spirit when it is not there in fact, and thus, when it returns at the end, precipitating not just the fulfillment of the doom but also our sense of the poetic rightness of that conclusion. It is typical of Morris's unflinching interest in the physical that he should have chosen the gut as his main leitmotif for this dance. It is also typical that out of this low-down material he made so lofty a work.

But if half of Morris's works are set to vocal music, this leaves another half that are not. Where does he get his story when there is no Dido, no doom? He finds the doom in the music. Or rather, he reveals it, for by the time he has chosen to choreograph a dance to a piece of music, he has already heard a kind of story in it. Remember the words of his childhood friend Chad Henry: "By the time Mark told you about a piece of music, he had already been inside it, thinking about it, for days, weeks. So in his mind it had already collected all this back-story, this subterranean stuff, from his emotional response. That part is what came out in the dances." That part, actually, is what comes out in the work of any musical choreographer, but with Morris the drama is unusually forthright.

In 1991, for Mikhail Baryshnikov's White Oak Dance Project, he created a large ensemble piece called *A Lake* to Haydn's second horn concerto. This concerto is not program music, nor does it contain any obvious dramatic cues—no lullabies, no fate knocking at the door. The only story in it is a music story, about the horn's relationship to the orchestra: how the horn is alone while the orchestra is many, how the horn comes and goes while the orchestra stays, how the horn has a distant, pure sound in contrast to the orchestra's meshing, threshing, blended sound. So there is something that is solid and busy and big, and it is visited by something small and elusive and pure. One might think of a ray of light falling on a forest, or a memory returning to a busy mind. But the situation is more general than that, and Morris keeps it general, while at the same time making it intimate and profound.

In the first movement the music is mostly horn-and-orchestra, and the dance is mostly walking, with a note of decorous cheer. But the dancing always changes when the horn enters. On the horn's second entry, in particular, something interesting happens. A man is carried in out of the wings and flies over the stooping body of another dancer—an action that is repeated four times. This business of something shooting out into the air is of course an imitation of the voice of the horn, but it has an internal drama as well. Someone being carried by someone else, someone flying, someone bowing down: this suggests a wholly different emotional world from that of the nice, jaunty walking, with everyone equal and independent, that we saw before. That walking soon returns, and the horn goes away. But on the last note of the first movement, a body falls in from the wings—it is the same man who flew in on the horn—and lands, unconscious, on the floor. The horn has spoken.

When the lights come up again for the second movement, the "dead" man has a circle of people around him, and a lone woman on the other side of the stage begins a slow, mournful solo. What is going on? Why did the man die? Actually, it is not a death. (The man reappears, in good health, in the third movement.) It is Morris using a frankly illustrative action to signal a change in his half-narrative. What he is saying is "The horn has something to tell us. You got a taste of it before. It is solemn and difficult. Here it comes." And now we get the second movement of the concerto, the slow movement, in which, after a brief introduction, the horn plays the whole time and the dance tells the horn's story.

The dance is done by two small groups at opposite ends of the stage, each performing much the same steps, almost all of which involve a risk-and-catch maneuver. Before, we saw a fall. Now we see how people manage not to fall: by depending on others. A woman sits down—in the air, it seems—and the people around her loop their arms down to support her. A man keels over, and the person next to him catches him and rights him. A woman goes into a split, and another person catches her front leg and holds it, so that she is suspended in the air. What all this adds up to is a sort of sixties-type "trust game," but it is conducted with no sentimentality, no emoting. The tone is like that of Love Song Waltzes: respectful, sober. (As Baryshnikov has said, Morris's work is "never drooly.") It is not a tragedy but a dark comedy, where death is not fatal but simply threatened, so that we will understand that life has a somber underside. Having learned that, we are allowed to pick up and go on.

And that is what happens in the third movement. The horn recedes, the orchestra takes over again, and the man who died returns, leading the ensemble in a dance full of happy skips, leaps, and kicks. But the horn's message is not forgotten. Toward the end, the horn returns, and goes into a long, elaborate cadenza, during which one woman reiterates most of the key motifs connected with the horn. (This is another instance of Morris laying his cards on the table.) She does the dead man's sound-of-the-horn entry, the flying lift; she does the sit-in-the-air, the split-in-the-air, the keeling over. She remembers. They all remember, and help her do it. Then the cadenza breaks, the orchestra returns, and the third movement concludes on the same joyful note with which it began. At the end, most of the dancers fall to the ground, repeating the "dead man" motif, but this time they haven't died. They're just tired from dancing so hard. They've gone to sleep, as it were—wiser than when they woke up.

People seeing *A Lake* for the first time will not grasp all these elements. Furthermore, my description of them, like all descriptions of meaning in dance, has been overliteral. But the audience will know instinctively, from hearing the horn and the orchestra, and from seeing what the dancers do in relation to them, what the story is. Actually, it is not a story but a drama of moods, and that is true in most of Morris's works to non-vocal music. All his works are semi-narrative, but in the dances to vocal music the narrative, logically, is more specific than in the dances to non-vocal music. As he has said, he goes for the obvious. If what he has is a queen in love, he goes for the kind of story she can tell. If what he has is a horn, he tells the kind of story a horn can tell.

On the evidence of his musical choices—half vocal, half instrumental—he likes both kinds, but I suspect that he is marginally happier when he has a text. He has made wonderful dances to instrumental music, but these do not stack up to quite the same height as his recent works to vocal music, which include *Dido* and *L'Allegro*, two of the finest dance works of our period. Vocal music seems to feed him in a way that nothing else does. The sound of the voice thrills his brain, at the same time that the words the voice is singing conjure up a whole world —queens and witches, rain and wind and fire—for his imagination to run around in.

Vocal music also seems to liberate him. If Morris has an important artistic fault, it is that he sometimes shows a certain structural doggedness.

As Arlene Croce put it, "Once he has got hold of a structural device nothing on earth can make him let go." This does not happen in all or even most of his works, and when it does happen, it is by no means fatal—*Stabat Mater* survived it—but it is a weakness: he starts laying down rules and following them stubbornly, with the result that the dance can come to look tight and hard. In general, it is instrumental music that brings out this tendency in him—not surprisingly. Instrumental works are more likely to have a grand architecture that he will be tempted to imitate. Furthermore, it may be that without the complication of the vocal line, the structure of the piece, grand or otherwise, reveals itself to him too nakedly and mesmerizes him. (Remember his capacity to lose himself in music.) And perhaps, without the "sense" that the vocal text makes of the music, he feels an anxiety to make sense of it himself, and then makes too much sense.

In any case, with a few exceptions (e.g., *Stabat Mater*), this does not happen when he is working with vocal music. What happens is the opposite. This powerful, muscular instrument, the voice, reassures him that it will hold the piece together; indeed, it is telling a story that will hold the piece together, no matter what he does. At the same time, he gets interested in the story, and so he is partially distracted from the seduction of the music. A happy balance is thus created: the music on one side, the story on the other, and Morris in the middle, free to answer now the one, now the other, now the logic of his own imagination.

The kind of elasticity he shows in handling the music will be a subject of the next chapter. What he does with the text is to make it his own. At times he follows the words obediently. At others, he puns with the words, moves them, superimposes them on one another, changes their meaning, strips them of their metaphors, dresses them in his own metaphors. One minute, a given dancer will be representing a given character; then, in a flash, he or she is something else altogether. In 1992, Morris made *Bedtime*, to three Schubert songs, "Wiegenlied," "Ständchen," and "Erlkönig." The last of these, Schubert's most famous song, set to Goethe's most famous lyric, is a romantic ballad, a fast-paced and exciting ghost story. A man and his son are riding home on a dark, windy night. A spirit—the Erlking, with a crown and a tail—appears to the boy and bids him come away with him. He promises him a thousand delights. He will play games with him; he'll pick flowers with him on the shore; he'll show him his mother's golden gowns. He has daughters who will wait on him, dance with him, sing him to sleep. With each of the Erlking's approaches,

the frightened boy appeals to his father: Do you not see the Erlking? Do you not hear him? And each time the father says no, no, that's not the Erlking—it's just the mist, the wind, the leaves. Finally the Erlking threatens force. The boy screams. The father, now shaking, rides faster and faster. Finally, breathless, he arrives home. The boy is dead in his arms.

Morris follows the story faithfully. He has an Erlking (himself—another daimonic role), a father, and a son, together with a sort of storyteller and an ensemble, and they act out the events down to the smallest detail. But what the characters are doing at any given moment may be a response to any one of a number of different cues. The father and son start out together, embracing. They are riding on the horse, the way the song says. But soon the horse is forgotten; they are dancing. The boy is doing

Bedtime. The father (Guillermo Resto, right) grips the dying boy (Kraig Patterson, center). The Erlking (Morris, left) waits for his prize *(Tom Brazil)*

153

stretches, reaches (the reach of his emotions and of the singer's voice). Then he is trying out the Erlking's games. Then he is running in a huge, tearing circle around the ensemble (his own scream and that of the music). Meanwhile, the father is holding the boy, drumming out the hoofbeats of the horse, imitating the mist, the trees, the Erlking. At the same time, the ensemble dancers are now the music, now the mist, the games, the daughters, the wind, the willows. Periodically, they drum their feet on the floor (the music, the horse, the terror). At the end they fall to the ground (the end of the dance, and of the boy).

As for the storyteller, if you tried to chart the planes of her action, you would end up with something like a cubist sculpture. She begins by miming the story—pointing to the father, the son. But soon she is part of their dance. Then she is on the floor (the coming death), drumming her feet (the horse, the music, the doom). Then she is in league with the Erlking, playing in his games, dancing with his daughters, being held up by him on the words "golden gowns." (She is wearing gold-colored pajamas.) Then she is twirling again (the music), then jumping (the vocal line shooting up). As the terror mounts, she becomes scared of her own story. When the boy leaps into the father's arms, she too leaps—into the Erlking's arms. When the boy dies, she throws her head back (the audience's emotion).

So the dance is simultaneously the music, the text, the three main characters' emotions, and a dance—a rich, elastic thing, full of turmoil, displacement, and metamorphosis: a quintessential nightmare. At the same time that it is filling in all those things in the song, it is also filling in Morris's own personal reading of the song, his sense (as usual) of its double-sidedness: how it is both childlike and profound, how it reflects both the fear of death and the love of death. On the last notes of the music, when the boy falls out of the father's arms, the Erlking falls into the father's arms and stares him straight in the eye. What is he saying? "Now, perhaps, you believe in me"? "*I'm* his father now"? "You're next"? Whatever— the father is looking the irrational in the face. This showdown is not in the story. Morris added it, a mark of the freedom he feels when he has a vocal text.

It is not only the "abstract," musical treatment of narrative material that makes Morris's work half-narrative; it is also the narrative treatment of abstract material. While many of Morris's key motifs are forthrightly representational (falling = death, stamping = hoofbeats), others are not. Furthermore, the motifs are embedded in or developed into a great deal of what looks, at first glance, like "pure dance" material. But this too has a story, and you can read it. *One Charming Night*, to four songs by Purcell, is, as we saw, a dance about a vampire eloping with a child. (The piece is a cousin of "Erlkönig.") The first song is danced by the little girl alone, as she waits for the vampire to arrive. At the beginning of the second song, he arrives and launches into a dance that begins with a phrase consisting of six basic steps:

1. *He travels across the stage with his arms extended, "flying."* "I am a creature that flies." Also—in view of the fact that the girl was performing this same gesture during the preceding song—"I know you want to fly. I am here to help you."
2. *He does nine tiny hops to the side, meanwhile keeping his arms down and patting the air with his hands.* "I understand children. I'm a bit of child myself. We will play games."
3. *He does a juicy dip, facing her, then springs upward, executes a perfect* gargouillade *(the flickety-flack with the legs), and lands.* The dip: "There will be something physical between us." The gargouillade: "I can do wonderful things, and teach them to you. We will have an interesting life."
4. *He performs two* piqués arabesques *(step onto one leg, then stick your other leg out behind you), with his arms stretching outward. On the second arabesque, the leg he is about to step on undergoes a momentary "catch," or spasm.* The stretch of the arms and legs in arabesque: "We will go far, far away." The catch in the leg: "I must warn you, I am a vampire"—and since she did that same little catch during her pirouettes in the preceding dance—"but you have a little of the vampire in you too, don't you?"
5. *He does another arabesque, with arms and face aimed directly at her.* "It's you I want."
6. *He does a back bend in which he seems to bite his hand, but very elegantly.* "I must tell you again, I am a vampire, but it's not so bad. Really, it's nice."

The phrase is only 25 seconds long. Except for the flying arms, there is not a single representational gesture in it. It is all pure dance, a matter of shape, accent, speed, rhythm, and dynamics. And in it the vampire tells the girl who he is, who she is, and what their life together will be. No one doesn't understand what he is saying, but he does it one more time to make sure.

This fusion of abstraction and representation seems to Morris perfectly natural. In his view, every dance is to some extent narrative, because the movements of the human body mean things to us whether we want them to or not. Even Merce Cunningham's dances, which Cunningham has tried to disinfect of narrative by assembling them through chance procedures (dice rolling, coin flipping), seem to Morris to tell a story: "If Cunningham's work doesn't add up in a linear way, that doesn't mean it's abstract. It means that life doesn't add up in a linear way. Like, things happen in the wrong sequence, or they happen in an exaggerated way. But they're still those things happening. It may not look like Red Riding-hood and the wolf, but that's still who it is." At the same time, because the dance consists of movement—and thus follows the laws of movement, not the laws of language—it can never be wholly narrative. It lives a separate life, as an abstraction. "There's a war between abstraction and realism that I don't think exists," he says.

But it does exist, and since the mid-nineteenth century, when romanticism forked into realism and symbolism, it has exerted a formidable influence on art. Modernism, the child of symbolism, took as one of its basic tenets the symbolist claim that art did not have to represent life or comment on it: art was its own world, separate from reality. "Ceci n'est pas une pipe," as Magritte wrote on his painting of a pipe. It was not a pipe; it was a painting. Likewise Stravinsky: "Music can express nothing but itself." Likewise Archibald MacLeish, speaking for poetry: "A poem should not mean / But be." Meanwhile, of course, representation did not die. Paintings that depicted things, music that expressed things, poems that meant—these went on being produced, for they were what most people wanted. Hence the highbrow-middlebrow quarrel between abstraction and representation that has so dominated art in our century.

In dance, this quarrel has had a life all its own. In some measure the history of dance has been a history of alternation between abstraction and representation, the abstraction of the seventeenth-century court ballets being followed by the storytelling *ballet d'action* of the late eighteenth century, the abstraction of late nineteenth-century Russian classicism being followed by the dance dramas of Michel Fokine in the early twentieth century. And throughout the twentieth century the quarrel has continued, with "realists" periodically rushing in to rescue dance from vacuity, and "classicists" then returning to rescue it from melodrama.

When Mark Morris walked on the scene in the early 1980s, dance aesthetics—and particularly the aesthetics of dance critics—had for several decades been divided between these two camps. The realists argued that the power of dance, as of most other arts, lay in representation: character, incidents, a good story, about life. The classicists argued that the only kind of story dance could tell was a dance story, a construction of open symbols created by formal means: rhythm, shape, phrasing, and so on. "Literary" ballet, to the classicists, was a contradiction in terms, or at best a bastardization. The classicists liked Balanchine and Cunningham; the realists liked older, more literary styles (Graham, Tudor) and favored European ballet (Kenneth MacMillan, John Cranko) over the more classical American ballet. The realists regarded the classicists as snobs and phonies; the classicists regarded the realists as people who didn't like dance. These are bald generalizations. They apply more to the critics than to the audience—the public flocked to Balanchine but not to Cunningham, though both were "classical" favorites—and critics too crossed over when they wanted to. Nevertheless, sides were taken.

By the mid-eighties, however, this division had begun to ease somewhat. The realism camp felt less suspicion of Balanchine and Cunningham. One was dead, the other old. Furthermore, once Balanchine died, so that his place in history was consolidated and his privacy less in need of protection, his classical-minded critics were much more willing to talk about the real-life roots of his work: his youth, his loves. (And as, following his death, the biographical material began to be collected, those roots became clearer.) A similar thing happened with Cunningham. People began discussing what his work was *about*, partly, in his case, because his work now swerved in that direction: it seemed to be more about things, more emotion-laden. Twyla Tharp, another classical-camp favorite, began making dances that were not only more emotion-laden but frankly narrative, with heroes and heroines, families and quarrels.

These shifts, artistic and critical, were part of modernism's yielding to postmodernism, but the change of mind on the part of the critics, at least in the classical camp, was also a realization that the lines had been wrongly drawn. The crucial distinction was not between the representational and the abstract. (Balanchine, for one, claimed that he didn't know what people meant by abstract dance. "Put a man and a girl on the stage, and there is already a story," he once said. "A man and two girls, there's already a plot.") What mattered was whether the dance was symbolically potent or not, regardless of whether it represented things. In other words, something could be an open symbol—a dance, with a full, autonomous movement drama—*and* a closed symbol: a princess, a pipe. Today, the word "literary" as a term of derogation is rarely seen in dance criticism. The literary has been absorbed into the classical.

And so it has in the work of Morris. In his dances, as he claimed, the war between abstraction and representation doesn't exist. When Dido presses her chest, then presses her abdomen, then opens her legs—one, two, three—we no more ask ourselves whether this is an abstraction or a representation than when Rigoletto, at the end of Verdi's opera, opens the sack, sees his dead daughter, and sings "Ah! la ma-le-di," and then, on descending notes—one, two, three—"zio-o-ne!" We understand the literary sense (that *maledizione* means "curse"), and it helps us figure out what is happening, but only from the musical values, the three notes falling slowly, like something locking into place, do we grasp the full meaning: Rigoletto's life is ruined, and he did it. Similarly, we know from the representational character of Dido's gesture that she is in love, but only from the dance values—the grave composition and timing—do we know that she is also a queen, and can't have this love, and will be destroyed.

It is no accident that Morris likes vocal music. His work is very much like song, a fact that has probably made him more popular. He can pull in the people who like the words and the people who like the music. This is no shrewdness on his part, however. Dance story, storylike dance: it is really all he knows how to do.

MUSIC

When Morris was young, music was his game, his hobby. What basketball is to some children, the piano was to him. After the Morris house burned down in 1971, and the piano with it, he bought a new piano as soon as possible, with his own money—$75—and was back at the keyboard, working away. That he had so little formal training is unfortunate, and also not unfortunate, for it meant that music was wholly his, not something imposed on him. And it was endlessly rich and flexible. It could be easy when he was young, harder as he grew. It could be a game that he played with his friends—clapping songs with Page Smith, round-singing with Chad Henry and Maureen. At other times, it was a territory that he entered alone, and where his mind could be completely occupied. The mathematical intricacies of Bach, the slippery jazz rhythms of Gershwin, the make-it-fit puzzle of rounds and madrigals—however big his curiosity, music was bigger. The piano was also a link to his father. It was Bill who had taught him to read music, and whatever Bill felt about ballet dancing, he took great pride in Mark's piano playing.

So music became, in large part, his life. The other large part was dance, though this was music too. In his ballet classes, and especially in his studies of Spanish and Balkan dance, with their subtle rhythms, he built up his rhythmic intelligence, he saw how dance was created on a musical structure, and he learned how to make music not just with his hands or his voice but with his whole body and personality—that is, in a way that was both intimate and complete. In Koleda his ideas about life and love grew up in relation to music. Eventually he took from music his choreographic method, motif development, a way of working that he refined as an adult but which at that point was completely natural to him, for by the end of his childhood the whole pattern of his mind—his intelligence, his emotions, his worldview—was woven on the web of music.

It is no surprise, then, that Morris's choreography reflects the music to which it is set. The dance is not just accompanied by the music; it is a reading of the music. When the musical structure is A-B-A, the dance structure is A-B-A. When a musical phrase is repeated, the dance phrase is usually repeated. When the music takes the form of fugue or canon, the dance is fugue or canon. When, in Baroque scores, there is a *ritornello*, an introductory instrumental section that keeps coming back, the dancers who danced to that music the first time keep coming back. When there is soprano-alto-tenor-bass counterpoint in a chorus, the ensemble will often dance in four-part counterpoint. When, in the music, the orchestra is heard in alternation with a solo singer, the ensemble moves in alternation with a solo dancer, or the dancers' arms move in alternation with their legs. When two singers sing polyphonically, two dancers do different dances; when two singers sing in parallel thirds, two dancers, close together, do the same dance. In the music of *Dido*, the Second Woman's Diana and Actaeon story is a vocal solo sung over a ground bass, a constantly repeating thematic motif in the bass line; in the dance, the Second Woman stamps out the ground bass with her feet while her arms dance to the vocal line.

Morris's choreography of course attends to the rhythm of its music; almost all dances do. But it also discovers and reflects internal accents, half-accents, little rhythmic surprises. When there is hemiola (two notes played in the time of three, or vice versa) in the music, as there is in so much of the Baroque music that Morris uses, there is usually hemiola in the dance. When, in *Dido*, Purcell uses a "Scotch snap" (a short note on the downbeat, followed by a long note), Morris mirrors it in a skip that does the same thing, going up fast on the downbeat and then sailing in a long arc over the remaining time. When he is faced with a jazz score, as in his *Three Preludes* (1992), set to Gershwin's Preludes, the body, with its snapping, dragging, deep-digging line, imitates the witty, flexible rhythms of jazz.

Musical attack and dynamics go into the mix. When a hand comes down hard on the piano, someone does something hard—lurch, leap, fall—on the stage. When the vampire in *One Charming Night* takes his nine tiny hops to the side, he is imitating the nine steady, sharp accents of the vocal line. The music's key structure is also there in the choreography. Dido's dance moods reflect the changing keys of her different scenes, and when, in Acts I and II, Aeneas' singing ominously violates the key, Aeneas' dancing disrupts the established mood of the dance. Even cadences are illustrated. In *Jealousy*, when Handel's sopranos sing "Tyrant of the human breast!" (they are describing jealousy) in a rising line, on four lurching beats, Morris's leg rises upward on four lurching beats. Then, as the altos repeat the line, his left arm rises in four beats, and when, following that, the tenors take up the line, his right arm rises in the same four beats. The choreography is a physical act of musical understanding.

If Morris's habit of developing his dance out of a limited number of movement motifs gives his work an unusual clarity, this other habit, of mirroring the music, redoubles that clarity, and since the two methods are entwined—the movements motifs are often attached to musical motifs, and thus appear, disappear, and develop as the music is mirrored—the dance is clearer still. To add yet another dimension, Morris often *chooses* his music for its clarity. His long, happy self-education in music left him with an extraordinarily catholic taste, and this is reflected in the list of composers he has used in the works he has presented since 1980: Purcell, Couperin, Vivaldi, Domenico Scarlatti, Handel, J. S. Bach, Pergolesi, C.P.E. Bach, Boccherini, Mozart, Sri Tyagaraja, Beethoven, Schubert, Haydn, Verdi, Brahms, Ponchielli, Saint-Saëns, Tchaikovsky, Satie, Schoenberg, Kreisler, von Dohnányi, Bartók, Stravinsky, Virgil Thomson, Henry Cowell, Gershwin, Poulenc, Alexander Tcherepnin, Harry Partch, Shostakovich, Jean Françaix, Conlon Nancarrow, Lou Harrison, Harold Budd, and Herschel Garfein, together with a great deal of country-western music, some traditional songs (Bulgarian, Romanian, Tahitian), Indian and Thai pop songs, a few jazz and rock 'n' roll songs, some old calypso songs, three parlor songs, and a piece of roller rink–type organ music. He has also made dances for operas by Gluck, Mozart, Johann Strauss, Richard Strauss, and John Adams.

This is a heterogeneous list, but still a personal one. There are clear favorites: vocal music, popular music, the West Coast experimentalists (Partch, Harrison, Cowell), and above all Baroque composers. And there are other composers who, relative to their output of danceable music and their popularity with choreographers, are notable non-favorites. There is little Mozart, no Chopin. Morris prefers the eighteenth century, especially the early eighteenth century, to the nineteenth. As for the twentieth century, he tends to pick those who came after the neoclassical revolution (Poulenc, Françaix, Thomson) rather than the still-romantic composers who came before (Debussy, Ravel). In view of his love of popular music, there is very little jazz and very little rock. There are exceptions to almost all these rules—despite his relative neglect of romantic music, he has made three dances to Schubert—but they prove the rule.

The rule is a love of melody and a love of strong, clear structure. A comment that he once made on Mozart is revealing: "I love Mozart . . . but I find that the structure of his works is often too fragile, too sophisticated for dancing." So over Mozart he will choose, for example, Haydn, because the form seems to him more legible. Above all, he will choose Baroque music, which is ultra-legible. Baroque scores are ideal for dancing, in any case, because in the seventeenth and early eighteenth centuries concert music was still based on dance music. In the operas of Handel and Purcell, in the cantatas of Bach, you still have, as Morris appreciatively notes, "dance rhythms and dance tempi—there's still minuet and gigue and bourrée and passepied . . . The basic thing is still human rhythms." But the critical thing about these scores, in his mind, is the clarity of their structure. Baroque music, as he says, has "perfect architecture."

Why is he so concerned with structural clarity? One reason is his wish to communicate. All human activity involves some element of mess or imprecision, but dance has a special problem in this regard, for the material of dance is the body. Whatever the rules of the dance, the body has a life of its own, full of vagaries and personalism—the fact that it has hair and pores, that it is big or little, fat or thin, that it sweats and gets tired, that it has a face that reminds us of somebody, indeed, that it has a personality that colors all its actions—and these facts will alter the dance, blur its edges. Furthermore, however pure the body's action, that action is gone in a second; the dancer is in motion. All this is fine. We forgive the body its imprecision for the sake of its poetry. Still, something is needed to prevent the body from resolving into sheer blur, its movement into sheer excitation. All good dance has some obvious principle of order that stands between it and entropy. In ballet the principle is the academic technique: the five positions of the legs and arms, the vocabulary of steps elaborated on that base. In much of Indian and African dance, the principle of order is rhythmic logic. In Mark Morris, it is musical clarity. If he can keep his music clear—choose clear music to start with and then reflect it in the dance, so that we never lose track of where it's going—then the music itself will order the dance, and the eye and the ear, each experiencing the same thing, cannot, between them, miss what he has to say. This is all the more important to Morris, for as we have seen, he has very specific things to say, and he likes his bodies messier than the average.

So part of the reason is his wish to get his points across. At the same time, it is obvious that he also loves structural clarity just for its own sake. He would love it even if he weren't a choreographer. "Beauty for me is usually structure," he has said. When he speaks of the formal probity of Baroque music, his words take on a kind of warmth and glow. "Handel's work is a perfect system. It's complete. It's a microcosm." "Bach's music sounds to me pretty close to a perfect thing, a perfect system." "Bach is God's favorite composer." He is ravished by them, and when he himself creates something that looks to him like a perfect system, he is ravished by himself and will describe his achievement to you with immense pride and enthusiasm. Here he is speaking about *Behemoth*:

Rob Besserer in *The Death of Socrates* (Tom Brazil)

There's a part of Behemoth *that's a beautiful machine. Everybody comes in, seven from one side, seven from the other, and they're all doing a seven-beat phrase, except everybody's doing it one phrase behind the person in front of them. And they're traveling in fixed floor patterns. One is a zigzag. The other's like a loop. But it's a loop or zigzag from the left or from the right depending on where you entered, and sometimes the loop and the zigzag are happening at the same time. So you've got fourteen people all doing this completely symmetrical and completely complicated thing, and everybody at a different point in it, and nobody bumps into anybody else. That whole movement—it's a perfect system.*

On his 1983 *Death of Socrates*:

I couldn't afford the score. I had to send to France for it, and I couldn't afford it. It was like 150 dollars. So I said, the hell with it, and I listened to the music and I counted it out and divided it numerically into equal units of time. So everyone does a 96-beat phrase six times. The way the dance overlaps, it starts with one dancer and adds up and diminishes so that, at the most, there are six people on the stage . . . So that's how many units of 96 beats it is. And everybody does exactly the same thing with their patterns—reverse from front to side. Some people have the side as the front. Some people have the front as the front. But it all fits.

It is no coincidence that both these systems involve canon, in which different dancers do the same dance at different intervals of time. (A canon is like a round, cf. "Three Blind Mice.") Canon is the strictest form of contrapuntal imitation, and therefore the clearest, and therefore dear to Mark Morris. When there is canon in the score, there is almost always canon in the dance, and when there is no canon in the score, there is often canon in the dance anyway. It is his favorite structural device, probably because it does two things that he wants to do—clarify (by repeating) and complicate (by repeating at different intervals)—at the same time. Also, a canon is like a puzzle. You have to work on it to make it come out right, and he loves that kind of game. "It's very satisfying to make up a canon that works perfectly," he once said,

something where, because of the way I designed the steps, I can combine them without making exceptions and everything comes out right. Like those canons I was working on today [he was choreographing Motorcade, *1990]—I made up the steps two weeks ago, and I know how they work.*

So now I can put them into different configurations, and they will take you to a certain place and then get you out of that place, and yes, you go there and that will curl you around, and of course, because of the way everyone is traveling, one space per two bars, that puts you through this hole instead of that hole, and nobody has to cheat.

If two or three of his brain cells had been wired up differently, he would have been one of those children who takes clocks apart, and grown up to be a mathematician. In any event, this habit of mind helps to account for the structural firmness that so distinguishes his work and for the structural doggedness—the defect of his virtues—that occasionally mars his work.

It is not just a quirk of mind, however. It has important psychological underpinnings. Why do people prize clear structure? Because they like to understand what they are seeing and because this makes them feel that life is understandable. There is a another, well-known reason: structure gives them freedom. The clearer the rules, the more flexible the situation. One can test the rules, bend them, even break them, without having to worry that the whole thing is going to fall apart.

This rhythm of rule setting and rule testing is the dominant pattern of Morris's personality. He is a great *provocateur* and a great traditionalist, and his work repeats the pattern: two opposing forces challenging each other. One can see it in the choreographic style, in his habit of making beauty out of "ugliness." One can see it, too, in the tone: the mixing of nastiness and cheerfulness (*Dogtown*), rage and elegance (*Jealousy*), horror and comedy (*Lovey, The Vacant Chair*), satire and endorsement (*Ten Suggestions*), pathos and sobriety (*Love Song Waltzes, Beautiful Day*). At times it is a matter of tension between the choreography and the music: agony versus sweetness in *Stabat Mater*, prostration versus exultation at the beginning of *Gloria*. It may indeed be the subject of the dance. Morris's two most ambitious works are both about things and their exact opposites: Dido and the Sorceress, L'Allegro and Il Penseroso.

But the clearest demonstration is his treatment of musical structure. The only thing more remarkable than his dependence on his scores is his independence of them, his free play within the rules they set down. Cadences he mirrors only when this is useful to him; otherwise, the dance goes its own way, up or down, depending on its own needs. He also likes to play with time values, for dramatic ends. In the "Destruction's our delight" chorus in *Dido*, the Sorceress and the witches all do the same movements, but the witches do two to every one of the Sorceress's. This

166

sets her off and at the same time gives the dance a hot, febrile quality that accords well with the sentiment under discussion, the love of evil. Rhythm is Morris's very special care, and one that he manages with a deftness worthy of a student of Spanish and Balkan dance. He often uses it, as he uses duration, for dramatic purposes. In *Lovey*, at the opening of the "Country Death Song," the mother, the father, and the child all move in different rhythms simultaneously, each rhythm giving a different character to each, and when the father leads the child out to the mountain, he moves in twos, she in threes, thus letting us know that she is smaller —a victim already before the crime. At other times, he seems to play variations on the music's rhythm—laying threes over fours, fives over threes—simply for the sake of vitality. Of all the elements of dancing, rhythm is probably the one most crucial to the spectator's attention. Variation or surprise in rhythm can force the eye (and hence the mind) back into the dance when otherwise it would glaze over. Morris knows this, and uses it.

Structure too is mirrored only in part—mirrored enough so that we hear the music's rules, then varied according to the dance's developing logic. In *Gloria*, two female dancers may dance while two female voices sing, and the dancers may enter when the voices enter, dance in unison when the singers are in unison, dance in counterpoint when the singers are in counterpoint. But when, later in this dance, Morris wants to enlarge the stage picture and the sentiment—it is the joyful "Laudamus te" section—by bringing in more dancers, he doesn't wait for the music to bring in more voices. (It's not going to.) He simply brings back the two dancers who, at the start of this section, were identified with the *orchestral* music. Shedding their former identity, these "orchestral" dancers now join the two "vocal" dancers, working in counterpoint to them. So where, before, we had one dancer per voice, now we have one two-dancer dance per voice. Okay, but now comes a twist. In the music, the orchestra reenters and the voices cease. What will he do now? Will he make the vocal dancers exit? No. They let the orchestral dancers join in their section; in return, they now get to join in the orchestral dancers' section. At the end, all four exit, with one trailing behind, as a kind of punctuation mark. What began in imitation ends in variation. Morris has built a wing onto Vivaldi's house, because he wanted to expand and complicate the dance.

This happens in all his works, and sometimes the deviations are far more extreme. In rare cases, such as the slow movement of *A Lake*, with the risk-and-catch maneuvers, the dance and the music have almost no structural relation whatsoever. In other cases, he will mirror the music for a while and then just stop. In *Dido*, once Aeneas has left, Dido has two lines—lines full of music to mirror—before the choral singing begins. But she mirrors nothing. She simply walks back to her bench and sits down, pulling her body tightly inward. In doing so, she gives us the meaning of those lines—"But Death, alas! I cannot shun; / Death must come when he is gone"—better than dancing could have. This is the first we have heard of the fact that Dido is going to die. Morris wants it to make an impression, and he achieves this by calling a halt to the dance. He does the same thing in the opening section of *Gloria*, this time going all the way, with the blackout. In showing us the two figures, the man and the woman, struggling forward, he has given us the rhythm of the music and the basic theme of the piece. But once the man falls and the voices enter, singing "Gloria! Gloria!," Morris just wants us to hear what the singers are saying. Also, as the critic Alastair Macaulay observed, he may have wanted to stamp the man's crucial fall on the viewer's memory. So he turns out the lights. As we know from power failures, people don't forget what was happening when the lights went out.

Given the extent of his music illustration, one is tempted to think of these deviations as music violation. In other words, he thought of following the music but then decided not to. But the process is probably less conscious than that. The deviation begins at the beginning, in his personal, idiosyncratic response to the music. Morris listens to a great deal of music. Only some of it evokes in him the kind of complicated emotional response that, for him, is the beginning of a dance work. There are other crucial considerations that are factored into his musical choices. (Is the music danceable? Is its structure clear? How does it fit in with what he is contracted to do in the near future? He can't choose a flute solo if he's supposed to be doing a large ensemble work.) But his emotional engagement with the music is the fundamental thing. "You can't just choose any old piece of music and lay choreography over it," as he said to an interviewer. "The choice has to be motivated." As Baryshnikov has described it:

With Mark, it's never just "Oh, I like that music. It's pretty. I'll do it." There is a need. Like, it must be done, almost, except that at the beginning he doesn't know why. He says to himself, Why do I like this music so much? He digs in it, in him. He goes through this angle and that angle. Then, when he finds the answer, everything is easy. The piece comes. But that is how it comes, from his searching in himself why he is so interested in this music. It is a very strange, very unusual attitude.

In the discussion, earlier, of his musical choices, one important point was not discussed: Morris has used almost no commissioned music. Cost could be a factor here, but he finds ways to meet costs when he cares enough about the thing he is buying, such as live singers. The primary reason for his failure to commission music seems to be that, for him, the music must precede the very conception of the dance. He cannot have music handed to him; he might have no response, or a shallow response, to it. The proof of this is the choreography he has produced when he *has* had music handed to him: for example, his dances for the Peter Sellars operas *Nixon in China* (1987) and *The Death of Klinghoffer* (1991), to music by John Adams, or *Striptease* and the other dances in *Mythologies*, to music by Herschel Garfein, or *Home* (1993), to a beautiful score by the Texas songwriter Michelle Shocked and the bassist Rob Wasserman. Some of these dances are not particularly interesting (*Home*, *Klinghoffer*), and some are inspired, but even the inspired ones are not wholly characteristic of him. They are theater more than dance, and their main thrust is wit, irony. His emotions are less engaged. Fundamentally, Morris is not a collaborator, or not when it comes to that paramount thing, music.

Not only does Morris rarely commission music; he seldom goes in search of music for a dance. Many choreographers, perhaps most choreographers, come up with an idea for a dance and then look for music that will go with their idea. Morris has done this once or twice—for example, with *One Charming Night*. He got the idea for making a vampire dance from reading Anne Rice's *Interview with the Vampire*. He then looked for music and found the Purcell songs. But this is the exception. Almost always, the idea for the dance is born from the music.

The centrality, for him, of emotional involvement with the music is one of the reasons he favors Baroque music. He loves its "clarity of expression," as he puts it: "that emotional stuff that just hits you in the face, like an air cushion in a head-on collision." Where the emotion is less direct, he loves the thrill of listening to the music deeply and hearing it give up its secrets. "The more you listen to [Baroque music], the more secret and rich things you can find dramatically. You realize that the phrase lengths are not all the same. You realize that the ways the keys relate changes completely how you feel what's going on. Within this

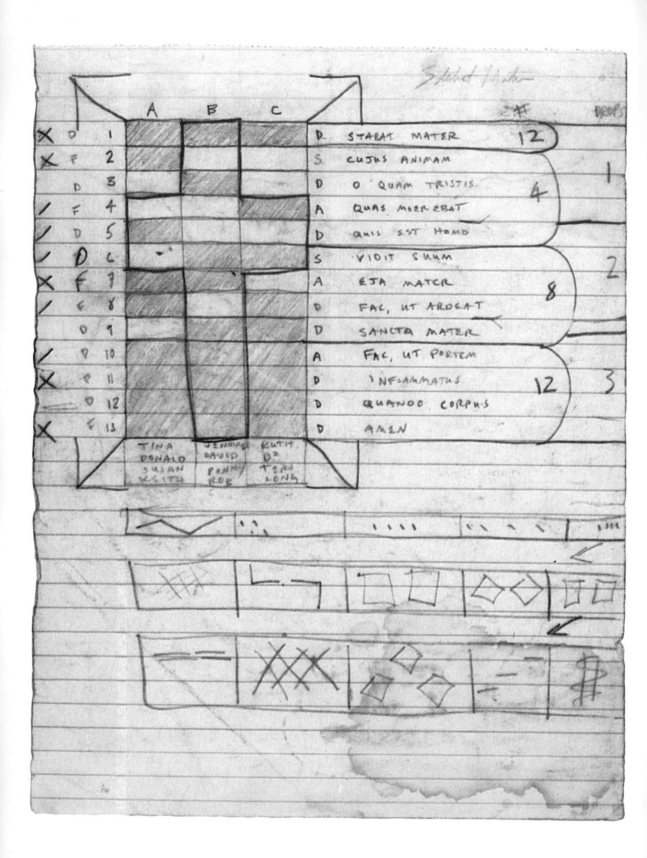

Stabat Mater

				A	B	C					#	DROPS
X	D	1					D	STABAT MATER			12	
X	F	2					S	CUJUS ANIMAM				1
	D	3					D	O QUAM TRISTIS			4	
/	F	4					A	QUAS MŒREBAT				
/	D	5					D	QUIS EST HOMO				
/	D	6					S	VIDIT SUUM				2
X	F	7					A	EJA MATER			8	
/	F	8					D	FAC, UT ARDEAT				
	D	9					D	SANCTA MATER				
/	P	10					A	FAC, UT PORTEM				
X	P	11					D	INFLAMMATUS			12	3
	D	12					D	QUANDO CORPUS				
X	F	13					D	AMEN				

TINA	JENNIE	RUTH
DONALD	DAVID	D^2
SUSAN	PENN	TERI
KEITH	ROB	LONG

seemingly very strict form, incredibly dramatic and terrifyingly powerful emotional stuff comes out."

This statement is probably a good description of what happens at the genesis of a Mark Morris work. He is listening to the music very hard, analytically—phrase lengths, key changes—but as he does so, an emotion is being born in his mind, an emotion that gradually eats the music, makes it his. That emotion, and not the music, is what he then mirrors in the dance. When, in *Jealousy*, he reflects the three successive rising lines of the chorus's song ("Tyrant of the human breast!") with three successive risings of his limbs, it is not because that is what the music is doing; it is because the music, by doing that, sounded to him like a seizure. It told him something emotionally (and the text is telling it to him at the same time): that jealousy is like a seizure of the mind. It grabs you, courses through you. And that is what he portrayed in the dance, something running through the body, grabbing it bit by bit. The seizure of course follows the lines of the music, but it is not a direct translation. (For one thing, the vocal line rises four times, not three. But Morris can't raise his fourth limb; he's standing on it. On the fourth line, therefore, he just bends over. So much for music mirroring.) The choreography is a translation of the emotional idea or—because he is a choreographer and thinks in move-ment images—the emotion/movement idea generated in his mind by the musical structure.

Once Morris knows that he is going to make a dance to a certain piece of music, he listens to the music again and again, often over a long period of time (three years in the case of *L'Allegro*). While listening, he will do certain preliminary work. He will decide how many dancers he wants, and which dancers. If it is a large ensemble work, he will figure out traffic patterns and sometimes draw them. Generally, he will also work out at least one movement idea. In the case of *Gloria*, for example, he came into the studio with the stomach crawl. For *Motorcade* and *The Death of Socrates*, as we saw, he had all the steps of the canons involved, but this is rare. Usually it is just a germ of material: a step, a phrase, a motif.

Now he goes into the studio with the dancers. Despite the fact that he already has certain dancers in mind, he often has the whole company learn all the material. Watching the dancers' different ways of doing the steps gives him ideas, or refines his ideas. (E.g., "All of you, do it the way Kraig is doing it.") Furthermore, he may change his mind about the size of the piece—his tendency is to enlarge. (He starts to feel sorry for the understudies and ends up putting them in the dance.) Finally, even if he

Opposite:
Morris's preliminary
sketch for *Stabat Mater*

171

sticks to the dancers he had in mind, making all of them do all the material helps him sort them into roles.

So he begins. He teaches the company the step he has brought in, which is already attached to a point in the music, though not necessarily the beginning of the music. Once they have learned that step, he starts developing it. As he proceeds, two things are guiding him: the emotion, which is in his mind, and the score, which is in his mind, in his ears— the rehearsal pianist is playing—and, almost always, in his hand. It is rare for a choreographer to work with the score in hand. (A number of good choreographers don't read music.) But because of his concern with musical structure, he needs the score: "When you're just listening, you can't hear every part. Also, there are subtle things, mathematical things: harmonic progressions, phrase lengths. You'd end up having to make a chart, and there already is a chart—the score."

To say, beyond this, what he is thinking as he makes the dance is to enter a slippery territory, but one can at least describe the planes on which his mind is operating. First, he is responding to the imaginative tug of the kernel material. As Balanchine said, steps have family relations. From the stomach crawl in *Gloria* it is not far to the leg-irons walk. They are roughly the same step, each a crippled, lurching progress, one horizontal, one vertical. Similarly, the risk-and-catch maneuvers in the second movement of *A Lake* are all cousins of each other, and all of them are descendants of the big lift in which the man who "dies" entered during the first movement. That was a case of total support; these are cases of partial support, and together they form a kind of analysis of that big gesture.

Second, he is responding to the laws of the body. The body is a specific instrument. It has only four limbs; the leg can rise only so far; the neck can bend only so far. Because of these facts, the body "wants" to do certain things, and if you work against those preferences, you get certain effects, some of which you don't want and some of which you may want. In *Motorcade*, the first piece that he made for Baryshnikov's White Oak Dance Project, Morris at one point had the dancers do a series of half-turns in the air that, because they worked against the body's momentum at that instant, came out looking very abrupt, as if an invisible hand had picked the dancers up and then plopped them down again. The turns didn't flow—and for that reason Morris liked them and kept them in. "In that step," as he said later, "you don't turn in the direction you want, and you don't use the leg you want. So the movement sort of 'pops.' That's what makes it interesting."

Connected to this is another consideration: rhythmic interest, the constant play of rhythm in his mind and his effort to transfer that to the dance. When, in the dance, an internal accent sneaks up within a larger rhythmic pattern, the viewer's mind is engaged. What is the relation of the little pattern to the big one? Will it disrupt it? Or when the dance rhythm departs from the musical rhythm—when three five-count phrases in the dance are laid over five three-count phrases in the music—the mind, again, is snagged. Will the two things come out even in the end? "You need suspense," Morris says. "Or not suspense, but suspensefulness, suspension. It could be a rhythmic thing or a tempo change or whatever. But for example, when all the dancers lunge to the side [he is talking about *Motorcade*] and suddenly they go slow, it's a way of setting up a theme that you're about to hear that you've never heard before. So you see this change, and it's like 'What is going to happen?' Then whap! It happens." And because it comes as an answer to a question, you pay attention.

Those suspensions are reflections of the music's suspensions, the musical story. But in many dances, Morris has a literal story to tell, with characters and incidents, so another consideration is how the musical facts will be distributed among these other elements. In "Erlkönig," for example, there is a roiling bass line that is a constant in the song, and a steady source of tension: the hoofbeats, the terror. How is this to be reflected in the dance? The father has to hold the boy; the narrator has to tell the story; the ensemble has to be flowers and mist, willows and wind. The answer is that the bass line gets assigned as Morris wants to localize or generalize terror in the dance, and also as the characters are freed up from their other tasks.

Sometimes the demands of the drama will temporarily wipe out the demands of the music, or part of the music. In *Dido*, as we saw, the Second Woman's Diana and Actaeon story is a vocal solo over a ground bass, and the dancer mirrors this by dancing the melody with her arms and the bass line with her legs. But *Dido* has two other big arias over a ground bass, and in neither of them is the bass line danced. This is because both those arias belong to Dido, and she says crucial things in them, in the vocal line. (One is the "press'd with torment" aria; the other is her death lament. These are her only two arias.) So Morris has Dido dance the vocal line only. Of course, he could have assigned the bass line to the ensemble, but he doesn't. Nothing should distract us from what Dido is saying.

All these considerations are being factored in at any given moment as Morris makes the piece. At the same time, like any artist, he allows himself a measure of free association, and this plays a large part in the production of the actual steps. *Motorcade* was not just the first piece that Morris made for the White Oak Dance Project; it was the first piece the White Oak Dance Project ever danced, their debut piece. So Morris wanted it to have a bold, here-we-are quality. He chose his music accordingly: Saint-Saëns's Septet. The piece is full of big flourishes on the trumpet, big runs on the piano, and the dancers echo these in lots of flourishing lifts and happy runs. Toward the end of the dance, though, something strange happens. We get an image of danger. Four dancers line up on the diagonal with their arms sticking out. In order for the other four dancers to run onstage, also on the diagonal, they have to push through these arms, and when they do, the arms swing around like revolving doors, almost hitting them.

This is a wonderful touch, a tiny note of skepticism. All through the music, things have been pushing for dominance—the trumpet, the piano, the strings—and the dancers have mirrored this good-natured pushiness. Now, however, we see that pushing through things can be dangerous: the thing you're pushing could hit back at you. Morris says that he didn't know beforehand that he would end up with doors. (Once he got them, though, he knew what they were. To keep the dancers moving briskly through this section, he said, "Doors are scary. You're not scared, but doors are scary.") Where did the image come from? Possibly just from a choreographic accident, an arrangement of arms that stood in the way of a running path. But the path didn't have to run so close to the arms; there was plenty of room on the stage. Morris clearly wanted to throw in a little difficulty, a little grit, to give the piece emotional traction. And revolving doors were what he came up with. This is not something that the music provides. It is something dragged up from the mind in the backwash of the emotion. Likewise the sense of when to illustrate the ground bass and when to ignore it, when to go with the rhythm and when to violate it. So Morris's relationship with the music is one of constant give-and-take.

This elasticity has increased over time, which is not to say that he has become less dependent on the music, but more dependent and more independent at the same time. His habit of illustrating the music began in earnest with *Gloria*—in other words, very early: 1981. (And in that same year he did his first parody of music illustration, *Ten Suggestions*.) As he became more interested in illustrating the music, he began choosing more architectonic music. The folk music and the Thai pop songs dropped out; the Baroque phase dropped in. From 1985 through 1988 he never made fewer than two pieces a year to Baroque music, and in 1988–89 he capped this by taking on two hugely ambitious Baroque scores, *L'Allegro* and *Dido*. His work with the Baroque began in strictness. *Marble Halls*, the kickoff of the 1985–89 Baroque run, is a classic example of his "perfect system" choreography. But as he came to know Baroque music, and music in general, better, his hold on it became less rigid. He could grasp the musical structure and also let go of it, or grasp other things at the same time: dramatic needs, theatrical needs, his own winding thought. Accordingly, he began permitting himself (though very rarely) to tamper with his scores. From 1984 to 1988 he never made an internal change in any piece of music that he used. But in 1988, in *L'Allegro*, he made important alterations in the score. (They are noted in the chronology.) In 1993, in *Grand Duo*, he dropped the fourth movement of Lou Harrison's five-movement piece. "It would have made the dance too long," he said simply. He is giving himself more leeway.

Nevertheless, music has never ceased to be central to his work and even to his managerial decisions. Certainly one of the main reasons he moved the company to Belgium was so that he would have the musical resources to produce *Dido* and *L'Allegro*. He still insists on dancing to live music whenever possible, and a large portion of the company's budget goes toward paying for that music. For the live-music nights of his 1992 New York season, the musicians' bill was $11,000 a night. He also tries to get the very best musicians. (The band for that season was the Orchestra of St. Luke's, one of the finest small orchestras in the United States.) When he can't count on live music, he would prefer to choreograph to a record—that is, not just a recording, but a piece of music that was made, and intended to be heard, as a recording, such as the Violent Femmes songs for *Lovey* or the many country-western songs he has used. This is one reason for the persistence of popular music in his repertory.

The degree to which Morris is true to his music has put off certain of his critics. "Too often his choreography shows us nothing more than the notes printed on the page," wrote *Newsweek*'s Laura Shapiro in 1988. Likewise Clive Barnes of the *New York Post*: "He usually choreographs [to a score] with a literalness that some apparently find musical but I consider Disneyesque." (Earlier, Barnes had written that Morris had "all the musical sensibility of a frog faced with ice cream.") Anna Kisselgoff of *The New York Times* has also described him as having a "step-to-note style." What these critics are talking about is "music visualization," or, as it is sometimes called, "Mickey Mousing" (so named because, in those cartoons where he danced, Mickey Mouse would go down on the low notes, up on the high notes—in other words, mirror the cadences). The reason music visualization is looked down on is that presumably it is a renunciation of the choreographic task: the score, not the choreographer, determines the steps. Actually, it is hard to see how music could determine steps. If it could, then *Liebeslieder Walzer* and *Love Song Waltzes/New Love Song Waltzes*—dances created by two *echt* "visualizers," Balanchine and Morris, to the same score—should at least resemble each other instead of looking, as they do, as if they had flown in from two different planets.

Of course, the consideration should not be—and, for these critics too, it is not—whether a choreographer is guided by the score, but whether there actually has been a renunciation of imagination, so that the music is reduced to a set of rules and the dance becomes simply an obeying of those rules, with nothing to tell us beyond the fact that the choreographer knows how to read a score. At rare times, this happens in Morris's work, even his recent work. When, in his 1990 *Ein Herz*, the female corps returned on the *ritornello* for what seemed the eightieth time, and with the same step—a *développé* front that looked as though they were taking aim to shoot the audience—one felt like shooting them instead. But in the great majority of his works, even his lesser pieces, Morris's imagination is working at full tilt within the musical structure. Because the musical structure is never forgotten, the fit of dance and music seems perfect. "Of course," you say, "given that music, it had to be that dance." But it didn't have to be that dance. There were a thousand different ways to imagine a dance to that music, even a "visualization" of that music. It took this choreographer to imagine it this way. As Morris has said, "People forget that somebody actually choreographed what Mickey Mouse does."

Behind the music-visualization charge lie certain historical facts. Of all known forms of dance, there is only one that has mixed feelings about music: European-American modern dance. From its beginnings, modern dance had a strong musical tradition. One of the major forces in the founding of modern dance was Eurhythmics, a system of music education invented at the turn of the century by the Swiss music teacher and theoretician Emile Jaques-Dalcroze. The Dalcroze system was designed to inculcate musical sensitivity by having students translate musical rhythm into bodily movements, often one rhythm in the arms, one in the legs. (The Second Woman's dance in *Dido* is thus a sort of Dalcroze exercise.) Eurhythmics was immensely popular. In the years preceding World War I, students of the Dalcroze system numbered over 7,000 per year, in more than 120 schools, and many of those students went on to become modern dancers, building their work on Dalcroze's musical base. Music was also of paramount importance to Isadora Duncan; her dances were essentially music interpretations. As for Ruth St. Denis, the other American "mother" of modern dance, it was she who, inspired in part by Dalcroze's system, invented strict music visualization as a mode of theatrical dance. In its ideal form, as she described it in her 1925 essay "Music Visualization," this would take the form of a "synchoric orchestra," with one dancer for each instrument in the score. When the violins played, the violin dancers would dance; when the clarinets chimed in with the violins, the clarinet dancers would join in with the violin dancers, and so on.

St. Denis staged such performances in the twenties, but not for long. They were not popular. More important in carrying forth the musical tradition was St. Denis's pupil Doris Humphrey, who had collaborated on St. Denis's music visualizations and whose knowledge of music (and of Dalcroze) was greater than St. Denis's. In 1928 Humphrey left St. Denis and went off to create freer music analyses: abstract dances to Bach and other composers in which she used choreographic counterpoint and harmony, based on the scores, as metaphors for her ideas about human society and the human spirit. Humphrey passed her methods on to her protégé José Limón, and she taught extensively.

Yet at least by the twenties, modern dance was also nurturing a strong anti-musical tradition, a movement to liberate dance from the dominance of music. The whole effort of the early modern dancers was to rescue dance from what they saw as the dead hand of opera-house conservatism—to give it a new creative force, to establish it as an independent art. And according to many of the pioneers, this could not be done as long as dance remained dependent on music. Mary Wigman, the leader of the early modern dance movement in Germany, decided that even the rhythm was not to be taken from music: "It is the rhythm of the dance which . . . engenders the musical rhythm. The musical accompaniment ought to arise from the dance composition." These principles were seconded by the composer-pianist Louis Horst, the most important composition teacher in American modern dance. Horst served first as St. Denis's music director, then as Martha Graham's—he was a crucial influence on Graham's style—and in the thirties, forties, and fifties, that is, the period of "middle" modern dance, he taught dance composition to literally thousands of students. Horst based his teaching on musical principles—statement and development, A-B-A—but the goal of these lessons was to inculcate *choreographic* craft. (It was Horst who set up the Juilliard choreography course in which Hannah Kahn learned the respect for craft that she passed on to Morris.) Once the students learned music-based principles, they were expected to apply them independently of music. To Horst, choreography inspired by music belonged to an early stage in the development of the art. Dance had now grown up; it no longer needed to borrow its ideas from composers. Therefore, like Wigman, Horst believed that a dance score was best composed *after* the choreography— a "frame to the picture," as he put it. John Martin of *The New York Times*, America's most influential dance critic in the thirties and forties, also reiterated again and again that dance should not let itself be bossed around by music. Though he admired Doris Humphrey, Martin disapproved of what he saw as her music visualizing. (Of her 1942 *Four Chorale Preludes* he wrote, "The music dominates in feeling and form," and he meant this as a criticism.) On the other hand, he vigorously championed Graham, who was never a "visualizer." Even after she broke with Horst's principle of having the music composed after the dance, Graham still did not normally use her scores as compositional guides. To her, music was more an atmosphere than a structure.

Such principles occasionally touched the ballet world as well. It was partly because he took his choreographic ideas from his music that Balanchine for so many years was chided for coldness—"le ballet frigidaire," as one French critic put it—and that John Martin in the thirties and forties so often dismissed Balanchine's work, claiming that it lacked "matter." Balanchine has since been more or less canonized by the public, yet as recently as 1992, a writer for *The Village Voice* characterized his legacy as "abstract patterns that please through their intricacy and precision." The greater the musicality, the less the substance: the notion is not dead.

But it is rare in ballet. In modern dance it is common, and while there continue to be musical modern dance choreographers, the direction of innovation is usually against music. Merce Cunningham won a great deal of prestige in the fifties and sixties by liberating his dances from music. (He creates the dance independently of what will be its accompaniment —music and dance usually do not meet until the first performance—and he gives the composer no instruction other than the length of the piece. Furthermore, his scores rarely make any pretense to being danceable in a conventional sense.) Paul Taylor, the other pioneer of the post-Graham generation, takes the rhythm and spirit of his dances from the music he is working with, but the structure of the score is not a primary concern of his. The same is true of Twyla Tharp, who on a number of occasions has switched scores in the middle of choreographing a dance. The Judson Dance Theater group frequently did without music altogether, both in their Judson years and after. Trisha Brown had been making dances for twenty years before she used a musical score, and she only made the switch, she once said, because she got tired of hearing the audience cough. Today, among young modern dance choreographers in America, dancing that is rooted in musical structure is rare. Among their European contemporaries, dancing to music is rare.

So what Mark Morris does has little counterpart in recent modern dance. Its counterpart is ballet, where dancing to music has always been the rule and where, under the influence of Balanchine, an analytic approach to music has become the rule. Hence the repeated comparisons of Morris to Balanchine. This comparison is a sore point with some critics —an example, in their view, of how Morris has been overpraised—and they are certainly correct that in terms of achievement it is not useful to measure a thirty-seven-year-old choreographer against a man who died at the age of seventy-nine, leaving behind a catalogue of 425 works. In other respects, crucial respects, the two men could hardly be more different: one Russian, the other American; one born under the czar, the other under Eisenhower; one bred in ballet, the other in folk dance; one a classic modernist, the other arguably a postmodernist. But in a very limited sense—not achievement or style but simply choreographic approach— the comparison is apt. It says what Morris is attempting to do that is different from other modern dance of our period: analytically musical choreography. Indeed, it says what he is doing that is different from *ballets* of our period, even ballets by choreographers who are strictly school-of-Balanchine. For aside from musical analysis, the thing that at present most distinguishes that school is a marked dryness, an academic quality. What Balanchine tried to do was to express in the open symbols of dance certain general truths born of a passionate response to musical form. Morris, though his primary inspiration was not Balanchine (it was music itself) and though he may succeed or fail, is trying to do the same thing, a goal unshared by any other prominent choreographer today. It is possible that this approach—the conjuring of a full-scale theatrical dance out of its music—is on its way out. It was born in the twentieth century, and it may die with the century. In any event, it is not the only way to make a dance. Martha Graham did fine without it. If it were to vanish, a rich and beloved art form would vanish, but such things have happened before.

The similarity of method points to another similarity: like Balanchine, Morris shows a classical temper. Modern dance's ambivalence about music is part of modern dance's intrinsic romanticism, its emphasis on original inspiration, with the artist creating his or her work alone, undictated to by any academy, any technique, any rule at all, including the rule of musical structure. It is no surprise that modern dance has an anti-musical tradition; the wonder is that it has a musical tradition. By contrast, Morris's approach is classical. He is willing to obey rules, to raise up his art on the art of others: old dance styles, old music. For him, as for many classical-minded artists, this has helped with productivity. (Since 1980 he has averaged over six works per year—an enviable record.) There is a great deal of music in the world. If you get your ideas from music, you can get a lot of ideas. There is also a great deal of *different* music in the world, and this helps to account for the variety of Morris's repertory, the fact that, for example, on a given night in Boston in 1992—a typical night—his company performed a piece that looked like a ballet, to Haydn (*A Lake*), a bluesy jazz solo to Gershwin (*Three Preludes*), a poignant duet to Bach (*Beautiful Day*), a nightmare fantasy to Schubert (*Bedtime*), a great Hymn to Man, set to Vivaldi (*Gloria*), and a piece to Lou Harrison that looked like a bunch of people getting ready to go out and kill somebody (*Polka*, 1992). And that was just Program A. Two nights later, the company performed Program B, which was an entirely different story.

There is no question that for Morris this music-based method is a metaphor for life, or for the mind's life in the world—the fact that things find their reality by attaching to other things. This, it seems, is the lesson he learned at the piano when he was young: that a melody becomes eloquent by being cycled through harmony and counterpoint, that emotion becomes powerful as it is seized by intelligence, that his own emotions could become useful to him—a source not just of turmoil but of creativity—as he found their counterpart in the emotions that other people, old composers, had had, and in the forms they used to contain them. In keeping with the old classical paradox, he found that this containment could free him. That is what happens as Morris listens to music. His understanding of the structure builds a floor and four walls around the emotion. Then the emotion is liberated, and not just into its bright center but into its dark corners: half-moods, internal beats, personal associations, fantasy. From these he makes the dance. As his pianist, Linda Dowdell, has said, "Sometimes the most personal thing he gives us is the way he hears."

IRONY AND SINCERITY

orris has a reputation as an artist of irony, and the leading example of this strain in his work is *The Hard Nut*, his *Nutcracker*. There is an irony already in the fact of the ballet's existence: this famously hip, bad-boy artist taking on the world's sweetest ballet, with its Candyland and Sugar Plum Fairy. And then there is the title of his version. He didn't invent it. "The Hard Nut" is the name of a tale-within-a-tale that occurs in the middle of the E.T.A. Hoffmann story, "Nutcracker and Mouse King," that was the original source of *The Nutcracker*'s libretto. This subplot takes on a special importance in Morris's version, so the new title was justified on grounds of content. Still, Morris no doubt liked its fortuitous associations. *The Nutcracker*, he seems to be saying, is a hard nut for a modern artist to crack.

In its traditional form, *The Nutcracker* presents two ideal worlds. Act I takes place in a snug, upper-bourgeois nineteenth-century German household—the home of Dr. Stahlbaum and his wife—where, on Christmas Eve, the daughter of the family is given a nutcracker and her brother breaks it. In Act II, the girl and her nutcracker, now transformed into a handsome young man, journey to a fairy-tale Candyland, to taste a thousand delights, which usually take the form of national dances (Arabian dance for coffee, Chinese dance for tea, et cetera). But the Hoffmann story was far darker and more grotesque than this. By the time Hoffmann's tale, written in 1816, issued out into the first *Nutcracker* ballet, premiered in St. Petersburg in 1892, it had been heavily edited, sweetened up. And though Tchaikovsky's score was keyed to this edited version, Morris decided he wanted to go back to the Hoffmann, which seemed to him, with its elements of Germanic horror, to have more poetic truth. So he hired a horror-comics artist, Charles Burns, to help him conceptualize *The Hard Nut*. Burns is best known for his "Big Baby" series—titles include *Curse of the Molemen*, *Teen Plague*, and *Blood Club*—in which a rather horrid-looking child, Big Baby, makes his way through a universe crawling with green monsters and mysterious, skin-curdling diseases. In the Big Baby comics, though, it is not just the events that are terrible; the victims are not very attractive either. Burns's world is something like that of David Lynch's movie *Blue Velvet*—a sanitized suburban sixties where people with teased hair and blank faces are constantly finding a severed body part on the linoleum. It is to that same world of the sixties that the events of *The Hard Nut* were transferred. And though the ballet is sweeter and funnier than Burns's comics, it does contain real horror.

The primary horror is simply the look of modern life. The Stahlbaum living room is a perfect suburban fright: white vinyl couch, white plastic drink caddy, white plastic Christmas tree with all the balls the same. Gone is the snugness and charm of traditional *Nutcrackers*. (The Yule log that burns in the Stahlbaum living room is on the television screen.) Gone too is nobility. Mrs. Stahlbaum is a big, fussy, hyper-femme redhead—she is played by a man, Peter Wing Healey—who has to take a big pill before her party. As for the Stahlbaum children, the eldest, Louise, is a horny teenager in go-go boots; the youngest, Fritz, is a truly loathsome little boy who runs around terrorizing people with a plastic submachine gun. The party guests are a pop nightmare: bouffant hairdos, push-'em-up bras, hip-huggers, skirts with slits. All the women think they're Barbarella; all the men think they're Robert Goulet. To Tchaikovsky's Act I dances—a march, a quadrille, the "grandfather dance"—they do the twist, the jerk, the stroll, and a very dirty version of the bump. In between, they drink, fight, burst into tears, make out, pass out, and steal back the presents they gave the Stahlbaums. When Drosselmeier, a family friend, arrives, the gifts he brings the children are not the dear little Columbine and toy soldier of yesteryear but a robot and a life-sized Barbie, in thigh-high silver boots. The robot tears Barbie's arm off. (Burns wanted him to tear her head off, but this would have necessitated a costume too difficult for the dancer playing Barbie to perform in.)

Opposite:
Carol singing at the Stahlbaums', *The Hard Nut*. Standing, left to right: Barry Alterman (Dr. Stahlbaum), Rob Besserer (Drosselmeier), Morris, Keith Sabado, Joe Bowie, Megan Williams, Guillermo Resto, Penny Hutchinson, Mireille Radwan-Dana, Peter Wing Healey (Mrs. Stahlbaum, obscured), Tina Fehlandt (Louise). Seated: Holly Williams, William Wagner *(Tom Brazil)*

It is all superbly, deliciously bad—an anti-party scene. And it stays bad. After the party scene comes the battle of the mice and the toy soldiers, which in most versions of *The Nutcracker* is a cute, mock-heroic business. Here it is a disorderly melee in which rats, not mice—big, hairy rats, with long, pink, phallic tails—do battle with a gang of G.I. Joes. This is followed, as in most *Nutcrackers*, by the Waltz of the Snowflakes, but Morris's snowflakes are not women in long white tutus. They are men and women, all costumed the same—satin halters, hats that look like the top of a Dairy Queen cone, puffy little tutus that make their rear ends look enormous— doing a half-awkward, half-charming dance while tossing out fistfuls of snow. (Half the women and several of the men are on point, the others in bare feet. Morris gave them their choice.) In Act II, the national dances are again pop updates. In the Arabian Dance, the Arabs wear sunglasses. In the French Dance, one of the dancers carries a baguette, another a whip.

The Waltz of the Flowers is a frankly biological number, with men and women, again all costumed the same, twining and chaining and coupling innocently to Tchaikovsky's famous waltz. The *grand pas de deux*, as we have seen, is an anti-*pas de deux* in which the lead couple is more or less forgotten while everybody in the cast runs onstage and has a terrific time doing big ballet steps.

Throughout, Old World quaintness, Old World assumptions are replaced by the things of the New World: the pop, the democratic, the lowdown. The style is broad, flat, and cheerfully crass. Mouths open wide, eyes bug out, things go pow. Burns's poster for *The Hard Nut* strikes the same note. "SEE the rat queen's horrible mutant offspring!" it says in big, bold letters. "SEE the bizarre dance of the oversized toys!" Everything is ugly, and laughs at its own ugliness. The tone is something like *Mad* magazine.

It is also something like the decade that produced it, the eighties. Much of twentieth-century art has been an act of irony, with the noble, preindustrial past being set alongside the tacky, low-down, democratic present—Ulysses *versus* Bloom, painting *versus* Campbell's Soup—but in the eighties what had been a trend became a conflagration. Mass culture invaded high culture. Artists made art in the form of comic books, greeting cards, ceramic knickknacks, electronic signboards, B-movie stills. In part, this plunge into mass culture was the result of the influence of the French school of criticism: Roland Barthes with his claim that a society's true meaning could be read in its billboards, Jean Baudrillard with his claim that our world now consisted of nothing *but* its billboards—that mass communications had brought us to the point where there was no reality left, only images. Another important factor, of course, was simply the expansion of mass communications, especially television. The young artists of the eighties grew up in the seventies and sixties. If their work looked like TV, it was no wonder. They spent their youths watching TV. Finally, the political battles of the eighties had a massive effect on the art of the decade. Many artists were not unhappy to break with a high-art culture that to their minds had served for centuries to support inequality: to increase the power of church and state, to perpetuate racism and sexism. That art and its canon and traditions—its claims of originality and inspiration, its transcendence of life's sorrows in the name of higher ideals—they could do without. They would make a non-original, non-inspired, non-transcendent art: an art that looked like the mass-produced world around them or an art that, if it relied on past models, did not carry on their tradition but instead flatly copied them, "appropriated" them, often in new, jarring contexts that made them look positively archaeological. If, as Baudrillard said, we live in an age of simulacra, these artists were willing to produce simulacra.

Much of *The Hard Nut* fits right in with these trends. A young artist taking on an old, idealistic form, classical ballet, and de-idealizing it with a flood of modern junk: what could be more eighties? Other things about the piece too, and about Morris's work in general—the scorching wit, the willingness to shock, the consciousness of historical styles and the ability to imitate them—seem quintessentially eighties. *The Hard Nut* also has the political edginess of its period, and not just in its fiddling with gender. In Act II Morris comments quietly on the ethnic stereotypes of the national dances by having his one Puerto Rican dancer, Guillermo Resto, dance the Spanish dance, and his three part-Asian dancers, Keith Sabado, June

Omura, and Olivia Maridjan-Koop, do the Chinese dance. Likewise, the Stahlbaums' maid is played by a black dancer, Kraig Patterson (another travesty role). To some extent *The Hard Nut*, like so much other art of its time, seems to be saying that the Old World is dead.

And to a very large extent, it is saying the opposite: that the ideal meanings of old art, including *The Nutcracker*, are still very much alive —indeed, the center of our existence. For in the middle of all the flash and pop of *The Hard Nut* stands its heroine, Marie, the Stahlbaums' middle child, innocent and noble. Marie is no stranger to *The Hard Nut*'s comic-book world. She wears a little pink dress, and she has a big, pointy hair bow, like Nancy, from the comic strip. Still, her character is a serious conception. (And it was played as such by Clarice Marshall, who, though she was thirty-nine at the time of the premiere, managed unsentimentally to make herself into a child.) Marie is truly excited and terrified by the big, ugly party, truly appalled when Barbie's arm is ripped off, truly in love with her Nutcracker, and steadfast in her love, even when, in a twist of Morris's complicated libretto, the Nutcracker is changed *back* from a handsome young man into an ugly toy. And Marie is our guide to the meanings of *The Hard Nut*: how everyone searches for love, how love must often be wrested out of ugliness, how love and beauty are there to be had in the world. For much of the ballet, Marie's idealism stands in contrast to the world around her. But even when Marie is not center-stage, there are events in the first half of the ballet—for example, the tender duet between Drosselmeier and the Nutcracker, with the hand-to-heart gesture—that clearly point to some ideal beyond parody.

Later in the ballet, the two strands, irony and sincerity, come together in earnest, and Marie's love for her ugly Nutcracker becomes a metaphor for the hidden sweetness of what had seemed an ugly, morally careless world. This is the point of the "Hard Nut" tale-within-a-tale that Morris went to such trouble to reinsert into the libretto. In the ballet, as in Hoffmann's narrative, "The Hard Nut" is a story that Drosselmeier tells Marie while she is recovering from the battle with the rats, and it is a grisly story, about a rat who bites a baby princess, Pirlipat, thus casting a spell on her that makes her monstrously ugly. The only way the spell can be broken, says the rat, is if a special hard nut is found and a young man cracks it with his teeth.

Morris acts all this out on his stage. We watch the rat jump into the baby carriage to do the vile deed. We witness the search for the hard nut, across the world. (This becomes the pretext for the national dances.) We see the great day when the young man cracks the nut and the ugly princess, now of marriageable age, is transformed into a raving beauty in a sequined dress. But all the major roles in this inner tale are performed by the characters in the outer tale. Pirlipat's parents, the King and Queen, are Dr. and Mrs. Stahlbaum. Pirlipat is Marie's sister Louise. Drosselmeier is the one who goes in search of the hard nut. His nephew the Nutcracker is the one who breaks the nut with his teeth, and breaks the spell. It is as if Marie, while listening to Drosselmeier's story, were imagining it in her mind, and casting it with the people of her world. In the process, the story becomes a comment on her world—on the ugliness of life and how to cope with it.

Eventually, however, the "Hard Nut" story ceases to be just a comment on Marie's world. It becomes her world. Because of a hitch in the spell, Pirlipat is no sooner transformed into a beauty than the handsome Nutcracker is transformed into an ugly thing. Pirlipat accordingly wants no part of him. At this point Marie stops the story or, rather, invades it, and offers her love to the Nutcracker—a selfless act that of course breaks the spell. The Nutcracker becomes a dashing young man again, and he and Marie run offstage together. This is immediately followed by the Waltz of the Flowers, a fertility rite in celebration of the couple's love. Then comes the grand pas de deux, in which we find out that this love was there all along, buried in the world, and that Marie and her Nutcracker learned it from the world.

It all happens a little too fast, though—this shift from the world's ugliness (a foil to Marie) to the world's beauty (a lesson to Marie). Furthermore, it is when the world is ugliest that it is most convincing artistically. The Act I party scene is the best thing in The Hard Nut: the most detailed, the most brilliant, the steadiest in tone, the most consistent with its music. In Act II there is nothing in Tchaikovsky's score to accommodate the terror of the "Hard Nut" subplot or, for that matter, the events of the "Hard Nut" subplot. Morris ends up, as he himself told an interviewer, having to "smash" his story into the music—not a formula for success. Elsewhere too his intentions jar with Tchaikovsky's. His grand pas de deux, however serious its intent, is still too comic on its surface to accord with the majestic sweep of its music. In other words, the thesis-antithesis (Act I) comes off better than the synthesis (Act II). Having set up ugliness as a satiric force in Act I, Morris never quite manages to convert it into the tragicomic force he needs it to be in Act II. He himself seems to acknowledge this when, at the end of the ballet, he sends that remote-control rat scuttling after Marie and the Nutcracker as they walk off into the horizon. The tone is a little odd. On the one hand, he believes in fairies. On the other hand, he doesn't.

This instability of tone is another thing that was common among artists of the eighties. In their use of mass culture, they were sometimes eyeing it coldly—"deconstructing" it, rooting out its hidden, oppressive meanings—and sometimes simply loving it, taking it for truth and beauty. Similarly, in their use of the past, sometimes the past was past—distanced, hedged all around with things that made it look arch, overblown, *past*—and sometimes, in a flash, it became real again, present and powerful. A leading example of this yes-and-no tone is in the work of Peter Sellars, the director who, in the eighties, imported the postmodern aesthetic into lyric theater, particularly with his productions of the Mozart–da Ponte operas. Sellars's *Don Giovanni* was set in a slum, his *Così Fan Tutte* in a diner, his *Marriage of Figaro* in Trump Tower, with Figaro as a chauffeur, Cherubino as a local hipster, and the guests at Figaro's wedding doing a rock 'n' roll dance to Mozart's fandango. Much of the time, in these violent transplantations, you couldn't tell what your attitude was supposed to be. On the one hand, Sellars treated the music with the utmost seriousness. On the other hand, no sooner did he get us through an impassioned aria than someone would be eaten up by a foldaway bed. Nor could you figure out what the attitude was toward the *pop*. Sometimes it was clearly there to deflate. (Don Giovanni, for his last meal on earth, had a Big Mac and a large fries.) At other times, it vaulted into beauty. In the diner where *Così* took place, every Jell-O cube, every Cool Whip florette was modeled with the same kind of passionate care that Luca della Robbia gave to the Madonna's cloak. The result was dazzling, and unsettling, for this was still a diner and everyone knew it.

Mark Morris and Peter Sellars are friends. Sellars, as noted, was the one who suggested Morris for the job in Brussels, and Morris has done the choreography for a number of Sellars productions. (It was he who made that rock 'n' roll dance for Figaro's wedding.) And *The Hard Nut* resembles Sellars's productions in many ways. Visually, for example. The Stahlbaum living room in *The Hard Nut* is the same witty conversion of junk-into-beauty as the *Così* diner: no surprise, since they were created by the same designer, Adrianne Lobel. The costumes too, by Martin Pakledinaz, are superbly vulgar. (The audience often laughs out loud when the party guests enter.) And all of this is in keeping with the acrid comedy of much of *The Hard Nut*. It is not for nothing that Alastair Macaulay called this piece "Morris' Peter Sellars ballet."

But again there is a difference between Morris and his postmodern counterpart, for while Sellars and many other artists of the eighties simply permit themselves their vacillations between irony and earnestness, Morris is constantly gnashing his teeth and pushing things around in the effort to resolve the contradiction. Hence the messy business of the "Hard Nut" subplot. He is attempting, mid-ballet, to modulate into a different moral key. He doesn't quite succeed, but you watch him trying. Likewise in all his work, when he sees—as he so often does—two things that oppose one another, he never just shuttles back and forth between them, adjusting his tone accordingly, as if such back-and-forthing were the fate of art in our time. ("How *can* we be serious, given our world?") He either unites them, or if he can't, he forces us to look at that fact, as a problem, a tragic metaphor. He has none of the deep cool of so much art of the eighties. His work is very hot, always sticking its face in your face and saying, "People die! People leave you! Life is cruel!"

This moral earnestness is related to another way in which Morris breaks the postmodern rule: his lack of self-consciousness about representation. Many of the artists of the eighties, with their sensitivity to mass communications, showed a considerable sophistication about the act of picturing things. Often, what they gave us were not pictures but pictures of pictures, meta-representations. Morris too goes in for meta-representation now and then. When the curtain goes up on *The Hard Nut*, the first thing we see is the Stahlbaum children watching *The Hard Nut* on television in the family den. In the last moment of the ballet, after Marie and the Nutcracker have gone off, we return to the den, and there, again on the TV, we see the happy couple kissing. (The credits then roll on the TV screen, and they are the actual credits for *The Hard Nut*. Louise points to her name with joy as it goes past.) But these are jokes—nods toward the world we live in and the medium through which we now acquire our dreams. They take nothing away from what has transpired in between. Morris's approach to representation is quite direct. He takes his dream as real, and he takes life as something real, which it is his job to make sense of. The illusoriness of the world is never an important subject in his work.

His approach to mass culture is *not* direct, and in this he is in line with his contemporaries. He, like them, is of the TV generation, and however much the artists of that generation may see through mass culture, they are usually not shocked by it. Many of them think it's funny, and fun. So does he. And there was nothing in his youth to discourage such enjoyment. There was no bohemianism in his family, no recoil from American middle-class life. They used Cool Whip. All through his youth, Morris absorbed mass culture together with high culture—above all, high musical culture—never thinking that the one might invalidate the other. And he didn't go to college, where the distinction might have been forced on him. So he never acquired either snobbery or a pop counter-snobbery.

His natural tendency is to love popular culture. For one thing, it reminds him of his youth. In many of his dances you can see traces of his childhood—cartoons, for example. The Sorceress in *Dido*, he says, is based in part on Cruella DeVil, the villainess of the Walt Disney movie *101 Dalmatians*. (The influence of Disney bumps up repeatedly in his work.) In *Championship Wrestling* one of the women in the bitch fight undergoes the same sort of virtuoso humiliation—a slow-motion head-over-heels tumble, five full revolutions—that Wile E. Coyote so often suffered in the Road Runner cartoons. Morris also uses a great many toys. *Lovey's* hard truths are played out on dolls. In *Deck of Cards* there is a whole, long solo, complete with pirouettes, for a little computer-controlled truck. In *The Hard Nut* he went further, devising a trio for remote-control rats, performing in unison. (They are controlled by three dancers, who stand in the wings manipulating joysticks in accordance with Morris's choreographic instructions.) Of course, *The Hard Nut* contains much, much more of his youth: the clothes, the dances, the Barbie, the robot. According to him, it also contains some beloved characters from his childhood. Mrs. Stahlbaum, in her more endearing aspects—the red hair, the elaborate behavior—is based on his old teacher Verla Flowers, and Drosselmeier, so dashing and so full of fun, is a memory of Uncle Jim. *The Hard Nut*, Morris says, is the most autobiographical piece he has ever made.

But the love of popular culture is not just a gesture of tenderness toward his youth; it is also a matter of temperament. Morris loves high style: things that are exaggerated, stylized, fancy. He loved this quality in flamenco. He loves it in Asian dance and in Baroque opera. And he loves it on television. When he was living in Hoboken, with all his friends around him, one of the things he liked to do was turn on the TV—*I Love Lucy*, as noted, was a special favorite—and act out all the parts. "He would laugh and scream and cry big crocodile tears and squeal with delight," says Robert Bordo, who often came over to watch TV with him. Exaggerated, to him, does not mean silly. (I once asked him whether the big flaming cross on the first backdrop for *Stabat Mater* was not a deliberate, pop vulgarity. "To me it looks like Fourteenth Street," I said. "To me it looks like the fourteenth century," he answered.) By the same token, he does not recoil from artificiality. In the loft in Hoboken he had a non-working fireplace, and at Christmas time, he would move the television into the fireplace and turn on the Yule log, just as at the Stahlbaums'. He gets the joke, but to him the artificiality of modern life is not a *cruel* joke.

The attraction to popular culture goes deeper still. As he said, one of the qualities that appeals to him most in Baroque music is its emotional directness, and this is something that he also likes about TV. "We would watch *Father Knows Best* together and cry," says Erin Matthiessen. "There's something deep in his psyche about normal American family life, an almost Christian vision of how people should live together and be together, that means everything to him." At the same time, he has an intensely critical mind and the keenest possible sense of the ridiculous, and he does not live a normal American family life. So he both experiences the emotion *and* criticizes it, or this is what happens in the work. "I think the more he goes in for parody," says Matthiessen, "the more fun he makes of something, the more he is deadly serious. Often, in his dances, when the audience is laughing really, really hard, that's when he's saying what he most truly believes." This is not a bad description of *The Hard Nut*, and it is a very accurate description of a piece like *The Vacant Chair*. The more he believes, the more he questions that belief, in a way that makes the audience laugh. Then he asks why the audience is laughing.

The critical point is that because an image is incomplete or sentimental, he does not take it for a simulacrum. Parlor songs may dress grief in ribbons, but they are still about grief. A Barbie doll may be a cheap plastic thing with a funny figure, but it is still somebody's idea of beauty. For that matter, traditional *Nutcrackers* may gloss over the cruelty of life, but they are still about finding love, a serious matter. So he takes these incomplete things and completes them, by yoking them to darkness and difficulty. He is trying to make them truer, but he is not doubting their truth. They are stabs at the "great themes"—the search for love, the struggle with loss—and he respects them for this.

This is probably Morris's most profound disagreement with the main line of postmodern art. Traditional humanism, the great themes: these are what the artists of the eighties turned their backs on. To them, the great themes were a lie, in that they claimed that all human beings were involved in a common fate, whereas in truth people's fates varied considerably depending on whether they were black or white, male or female, rich or poor. Hence the concentration of many artists today not on "human" themes but on women's themes, racial themes, gay themes. Morris, on the other hand, never swerves from his interest in a common human fate or from his belief in its poignant and heroic character. He may test that belief, press it to the wall, but he never discards it.

This raises the question of the politics of his work. Despite his old-fashioned humanism, he is often considered a *de facto* political artist because of his forthright homosexuality, and also because of his choreographic explorations of gender, so pertinent to the women's and the gay-rights movements. His transgressive spirit has won him praise from a number of political-minded critics. For example, Marcia Siegel, reviewing *The Hard Nut* in *Ballet Review*, described it admiringly as a deconstruction of *The Nutcracker*. By the end of *The Hard Nut*, she writes, "the *Nutcracker* ballet has been thoroughly demolished," and all its outworn conventions—"the romantic love, the power struggles, the patriarchy, the magic, the sensuous dancing and the illusion of safety"—consumed in the flame of Morris's irony. But this is probably more deconstructive credit than he deserves. The thrust of modern deconstructive criticism, broadly defined, is to read through cultural myths, such as *The Nutcracker* or indeed classical ballet, and expose their hidden meanings, particularly their hidden political meanings. The "mythology" is stripped away; the message that it was covertly selling is laid bare. But if, in *The Hard Nut*, Morris does dispose of certain culturally ingrained and politically suspect conventions—above all, romantic love and classical ballet's ideas about men and women—he replaces them not with a cold look at the division of power in the modern world but instead with an assertion that beneath its ugly surfaces the world is still full of love—that no matter what ignoble parts people are assigned to play in modern life, they are fundamentally decent, and that if you bring them together in a group they will naturally love one another.

This idealism of his, and its distance from deconstructive thinking, is clearest in his *Mythologies*, for the three dances that make up this trilogy—*Soap-Powders and Detergents*, *Striptease*, and *Championship Wrestling*—were based on essays from Roland Barthes's 1957 *Mythologies*, a book that anticipated modern deconstructive criticism. The essays in Barthes's collection cover a wide assortment of cultural topics—toys, detergent ads, strip shows, Greta Garbo—always with the aim of showing how petit-bourgeois culture enforces its laws, indeed, passes them off as the laws of nature. In the essay "Striptease," for example, Barthes argues that strip shows, while seeming to offer a release from prudery, are actually an exercise in prudery: "Evil is *advertised* the better to impede and exorcize it" with the revelation of the natural chastity of the naked body. Likewise, in the essay "Soap-powders and detergents" he claims that detergent ads, by disguising the abrasive function of detergents under the lustrous image of bubbles and foam, reinforce our preference for white over black, "purity" over "dirt," while denying that such prejudices cause any harm.

And what does Morris make of this Marxist analysis of bourgeois culture? A drama of humanistic faith. His *Striptease*, like Barthes's, is full of irony about the distance between the luridness of fantasy and the chastity of the flesh, but he sees this as a poignant human fact, not as a mechanism of bourgeois law enforcement. In *Soap-Powders* too, he unmakes Barthes's point. The dance is essentially a "toil dream," in which a harried housewife wanders forlorn among visions of laundry—sheets billowing, sheets flying, sheets coiled and stretched into machines, Maypoles, instruments of bondage. To construct this vision, Morris calls upon almost

Soap-Powders and Detergents. Mrs. Michaels crucified on her laundry. Left to right: Guillermo Resto. Donald Mouton. Penny Hutchinson. Ruth Davidson. Tina Fehlandt (Beatriz Schiller)

every device ever employed by early and middle modern dance to make cloth an extension of the female soul. But whereas Doris Humphrey's and Martha Graham's fabric-aided strivings were for spiritual illumination, the heroine of *Soap-Powders*, Mrs. R. Michaels of Joliet, Illinois, is only looking to get her wash clean. This is the joke, the comedown. But as Morris and his composer/librettist Herschel Garfein contrived it, Mrs. Michaels's struggle is no sooner made comic than it is given an edge of nobility. In one section of the dance, an interviewer arrives in Joliet to conduct a "test," just as in the television commercials. He takes away the Joliet housewives' favorite washday product, Era, and replaces it with an "ordinary detergent." This creates a terrible reversal in Mrs. Michaels's life. Her wash is ruined:

Look at Tommy's uniform . . . Oh, and Sally's jumper, all the linens . . .
My wash was once so bright, my friends would tell me.
Now it's like day and night; they never even mention it.

To hear the soprano sing these lines—Garfein's score for *Soap-Powders* is a cantata—while Mrs. Michaels roots disconsolately through her wash is very funny. Likewise her triumph when the man returns and she, refusing his tempting offer of one hundred dollars, chooses instead to have her Era back. At the same time, however, this little drama is reminiscent of other, nobler tales of fall and redemption, temptation and chastisement, and partakes ever so slightly of their moral force. Ruth Davidson, who was in the cast of *Soap-Powders*, compares it to Martha Graham's dark-night-of-the-female-soul dances—"This is a myth too," she says—and recalls that Morris told the company to dance it like Graham's *Night Journey*. What in Barthes was an analysis of the oppressions of bourgeois culture becomes in Morris a meditation on human hope and the difficulty of its fulfillment.

That is his big subject, and if, in pursuing it, he discards certain mythologies, he embraces just as many others. His work, as Siegel pointed out, may have little place for romantic love or power struggles or patriarchy, but as for magic and sensuous dancing and the illusion of safety, they are all there. Anyone who believes, as he does, that the more human beings you gather around you, the better off you are—that love is the natural function of the group—has a powerful illusion of safety. But that is the whole thrust of his politics: always to gather in, to universalize. Morris's service to women has been considerable. He has created a hero-

ically scaled style of female dancing that is not dependent on erotic themes—a great gift to the dancers and, as a symbol, to the audience—yet he cannot be called a feminist. Though his company is racially mixed, he has made no dances about race, and *The Hard Nut*'s national dances notwithstanding, he doesn't think in terms of ethnic division, that is, in multicultural terms. (For example, he has no anxieties about "transculturalism," the borrowing of artistic styles from other cultures. If he wants to use Indian and Indonesian dance styles for *Dido*—and use them "inaccurately," wed them to his own style, just like Ruth St. Denis—he does so.) He has a very strong democratic feeling, and this is part of what powers the ironies in *The Hard Nut*. By placing the heroine among vinyl couches and Barbies, he is saying, "Nobody is ridiculous. Girls who shop at the mall are also noble-hearted, and can be the star of a ballet." In other words, anybody can be President. But again, this is not an allegiance; it is one facet of a general sympathy.

The same can be said of his attitude toward homosexuality. His homosexuality must certainly have figured in his effort to extend the boundaries of male and female dancing, but that effort was not just for homosexuals; it was for everyone. (Ultimately he has pushed female dancing further than male dancing.) If he has remembered AIDS in his work, so have many other American artists of his generation, and the "Nicht wandel" section of *Love Song Waltzes* is not really about AIDS; it is about loss in general. Once, when he was asked by a writer for *The Advocate*, a gay bi-weekly, whether his work had a message, he answered, "There's not a lot I can do about, like . . . world hunger, as far as choreography goes. So it's more like people should be nicer to each other—better, kinder, clearer. *Better*. That's all."

Doesn't he, though, have a "gay sensibility"? There are certain qualities in his work—irony, parody, the love of high style, the embrace of taboo subject matter, a tendency to mix the comic with the horrific—that are part of what we think of as gay sensibility, though they have also figured importantly in the work of heterosexual artists across time. And perhaps two of those qualities—irony and the mixing of comic and horrific—are as central to Morris's work as its musicality, structural clarity, emotional breadth, physical bluntness, danciness, humanism, and fusion of narrative and symbolic expression, none of which has anything to do with gay sensibility. Does he use "camp"? He says no. "I have absolutely no sense of camp," he told an interviewer in 1990. "How could anyone think I do? I'm always dead serious." And in view of the fact that reviewers who dislike his work have often characterized it as camp—that is, *merely* camp—such a response is understandable. Actually, there is some camp humor in his work. If, in *Dido*, we can't use the word "camp" to describe the Sorceress's trashy imperiousness—the strutting, the hair-flicking, the I've-had-enough-of-this exits—then it is hard to know how to describe it. As with music visualization, the question is not whether there is camp in Morris's work but whether the work is merely camp, and whether the camp that is there is well done. Camp has a minor place in his dances, but when it is present, it is often exquisitely funny, carefully controlled in tone, and full of delicate detail. People should enjoy camp while it lasts. Like "gay sensibility," it is a product of the closet. As homosexuality becomes more accepted, camp will become obsolete.

The measure of irony versus emotional directness in Morris's work, and his success in fusing the two, varies from piece to piece, but according to certain laws. The most important, predictably, has to do with music. As noted, whenever there is any break in his emotional bond with the music, he will generally make a dance that is either notably ironical or notably uninteresting. In the case of *The Hard Nut*, where irony runs so strong, he seems to have chosen Tchaikovsky's score not so much because it appealed to him emotionally but because he wanted to make a *Nutcracker*. He says he loves the score, but on the evidence of the ballet that he made to it, he does not care about it in the deep, mind-snagged way that he cares about most of the music to which he sets his dances. Furthermore, he acknowledges that there are parts of the score he doesn't love, and these may be the parts where the dancing becomes weak. The concluding duet for Marie and the Nutcracker is underchoreographed: the two of them run around and whisper and kiss for what seems a very long time. Earlier, I suggested that the weakness of this dance might be due to Morris's lack of interest in romantic love. But his comment on this section of the music is worth considering: "I hate that part of the music. That's where the Chinese people usually come out and wave."

The link between musical disengagement and emotional disengagement is even more obvious in his work to commissioned music. Both of his major jobs on Peter Sellars operas have been to commissioned music, and the composer, John Adams, was of course chosen by Sellars, not Morris. The first of those operas was *Nixon in China*, for which he made a wonderful parody of Chinese Communist agitprop ballet, complete with rifle-toting ballerinas. The second was *The Death of Klinghoffer*, for which he made a series of unremarkable dances. Of the very few pieces for which he himself commissioned a score the most important is *Mythologies*, which is less a dance than a brilliant theater work, with irony as its dominant tone. In the case of *Mythologies*, furthermore, the idea for the dance was not his—it came from Herschel Garfein—and it is not typical of Morris. It is too intellectual. The music is intellectual too, long on concept, short on rhythm. (The score for *Championship Wrestling* is largely a collage of sounds—fans cheering, announcers announcing—taped by Garfein from TV wrestling and from live matches at the Boston Garden.) When the music he is using does not lend itself to dancing, what Morris produces, logically, is something other than dancing—a fact that has to do with feeling as well as with movement. Morris's specialty is the conjuring of great, knotty, *compound* emotions, for which dance, because it is so intimate and yet so non-specific, is perfectly suited. When he turns away from dancing to something else, the compound tends to come apart. The irony that is always present in his work, but as a test and support of "sincerity," breaks off from sincerity and competes with it. This can make for wonderful theater, but such theater is Morris's avocation, not his calling.

There is another factor that can affect the emotional integration of his work, and that is ballet. One of the reasons irony runs so strong in *The Hard Nut* is that the subject of this piece is not just Marie and the Nutcracker but also classical ballet, and Morris's mixed feelings about that form. His knowledge of it is long and intimate. He began ballet training at age ten, and he made his first ballet at age fifteen. Like his old teacher Verla Flowers, he regards ballet as a groundwork, and so do his dancers. Most of the members of the Mark Morris Dance Group take a ballet class every morning, and when they are away from their regular ballet teachers—on tour, for example—Morris fills in. In Brussels, he taught a ballet class for the company every morning, five days a week.

He loves ballet. For one thing, it's a "high" style, the kind of fancy, formal style he is so fond of. And like most Western dance professionals, he admires ballet for the fullness of its vocabulary and hence its expressive potential. But he has objections too, the same sort of low-church objections that many modern dancers have to ballet: that the dancers are skinny, undereducated, and immature ("dead virgins," he has been known to call them), that, too often, their dancing is showy and shallow, that it is completely frontal, aimed solely at the audience, and thus discourages feeling *within* the group. Ballet's emphasis on romantic love and therefore on partnering is alien to him, as is its hierarchical organization, its division of its populace into principal dancers, demi-soloists, and corps de ballet. The "star system," whereby all energies onstage are directed toward the display of the artistry and personality of a single featured dancer, is completely alien to him. Furthermore, he has practical problems in transferring his style to ballet dancers and in making the best use of their style. As he has pointed out, most ballet dancers' sense of timing is different from his. He is far less concerned with beauty of line, with the visual design of the body, than ballet dancers, and more concerned with the actual, muscular enactment of the dance phrase. Therefore, where he will often place the accent in the middle of the phrase, to highlight that part, they will shift the accent to the end of the phrase. In a sense, this is just an extension of an old argument about gravity. "Ballet dancers are antigravity," Morris says. "That's the big difference; it's not political anymore, it's about gravity."

Despite these quarrels, he is fascinated by ballet, and since 1986 he has made seven ballets, five for classical companies and two for his own troupe. But most of these works show a marked self-consciousness about *being a ballet*. In *Mort Subite*, which he made for Boston Ballet in 1986, the women were dressed in shorts and T-shirts; they wore ankle socks with their point shoes—a contest, right there, between the lowdown and the high up. In *Esteemed Guests*, also from 1986, for the Joffrey Ballet, he used a ballerina, the way ballet says one should, but he gave her no partner, so that in the slow movement she seemed to wander forlorn in search of the dance she was supposed to be doing.

On occasion he has managed to turn his mixed feelings into high art. In *Drink to Me Only with Thine Eyes*, which he made for American Ballet Theatre in 1988, he was again working against a ballet convention: the hierarchy. *Drink to Me*, like so many Mark Morris works, was a group piece—twelve dancers, no stars—the joke being that hidden in the group was the biggest ballet star in the world, Mikhail Baryshnikov. (It was Baryshnikov, at that time director of ABT, who commissioned the ballet.) At one point in the middle of the ballet, Morris played his ace. Baryshnikov came out onstage alone and launched himself into a pirouette combination more elaborate and more difficult than most other dance phrases he had performed in his career. He started with a triple pirouette, then stopped on a dime, with his leg still in the air, then swung the leg through to the side, then scooted around 180 degrees, still on one leg, then snapped the leg in and out twice, then finished off the phrase with a leap to the side, and then did the whole thing three more times, with variations, ending with two arabesques on the floor. "Surprise!" Morris was saying. "Look who's in the group." Then a second dancer came out onstage and performed the same phrase, also very well, in order to show us that no matter who's in the group it's still a group.

Out of this tension between virtuosity and cooperation, and other tensions as well—flow versus abruptness, elegance versus awkwardness—Morris in *Drink to Me* managed to distill a unique atmosphere, acerbic and tender, that was the perfect complement to the Virgil Thomson score. In other words, he did again the thing that he does so well: extract from music a complicated emotion and make a dance that re-creates that emotion. *Drink to Me* is the finest work he has made for a company other than his own, and it is arguably the freshest, most original ballet produced in America since the death of Balanchine. In many of Morris's ballets, however, what we see is sophistication warring with expressiveness. He is so busy reacting to ballet, showing it who's boss, that whatever emotion he feels in response to the music remains withheld, or obscured by the play of surface ironies. It is possible that Morris will always feel a little uncomfortable with ballet. Possibly, one has to have been a classical ballet dancer, and spoken that language day after day for years, in order to make ballets. Twyla Tharp's ballets show a reactiveness similar to Morris's. But if ballet is not for him, seven works in seven years—and almost all of them created for companies new to him, with unfamiliar dancers, under unfamiliar conditions—will not prove that conclusion. (In modern dance, he makes close to seven works in *one* year, constantly refining his skill.) *Drink to Me* suggests that all he needs is just to make more ballets, get comfortable with the form, but there are only twenty-four hours in a day. He has a company whose survival is completely dependent on his creating new work for them, and considering what he has created for them, in their native style and his—modern dance—it is hard to regret that he has not taken more time off to accept freelance ballet commissions.

In Morris's early works, irony was very strong. You could see a clear division between two things, with one commenting on the other: the son on the father in *Dad's Charts*, androgyny on sexual definition in *Deck of Cards*, romantic impossibility on romantic hope in *New Love Song Waltzes*. Then, gradually, a change occurred. The 1984 *O Rangasayee*, in which grotesquerie was so powerfully assimilated into spiritual transport, was possibly a turning point. In any case, he took a turn: the opposites began to leak into each other, absorb each other.

It is hard to say what precipitated this development, for when it occurred, in the mid-eighties, several crucial things happened to him at the same time. First, he lost Erin Matthiessen. Second, he became a professional: he made a commitment to his company and to his and their future. Third, he began his big plunge into Baroque music. Each of these events influenced the others, and together, all of them caused a change in his understanding of life. Newly alone, newly serious about himself but with no one to turn to with the questions that this raised, he lowered himself into the depths of Baroque music, and there, it seems, he found a world that was newly real to him, a world of huge emotional forces whose conflicts could be ordered, made beautiful, but no longer solved in such a way that one side knew better than the other.

For that is what irony is, in its classic form: a condition of knowing better. When Oedipus taunts Tiresias for being blind, we know that Oedipus is blinder than Tiresias—figuratively blind—and that he will soon be literally blind as well. When Emma Bovary and Rodolphe Boulanger exchange compliments at the agricultural show, with the pigs grunting in

The Waltz of the Snowflakes. *The Hard Nut (Tom Brazil)*

the background, we know better than Madame Bovary: we know that the feeling she takes to be romantic is also animal. And in those moments we know better than all who imagine themselves wise or in love. Such ironies can still be found in Morris's work of the late eighties and also in his most recent work. In *The Hard Nut*'s Waltz of the Snowflakes, we know, as the happy little snowflakes apparently do not, that men don't dance very well on point and that people look funny in hats shaped like Dairy Queen cones. But in most of Morris's dances since the mid-eighties what happens is that while there is still a division of feeling, one side does not know better than the other. Actually, one can say this even of the snowflakes. Our superior knowledge—that their dance is iconoclastic, a comment on ballet—lasts about thirty seconds. Then, slowly, it begins to seem that *they* know better. They are not a subversion of an old beauty, or not just that. They are a new beauty, a child's dream of winter—of ice cream and snowballs and things flying around, blinding and beautiful—and all of this spun into a gorgeous dance, as frenzied as a snowstorm, as organized as a snowflake. The dance shades from wit into magic. And at that point there is no longer a question of irony, of knowing better. There is no better to know.

BRUSSELS

For Morris's company, the move to Belgium in 1988 meant expansion, prestige, a decent working life. In New York they hadn't even had a studio to themselves. Now, in Brussels, they had a whole building: 103, rue Bara, the former home of Maurice Béjart's company and school. The place was not deluxe. Located in what is now the city's garment district, it was an old factory, and it looked like one. There were holes in the roof through which pigeons flew into the building. (To the dancers' alarm, the concierge, M. Barré, used to shoot the birds down with a rifle.) But to the Mark Morris Dance Group—now, after much negotiation, renamed the Monnaie Dance Group/Mark Morris—this was a palace. They had four studios for their exclusive use, plus an exercise room. They had their own canteen, with three cooks waiting to make them omelettes. Barry Alterman and Nancy Umanoff had their own offices, and in another office sat a luxury hitherto undreamed of, their secretary. Morris had a spacious dressing room with a brass plate on the door saying DI-RECTION ARTISTIQUE. And all to himself, in this same building, he had a crew of ten—a carpenter, a sound technician, two lighting technicians, a wardrobe director, two stage managers, two technical assistants, and a masseuse—awaiting his instructions. Formerly the boss of twelve under-paid dancers, he was now the director of a well-compensated company of twenty-seven, one of the largest modern-dance troupes in the world.

"Think of the biggest thing you want to do," Gérard Mortier, the director of the Monnaie, had said to him, "the very biggest thing—then do it." Morris didn't have to think. For years he had been wanting to choreograph a dance to Handel's oratorio "L'Allegro, il Penseroso ed il Moderato." Now he had the means. Immediately after the company's arrival, he gathered the dancers around him and set to work. "How do you feel?" an interviewer asked him soon afterward. "Like emperor-for-life," he said.

That mood was to be short-lived. In many ways it would be hard to imagine a poorer match than Mark Morris and the Belgian dance community. Not just Belgians but most Continental Europeans view dance somewhat differently from Americans. They regard it as theater. They expect it to have a story, or at least an obvious theme—an extractable, expressible idea about life—and accordingly, they expect the dancers to be representing something other than dancers. Furthermore, because it is theater, they want a dance show to be interesting as spectacle, to have vivid sets and costumes which, again, represent or symbolize something in life. European dance creates and supplies these needs. It is common on the Continent for new ballets to be full-evening works with titles such as *War and Peace* or *Malraux, ou les métamorphoses des dieux*, and these are often lavish productions, filled with grand staircases, brocade gowns, and starry skies. By contrast, American dance tends to be far more austere and abstract, and this is what American audiences expect. The United States too produces full-length story ballets, and they are well attended. But in general new ballets in America are short works, twenty to thirty minutes long, with titles like *Bach Duo* or *Haydn Concerto* and with simple, non-representational costumes. Often there is no set and no story, but even if there is a narrative, the real story is the choreography.

Such differences between Europe and America are even more pronounced in the case of modern dance. In America, modern dance has had a far smoother development than in Europe. It is now considered a form completely apart from ballet, and its basic medium, like that of American ballet, is dance, not theater. Though in recent years young, experimental dance makers have gone in for a great deal of talking and videotape-showing, most American modern dance choreographers still focus primarily on choreography. In Europe, on the other hand, the development of modern dance was brutally interrupted by World War II. The movement was centered in Germany. Under the Nazis, some modern dance choreographers fled; others collaborated, and discredited the movement. By the end of the war, European modern dance was all but wiped out, and it did not revive until the sixties, when a new form, the German *Tanztheater*, or dance-theater, rose from the ashes of German expressionist dance of the twenties and thirties. But German dance theater is far more theater than dance, as can be seen in the work of Pina Bausch, director of the Wuppertal Dance Theater and, since the seventies, the leader of the *Tanztheater* movement. Bausch's productions are generally full-evening shows that take as their subject the anguish or absurdity of life and in which the performers eat, speak, quarrel, wash clothes, dive to the stage from great heights, and do other things as well, sometimes to great effect, but rarely dance. Bausch's work has had an immense influence. In many European cities there are now young modern dance movements, but in keeping with the Wuppertal model, what they are producing, for the most part, is an updated theater of the absurd. To present extended passages of dancing to music is regarded as conservative, ballet-like. (The new dance-theater defines itself as against ballet.) In the words of Susanne Linke, one of the few prominent German choreographers still interested in dance, "If you dare to take one step that looks like dancing, [the critics] stamp you as old-fashioned."

Where Mark Morris fits into this picture should be obvious. He is squarely in the American tradition. His medium is choreography. Though his dances often have stories, the meanings are not laid out before you as a statement about life—they must be extracted from the dancing. No one speaks in a Mark Morris dance; no one jumps from a great height. The costumes are usually simple; there is rarely a set. All there is is musical dancing, exactly what Europeans today are not looking for in modern dance.

Nevertheless, Morris might have hoped to win an audience in Europe, as Pina Bausch has won one in America, and to some extent he has done so. *Dido and Aeneas* was a tremendous success at the Edinburgh Festival in 1992 (though British reviewers have more classical tastes than critics on the Continent). When the Morris company was in Brussels, they routinely received rave reviews from English critics. French critics too praised them warmly. From other non-Belgian Europeans, the response was mixed: some hate, some love, and a great deal in between.

But Belgium was different. Prior to Morris's arrival, the Belgian dance scene had been dominated entirely by Maurice Béjart. A Frenchman, Béjart got his start in the Parisian dance avant-garde of the fifties. In 1959, as a visiting choreographer at Brussels's Théâtre Royal de la Monnaie, he created a new version of *The Rite of Spring*, a bold, sexy piece that was a great hit. The Monnaie then asked him to stay on permanently, as director of dance. He organized a new troupe, which he called the Ballet of the 20th Century, and he remained at the Monnaie for the next twenty-seven years, during which time he evolved a kind of dance production that was wholly his own, full of themes from the sixties counterculture—youth, sex, Eastern mysticism—and featuring a kind of iconoclastic "modernity" that often consisted simply of juxtaposing old-fashioned tradition with new-fashioned energy and sex. Béjart used classical ballet, but he combined it with other idioms, and he was not a subtle choreographer. As he told an interviewer in 1989, "I don't work on little particular steps, I just work to touch people." Nor was he a subtle musician. As noted earlier, he liked to splice music, and he often chose his music on conceptual rather than musical grounds. (For example, in his recent *1789 . . . and Us*, a meditation on the French Revolution, he was inspired by the numbers 1, 7, 8, and 9 to splice parts of Beethoven's First, Seventh, Eighth, and Ninth symphonies into his score.) Béjart's productions were not so much choreography or music as they were spectacles—lurid, exuberant, grandiose.

As such, they were routinely execrated by the classical-minded American dance critics, and also by many English critics, but they were very popular on the Continent, where they satisfied tastes not unlike those that have drawn people to the new dance-theater. (Béjart, in a sense, is dance for the parents of Pina Bausch fans.) In Belgium, however, Béjart was not just popular: he was revered. To most Belgians, even those who had never seen his work, he was a source of national pride. And to dance lovers, as the Brussels critic Luisa Moffett has written, he was "the standard by which other styles of dance [were] judged . . . The Kirov? Too classical. Merce Cunningham? Too obscure. Balanchine . . . ? Too cold." In consequence, foreign dance companies rarely included Belgium on their touring schedules. Nor did Béjart have any native competition. Before he arrived, there was very little concert dance, let alone modern dance, in Brussels. The eighties saw the rise of a Belgian dance-theater movement, led by the young Flemish choreographer Anne Teresa de Keersmaeker, but its following was minuscule compared with Béjart's. In the words of Gérard Mortier, "Brussels was never a city of dance. It was a city of Mr. Béjart."

So Béjart was the standard by which Mark Morris was to be judged. But the situation was worse than that. Morris was replacing Béjart. Indeed, with a little blurring of the facts, Morris could be seen by the Brussels public as the *reason* they no longer had Béjart. Yes, there was a middleman, Mortier, and for several reasons—that he was a Fleming in what was traditionally a Walloon job, that he made no bones about what he viewed as Belgium's artistic mediocrity and, to remedy it, had spent massive amounts of public funds on the opera house—he was disliked by many important people, above all by the Francophone press, even before he managed to quarrel with Maurice Béjart. But once he did this, and Béjart left, a number of journalists had no hesitation about attacking the man that Mortier had been blind enough to prefer to Béjart. At the same time, there was a small but vocal group of young people who, while not necessarily sorry to see Béjart go—the reverence for Béjart was not wholly unanimous—felt that his successor should have been a Belgian, the obvious candidate being Anne Teresa de Keersmaeker. This nationalist resentment was aggravated by the fact that when Morris held European auditions to increase the size of his company, he hired only one Belgian dancer. ("I didn't check their passports at the door," he later explained.)

When Morris flew to Brussels in the summer of 1988, he was not ignorant of the enmity that awaited him, and he soon got a taste of it at the press conference that Mortier arranged in late September so that the Brussels critics could talk to the new director of dance. As usual, Morris did nothing to deflect criticism; he met it with defiance. *Who* are your dancers? asked one critic, concerned over the nationalism issue. "Who are the dancers?" Morris replied. "Here's who they are." And he asked the dancers, who were in the room, to rise as he called out their names. These were his dancers: human beings, dancers. Their nationality, in his opinion, was not an issue. Then, as we saw, he was asked to share his philosophy of dance, and he shared it: "I make it up, and you watch it. End of philosophy." (This latter question and Morris's answer to it in some measure encapsulate the difference between the Continental European and the American idea of dance.)

After the press conference, several of the critics drew Morris aside for little exclusive interviews. One of them, Laurence Bertels of *La Dernière Heure*, asked him what he thought of Béjart. In the months preceding his departure for Belgium, Morris had been careful in what he said to reporters about Béjart. ("Béjart was Belgium's most important export, next to endive," he told Robert Greskovic of the *Los Angeles Times*.) But the tone of this press conference had sapped his good will, and he told Bertels the truth: "No, I don't like Béjart. I liked him fifteen years ago, but not any more . . . I have the sense that he's tired." Bertels, in her piece, quoted Morris's words, and after them wrote, "No comment." The piece was headlined "No, I Don't Like Béjart!" and it was accompanied by two photographs, obviously chosen with care, of Morris making silly faces.

Swords, then, were drawn from the start. Still, Morris believed that his job was simply to make dances; beyond that, he could do or say what he wanted. This had worked for him before. Why not now? Barry Alterman too was confident: "I knew about all the problems. But I believed that if we went there with clear hearts and open hands, we would win them over."

For close to two and a half months, from the time of their arrival until the end of November, the company worked on *L'Allegro*. They were full of excitement. Here was this big new piece—two hours long, twenty-four dancers, forty-five singers, a full orchestra, beautiful sets and costumes—and with it they would make their entry into the Monnaie, a theater such as they had never danced in before, with velvet chairs and gilded balconies and a box for the king and queen. As the date of the premiere drew closer, the company moved from rue Bara to the opera house, where they were allowed six rehearsals with the orchestra—a thing almost unheard of in the United States. (Balanchine, in all his years at New York City Ballet, rarely had more than one or two orchestra rehearsals for a new work. More was simply too costly.) For the first time in its history, the company had everything it needed to put on a show properly.

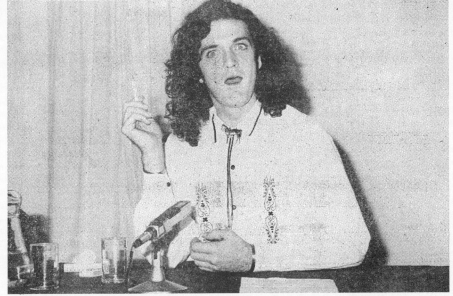

Le physique du successeur de Maurice Béjart est ingrat. Mais le charme vient avec la parole et le geste.

▬ L'ENTREE EN SCENE DE MARK MORRIS A LA MONNAIE

« Non, je n'aime pas Béjart ! »

« J'aime la musique, j'aime la danse, le romantisme, les gens qui dansent ensemble. Mais ce n'est pas à moi de décrire mon style. Certains le trouveront peut-être démodé. Vous me raconterez. J'aime regarder les gens danser et j'aime que les gens aiment regarder les autres danser. » Mais il n'aime pas Béjart !

Mark Morris, introduit par Gérard Mortier au Théâtre Royal de la Monnaie, s'est présenté au public belge et a accepté de jouer le jeu des questions-réponses. Il a surpris, séduit. Principalement grâce à son humour.

Il lui reste maintenant à plaire pour son talent. Réponse sur les planches dès le 23 novembre au son et au rythme de l'*Allegro* de Handel.

« Il est mon auteur préféré, dit l'artiste. Et l'Allegro est sa plus belle œuvre. Je l'étudie depuis trois ans, je sais ce que je fais. » Le successeur américain de Maurice Béjart nous donne tout, tout de suite. Pour séduire et conquérir le public européen, il se présente dans ce qu'il a de plus cher au monde, l'*Allegro* de Handel. Ensuite, il fera danser sa troupe la même soirée sur Stravinsky, Poulenc, Tchérepnine et Vivaldi. *Dido And Aeneas* de Purcell et *Mythologies* de Garfein sont les deux autres chorégraphies prévues cette année. Mark Morris ne quittera pas la Belgique en 1988, si ce n'est pour un rapide aller-retour en Hollande. Il a même décliné l'invitation de New York ! Le premier défi à relever, cette saison, étant de maîtriser les planches belges.

Dans la classe

Depuis qu'il a été rénové, le Théâtre Royal de la Monnaie est

Il ne dansera pas toujours, mais, quand il le fera, ce sera pour un véritable one-man-show.

un des sites les plus prestigieux de la capitale.

Gérard Mortier et Mark Morris ont préféré nous inviter, derrière la gare du Midi, dans la salle de répétition qui n'est autre que l'ancienne classe de l'école Mudra. Ce détail, très américain d'ailleurs, nous annonçait déjà un Mark Morris sûr de lui. Il nous attend dans son élément, dans son jeans et sa chemise blanche Far West, les cheveux toujours aussi longs et la cigarette aux lèvres. Les cernes sont également au rendez-vous. A ses côtés, Gérard Mortier, propret, cheveux

nets et col-cravate, rougit parfois des réponses de son nouveau chorégraphe.

« Le départ de Maurice Béjart a laissé le vide dans la ville et dans le pays. Mais il également provoqué des effets positifs, car certains chorégraphes ont enfin osé se présenter. Pourquoi ai-je choisi Mark Morris ? Car je l'adore. J'en conviens, c'est un choix absolument subjectif. De nombreuses discussions ont suivi son engagement, car il n'était pas belge, et ses danseurs non plus. On voulait que j'invite différentes troupes, les unes après les autres. Mais, selon moi, la danse et l'opéra sont deux formes d'art qui doivent se côtoyer, vivre ensemble. J'ai choisi Mark Morris pour son sens de la musique et pour son sens de l'humour, de la tragi-comédie. » Voilà pourquoi Bruxelles a donc choisi Morris. Mais, pourquoi Morris a-t-il choisi Bruxelles ? « La création est beaucoup plus dure à New York, nettement plus chère aussi, répond-il. Ici, on obtient plus facilement les moyens pour créer. Bruxelles est une ville très calme et idéale pour travailler. »

Vient alors l'inévitable question relative à la nationalité des danseurs. Non, ils ne sont pas belges. Ou si peu. « Les danseurs ont tous quitté New York, leur maison et leur famille. Ils se sont installés à Bruxelles et y vivent. Qui sont-ils ? Les voici » Pour narguer son public, Mark Morris les appelle et leur demande de se lever lorsqu'ils entendent leur nom. Voilà, les présentations sont faites.

De manière plus formelle, le TRM écrit : « Le Monnaie Dance Group/Mark Morris a été fondé en 1980 en tant que Mark Morris Dance Group et se produisit pour la

première fois à New York City en cette même année. » On ne peut être plus clair. La troupe existait déjà

L'orchestre sur scène

Mark Morris et Gérard Mortier ont tous deux insisté pour que, dorénavant, les danseurs soient accompagnés par les musiciens. L'orchestre reprend ainsi sa place d'antan. Comme à l'opéra, en somme. Cette présence musicale ne manquera pas de donner aux spectacles une dimension supplémentaire et réjouira tous les mélomanes.

C'est avec une impatience non dissimulée que les spectateurs se rendront donc à la première de l'Allegro qui sera plutôt pour eux la première de Morris. Aura-t-il le même succès qu'aux Etats-Unis ? Le press book dont il bénéficie est, en tout cas, un des plus enviables. Ces quelques lignes, extraites du Washington Post, en disent long sur sa réputation. En mai 1986, le quotidien américain écrivait ceci : « Quelle que soit la position que Morris finisse par occuper dans le développement historique de la danse, il est certain que ce chorégraphe est un phénomène sensationnel et que de nombreuses décennies se consacreront à l'étudier sous tous les angles. »

S'il aime qu'on soit tendre avec lui, le chorégraphe n'écarte cependant pas la dureté pour parler, en intimité, de son prédécesseur : « Non, je n'aime pas Béjart. Il y a quinze ans, je l'aimais. Mais ce n'est plus le cas aujourd'hui. Soit il a changé soit je le regarde différemment. Mais j'ai l'impression qu'il est fatigué. » Sans commentaire.

Laurence Bertels

On November 20 came the *répétition générale*, a preview that in European opera houses is given to an invited audience of critics, patrons, and theater employees. The performance was leafleted by young people protesting the Monnaie's hiring of an American company, but the show went well, and though there was some booing afterward, it was drowned out by the applause. As for the critics, their reaction was mixed. There was one unqualified rave, and it is an interesting review, for it came from the critic who was later to be Morris's most violent detractor, Charles Philippon of *Le Soir*, the largest newspaper in Brussels. Under the headline "Mark Morris's Joyous Entry into the Monnaie: The Naked Pleasure of Dance," Philippon wrote that just as Béjart had revolutionized ballet during his reign in Brussels, so *L'Allegro* gave reason to hope that Mark Morris too would initiate "a new era in the history of dance." In other words, the king is dead—long live the king. Some insiders in the Belgian dance world feel that the general hostility shown to Morris by the press during his stay in Belgium was entirely political, that the reviewers never gave the work a chance but simply hated it because they hated Mortier for letting Béjart go. According to this theory, even positive reviews of Morris's shows must be read between the lines: if certain critics were kind to *L'Allegro*, it was because they didn't want to give the impression that they were attacking Morris straightaway. But Philippon's review is not the sort of piece that is easy to back off from. (And he was to have a hard time doing so.) This article and several others suggest that some critics, on some occasions, did actually look at Morris's dances with a willing mind. It should also be said that if many reviewers disliked Morris because he was not Béjart, this was not necessarily a political judgment. Béjart had formed their tastes, which, mysterious as they might seem to some American critics, are nevertheless artistic tastes.

The qualities the Belgian critics remarked on in *L'Allegro*—and also in the repertory program that alternated with it—were indeed those in which he most differed from Béjart. To begin with, the reviewers couldn't believe there was all this *dancing*. Some of them liked it. To others—not surprisingly, in view of Belgium's lack of a modern dance tradition—it all looked the same. It wasn't ballet; it was just running around. Why, then, did there have to be so much of it? Aside from his curious insistence on dancing, the thing that almost all the reviewers noted was Morris's musicality, though this too cut both ways. Some praised him for it, but even they spoke of it with a certain detached interest, as if it were an exotic trait—again no surprise, in view of Béjart's legacy. Others saw no virtue in it. "Morris is musical? Handel is musical too, without dancing," wrote Nicole Verschoore in *Het Laatste Nieuws*, a Flemish daily. Several writers compared Morris's musicality to Balanchine's, not necessarily in praise.

Something else that struck many reviewers of the first two programs was that, again in contrast to Béjart, Morris's work seemed to have no philosophical program: no attack on the clergy, no decline of the West, nothing. For a number of writers from outside Belgium, this was a welcome development. "The hour of existential meditations has passed," wrote the critic for Bonn's *Die Welt*, with apparent relief. But many of the Belgian critics *missed* the existential meditations. What was the point of Morris's work? "Where is the profundity?" asked Claire Diez in *La Libre Belgique*. To these writers, Morris seemed naïve. *L'Allegro*, Diez wrote, showed a "dumbfounding simplicity, more American than European." It was like children's art, she said. Even those who liked this new style stressed its innocence. Philippon, in his second review of the company, listed the leading traits of Morris's work as "the expression of the wellsprings of movement and its musical significance, an omnipresent light humor, an infinite tenderness for humankind, and a wish to live in a world swarming with happy images."

In sum, after the first two programs, some of the critics saw Morris as simple and talented, a sort of noble savage, and some saw him as simple and untalented, a nonentity. So a trend was established. Even then, perhaps, it might have turned. Had the critics looked at his work harder, they might have discovered that the complexity they were seeking, and the profundity, were there, but in the choreography. Perhaps not, though. This work was indeed very different from Béjart's, and grieving over Béjart, the reviewers could not view that difference dispassionately. Most important, however, was the fact that Belgium had no real tradition of modern dance. Without that, it was hard for the reviewers to see in Morris's choreography the fine distinctions in weight and shape and rhythm and phrasing that are the vehicle of its meanings. To them, it all just looked like modern dance.

Nor would many of them ever try to see more deeply, for the next dance that Morris placed before them, *Dido and Aeneas*, disgusted a number of the daily reviewers to the point where they more or less gave up on him. "All of Belgium . . . stands speechless before the disaster," wrote Nicole Verschoore of *Dido* in *Het Laatste Nieuws*; the piece was a "hideous spectacle." Even those who had most admired *L'Allegro* could find nothing good to say of *Dido*. *Le Soir*'s Philippon, the man who had prophesied that Morris would usher in "a new era in the history of dance," described the new piece as "tasteless" and "debased."

Most of the critics were revolted by two things, things that are fundamental to Morris's work. One was his mixing of moods—in *Dido*, his juxtaposition of grave tragedy with obscenity and hilarity. The Belgian reviewers were confused by this, as a few American reviewers have been also, and they took it for a ruse: Morris was making fun of Purcell's opera and of tragic feeling in general. Many writers concluded that *Dido* was a parody. Others, more observant, noted with disgust its double character —its combination of "vulgar parody and syrupy pathos," to quote Verschoore. As Morris's Belgian years wore on, the emotional complexity of his work was to pose more and more problems for Belgian dance writers. In the words of René Sirvin, of the Parisian daily *Le Figaro*, "The art of Mark Morris apparently troubles the Cartesian spirit of the Europeans." They wanted something clearer—or at least the Belgians did.

But to judge from the reviews, a worse problem with *Dido* was its violation of decorum, above all the fact that Dido was played by a man and that Morris was that man. How dare he present himself as the Queen, asked Philippon: "Queen of what? Queen of whom?" Several reviewers compared the show to a transvestite act—"just competent enough for a disreputable café," as Verschoore put it. Why was the gender crossing so offensive to these writers? In Japanese and Indian theater, tragic female roles are routinely performed by men, as they were in Elizabethan England. And though this practice is now rare in the West, one does not expect Europeans to be so shockable in sexual matters. But Brussels is a staid Catholic community. Furthermore, Morris didn't just portray a woman. In the Sorceress he portrayed a woman doing obscene things—notably, masturbating. None of the daily critics could bring themselves to mention this, though Philippon noted that when Morris "pulls aside his little black skirt or rocks his pelvis, he topples inevitably into the ridiculous." But ridiculous was not all they thought it was. As Philippon added, Morris showed "a lack of respect for Woman."

More important, perhaps, was his lack of respect for the difference between men and women. To what extent did feelings about homosexuality affect the *Dido* reviews? Institutionalized hypocrisy—permission to do things in private as long as they are not announced in public—is not uncommon in the United States, but it is more common in Europe. Béjart's Belgian works had had an unmistakably homoerotic flavor. One of the qualities for which Jorge Donn, Béjart's foremost male star, was most prized was his androgynous allure. But Béjart never declared himself on the subject of homosexuality. He was "chic" about it, to use Mortier's word. Morris, as usual, wasn't chic about it. For his very first press conference in Brussels, he wore the pink triangle, symbolizing solidarity with gay rights, on his lapel; he also wore gold earrings. As usual, he was telling the press that he was homosexual. *Dido* undoubtedly seemed to the critics another announcement of this, and not a welcome one, particularly in the context of a revered tragic opera.

A month after *Dido*, the company presented *Mythologies*, and at that point what had been a problem between Morris and the press became a scandal. *Le Soir*, on its front page, above the fold, ran a special article entitled (in English) "Mark Morris, go home!" It reads, in part:

Provocation or suicidal anti-performance? Mark Morris, Wednesday night at the Cirque Royal, gave a preposterous demonstration of his creative poverty. The man who succeeded King Béjart laid himself bare. Which is to say that he not only took off his underwear but revealed an undigested mixture of old-fashioned vulgarity and intellectual pretention . . . See our reviews on page 18.

On page 18, in an essay entitled "The Pathetic Frauds of Mark Morris: Enough!" Philippon described *Mythologies* as a "sordid display of choreographic and cultural deficiency unprecedented in the annals of the Monnaie." Accompanying this was a second piece, written by *Le Soir*'s cultural editor, who deplored what he saw as Morris's distortion of Roland Barthes's essays:

Perhaps in the U.S.A. one makes such crude use of European thinkers, reducing them to undigested digests in the "fast food" of the "camp" intelligentsia. But we don't do that here, Mr. Morris. Your predecessor, Maurice Béjart, knew not only how to dance but how to read. What we have here are simply illiterates who shamelessly give themselves over to the most contemptible of intellectual swindles.

(Other *Mythologies* reviews had similar things to say about Americans.) Even the Communist papers hated the piece. "Obviously," wrote the critic for *Le Drapeau Rouge*, "Mark Morris's choreographic inspiration is to be found up his butt—which, incidentally, is not worth going far to see."

What could have provoked this reaction? Basically, the same things that provoked the reaction to *Dido*. First, emotional complexity. As I have said, *Mythologies* is a sharp, acrid, ironical work with a strong humanistic undercurrent. Some of the reviewers actually missed the irony. Others thought that irony was the only point, and particularly the point of *Striptease*. This brings us to the second problem: the critics felt, rightly, that Morris was again attacking an idea sacred to them. In *Dido* it was Woman, or the difference between men and women. In *Striptease* it was eroticism. As the above quotations make clear, the reviewers were deeply offended that the performers actually stripped naked. Béjart's work had often involved nudity, but partial nudity, alluring nudity. In *Striptease*, on the other hand, the dancers stood before the audience stark naked—breasts, penises, pubic hair, the whole thing. Not only was this not alluring; it seemed to undermine the very idea of sexual allure. That, of course, was Barthes's point. But to make such a point in writing was different from demonstrating it live on a stage. To many people these bare bodies were repellent—"painful images of ugliness," in the words of *Le Drapeau Rouge*—and Barthes notwithstanding, the reviewers were appalled at Morris's destructiveness.

A final and critical point is that Morris was one of the strippers. As usual, he gave his role a daimonic twist. All the other dancers in *Striptease* had a recognizable stripper identity—the bride, the dominatrix, et cetera. Morris alone was unclassifiable, a disreputable-looking character in a cheap, baggy business suit. If anything, he looked like a flasher, not something to which the audience would have any tender erotic associations. And he was the most obscene of the group, miming luridly as he disrobed and, once he was nude, bumping and grinding in front of the amazed spectators. This was the last straw. If in staging *Striptease* Morris had committed an offense against eroticism, in joining its cast he offended against his position as director of dance at the Monnaie. Having pulled down his pants in front of the Belgian people, he had nothing left to show them, Philippon wrote: "there remains nothing for him to do but get dressed and . . . leave, in search of other audiences." Other papers also called for his dismissal.

In the case of *Mythologies* the argument that the reviewers were just out to get Morris, no matter what, is hard to make, for at *Mythologies* the audience too turned on him—for the first time. At most of Morris's Belgian shows, there was some booing, but it was almost invariably followed by a volley of retaliatory bravos. Allen Robertson, a London-based journalist,

described a typical curtain call: "It's a three-ring circus, with the cheering squad trying to drown out the boos, while those who want to leave in a huff have to squeeze past those giving [Morris] a rousing, standing ovation." To the Americans present, the booing was a shock, but booing in Europe means something different from what it does in the United States. For one thing, it is far more common. (Americans generally do not boo at the theater; they consider booing rude.) Furthermore, booing in Europe is often done by claques, groups of people who come for the purpose of booing, and this was undoubtedly the case at many of Morris's performances in Brussels. But even a small claque can make a big showing. Because applause is what is expected, it takes a lot less booing to give an impression of disapproval than applause to signify approval.

For these reasons and one other—scandal makes a good story—the booing at Morris's Brussels shows was overstressed by American journalists. Almost all these shows were far more popular with their audiences than with the press. *Dido*, for example, which was so execrated by the critics, was very warmly applauded, a fact that actually angered certain reviewers. ("How much longer before we get a reaction from the willing Monnaie-audience clan?" asked *Het Laatste Nieuws* impatiently.) At other shows, many people neither applauded nor booed but simply sat on their hands. This is partly because most of the Morris seasons in Brussels— seven out of ten—took place at the opera house, as a dance "extra" inserted into the opera season, which was almost wholly subscribed, with very few seats available on a single-ticket basis. In other words, the audience for the majority of Morris's shows was upper-middle-class opera subscribers, not the general public. This arrangement, which effectively precluded Morris from building an audience in Brussels, also isolated him from the majority of the Béjart enthusiasts. For Béjart had had a different arrangement. He performed not at the Monnaie but at the Cirque Royal, a theater twice the size of the opera house. His tickets were available to the general public, and that was his audience, the great middle class. (At many of Morris's shows, the biggest Béjart fans were probably the critics.)

To most of the operagoers at the Monnaie, a night of American modern dance might be boring, but not infuriating. In the worst case, they could close their eyes and listen to the excellent music that this American person always insisted on providing. It was not until Morris's fourth show, *Mythologies*, that he gave a series of non-subscription performances in a large theater. These, at last, were performances that the Béjart fans could easily attend—indeed, that they were very likely to attend, for the theater was the Cirque Royal. And what they saw looked to them like a bunch of shaggy Americans, with no sets, no nice costumes, no ballet steps, no philosophy of life, making sport of their cherished beliefs in the temple of their banished god.

The audience response to *Mythologies* was violent even by European standards. Already before the final curtain, the show was repeatedly interrupted by catcalls and laughter, and when the curtain came down, the booing nearly lifted the roof off. On the second night, before the curtain went up, the company had a meeting to decide what to do if the audience started throwing things. (They never did.) The next day the reviews came out, and that evening the backstage area was crawling with reporters trying to get a story on the dancers' reactions—"to see if we were scared or shooting ourselves or something," says Alterman. Nor did the rage let up in the course of the remaining performances. One night, as Morris was standing near an exit during the last part of the show, a woman leaving early recognized him and stopped to scream at him at length.

So *Mythologies* was a disaster with the audience as well as with the press, which suggests that the response of the press was indeed to the show. There was, however, one extra-artistic circumstance that may have contributed to the reviewers' wrath. Even before *Mythologies*, Morris's Belgian operation was considered a story by American magazine editors. Several of them assigned features on the subject and sent reporters to Belgium to speak to Morris. Morris, as I have pointed out, has to make a prodigious effort not to say what is on his mind. Furthermore, these reporters came at what was a harrowing time for him, the period when he was making *L'Allegro*. If he arrived in Brussels in a state of ebullience, his mood quickly darkened as, with enormous stakes riding on his first Belgian show, he set out to create the first full-evening work of his career. This was more pressure than he had ever faced before (or has faced since), and he reacted to it as he often reacts to very difficult situations: he became nasty and imperious. "It was the worst I've ever seen him," says Clarice Marshall, one of the new dancers who joined the troupe in 1988.

That is the state of mind in which the early feature writers caught him. To one, Charles Siebert of *Vanity Fair*, he gave a particularly vivid interview. Asked about his nice new setup at the Monnaie, he said, "Yes, things have changed a little. It's weird. The Monnaie will give me anything I want. It scares me sometimes, and it doesn't. I'm not fucking around. I know how to use this stuff." He went on to insult the two choreographers most cherished by those Belgians who resented his arrival. "Béjart's work is shit," he said. "On my worst day, with the worst hangover in my life, I could never do anything that bad." As for Anne Teresa de Keersmaeker, Siebert noted that Morris liked to call her "de Tearjerker" and that he had recently walked out of one of her shows during the first act. "It was empty," Morris said. He even managed to insult the hairdo of Belgium's beloved Queen Fabiola (a "Maggie Thatcher hairdo of death").

This article, accompanied by Annie Leibovitz's photographs of Morris, nude and semi-nude, with his face heavily made up, was published in the April 1989 issue of *Vanity Fair*. The issue went on the stands in the middle of March, leaving the Belgian critics a month to get wind of it before the April 19 premiere of *Mythologies*. There is little doubt that some of them saw it, and it can have done nothing to warm their hearts toward that show. Those who didn't see it before *Mythologies* found out about it soon afterward. At the end of April, *De Morgen*, a Flemish daily, ran a special story on it, with the headline "Mark Morris: 'Béjart is shit.' "

At the same time that the company was being attacked from the outside, it was being torn apart from the inside. As we saw, Morris doubled the size of the troupe when he moved to Brussels. (During the Belgian years, the membership ranged from twenty-one to twenty-seven dancers, not counting Morris.) What he ended up with, however, was not one big troupe but two small troupes—one consisting of the old company, the other of the new recruits—and each resentful of the other. With the company's move to Brussels and its elevation in status, the old dancers expected a corresponding elevation. In the words of Clarice Marshall, "They figured they'd be up at the front of the stage in big silver outfits, with the rest of us running around in tiny little clumps behind them." Nor was this an unfair expectation. They were the ones who knew Morris's style, which the new dancers were only slowly learning. Furthermore, they were the ones who had toiled for eight years, on starvation wages, making the company good enough to be hired by a European opera house. What they got in their first year in Belgium, however, was not promotion but demotion. Thrilled by the means now available to him, Morris began making large choral works in which each dancer's time onstage was accordingly reduced. "In *L'Allegro* you didn't even have a chance to break a sweat before you were offstage again," says Donald Mouton.

But it wasn't just that they had less time onstage. It was that the dances were no longer about them. Morris's works before his Belgian period tended to be small group pieces in which the dancers and their personalities shone forth. Guillermo Resto, Penny Hutchinson, Tina Fehlandt, Jon Mensinger, Teri Weksler, Donald Mouton, Susan Hadley, Keith Sabado, Ruth Davidson, David Landis, Kraig Patterson—the audience saw them up close and felt they knew them, almost personally. The dancers, in turn, felt known, and this was satisfying to them, part of what they worked for. Equally important was the fact that the dances were about their group. Morris's communal vision was shared by his company, and to them, perhaps, that vision was less symbolic than to him. They were the ones who performed the dances, and while they were onstage, these ensembles were their ensemble—an image of the little world that they had built together. Two dances in particular carried this meaning: *Gloria* and *New Love Song Waltzes*, both of them early, tenderhearted pieces created for the entire company. The dancers held these dances very dear and performed them almost as rituals. But all the old repertory, in their minds, was a sort of hymn to the group.

Once they got to Belgium, however, their group was enlarged, and

with strangers. To make use of the new people, Morris was making big works, works that were no longer about their group, let alone its individual members. Furthermore, he started putting the new people in the *old* dances. In large companies, double-casting is standard procedure. One dancer plays the Swan Queen on Wednesday night; another steps into the role on Thursday. In the Mark Morris Dance Group, however, this practice was almost unheard of. Now it began, and soon it encroached on sacred ground. One day in rehearsal Morris quietly announced that he was double-casting *New Love Song Waltzes*. "He looked at me and said, 'Who do you think should do your part?' " Tina Fehlandt remembers. "I was speechless." Nor did Morris create an old-dancers cast and a new-dancers cast. He mixed them. This was his way of ensuring continuity. In each cast, the old dancers would fire the new, and the flame would rise again. But that would be a gradual process. In the meantime, the emotional ties that had held the dance together were severed. "Here I was onstage," says Keith Sabado, "looking somebody in the eye who had once been a person I had a relationship with, and now it was a person I had no relationship with, except that I had seen them at an audition." That experience epitomized the old dancers' situation in the new, expanded company. "Suddenly we were faced with ten other personalities that *he* wanted," says Sabado, "and it was *our* job to keep the thing moving while it was in the transitional stage."

Morris's position in all this is completely understandable. For him, the Monnaie job was a chance to do something big, and a big company was essential to this. Having hired these new dancers, was he not supposed to use them? Furthermore, many of them interested him artistically; that was why he had hired them. Also, they worked harder. The older dancers had joined the company when it was a small, struggling enterprise and Morris an obscure young artist who, in most cases, had been their friend before he became their boss. They had treated him as an equal, and now, though the troupe had changed, they still treated him as an equal. When he corrected something they did, they were as likely as not to say, "I'm sorry, that's how I dance." Many of them put in only rare appearances at the class that in Belgium he began teaching every morning. (Keith Sabado: "It's better for me if I don't spend that many hours a day with him telling me what to do." Jon Mensinger: "That class is incredibly difficult, incredibly structured, and Mark is so loud—always singing or yelling or just blah, blah, blah the whole time—that you can't hear yourself *plié* or think.") The new dancers, on the other hand, were mostly younger than

Morris, and when they met him, he was a well-known choreographer. They treated him with respect, attended his class, heeded his corrections, and thought the old dancers arrogant for not doing likewise. ("The tiara club," they called the veterans.) The new dancers were not just ambitious; they were genuinely interested, in Morris's work and also in him. In the canteen, and in the bar after work, they clustered around him, their young, eager faces lighting up at his jokes—a scene the old dancers viewed with distaste from afar.

In their unhappiness, the older dancers had no outside comforts to turn to. They were four thousand miles away from home—stuck in a foreign city where they had to struggle to converse with a store clerk, where the sky was overcast every day, where people booed them and reviewers called them names. And now they had to sit and watch while the company in which they had invested their hearts and, in most cases, close to ten years of their dancing careers fell apart. In the spring, four of the company's senior dancers—Teri Weksler, Donald Mouton, Susan Hadley, and David Landis—announced that they would be leaving at the end of the season, thus plunging the remaining older dancers even deeper into despair.

In May, soon after the *Mythologies* debacle, the company left on tour, and while they were on the road, they found out that they had yet another kind of trouble, this time with the Monnaie, and specifically with Gérard Mortier, the man who had brought them to Belgium. Actually, they had had some difficulties in this quarter from the beginning. Mortier, in setting up the company in Brussels, had wanted its administration to be headed by two people. Morris might bring Barry Alterman, but Mortier wanted a deputy of his own—Stanislaw Bromilski, who, as administrator of the Béjart troupe, already had an office at rue Bara—to share responsibilities with Alterman, an arrangement that would have placed the company under Mortier's direct control. Morris, however, did not want to work with Bromilski. His company would be headed in Belgium, as it had been in the United States, by Alterman as general director and Nancy Umanoff as managing director. Mortier conceded reluctantly. Bromilski moved out of rue Bara and went off to take another job in the Monnaie bureaucracy, but after this episode he presumably harbored little affection for Morris's administration, and he remained close to Mortier.

In the year preceding the company's arrival, Alterman had spent a great deal of time in Brussels with Mortier, working out the deal, and the two men had built up what seemed to Alterman an excellent relationship.

Mortier is a notoriously cunning politician. ("I am a Machiavellian," he once told an interviewer. "I have to be. If you don't fight with the same weapons as your enemy, they will surely kill you.") Alterman admired Mortier's political skills, together with his artistic taste, and he felt he could trust him. This faith endured through most of the company's first year in Belgium. Mortier seemed to love the troupe. Right after *L'Allegro* he offered to extend their three-year contract to five years. (They turned him down. "We didn't know yet," says Alterman. "We had just arrived.") And through all the troubles with the press, Mortier seemed to be on their side. Indeed, as they both knew, many of the attacks on the troupe were attacks on Mortier. They were in this together—partners.

As Mortier explains it, he felt the same way: partners with the troupe, partners with Morris (whose work, through all the troubles, he never ceased to admire), but not necessarily partners with Morris's administration. In all opera houses, public relations—wooing the press, dining with sponsors, making the right phone calls—is part of the administration's job, and in Europe, where the press is generally more wooable, it is a bigger part of the job. Morris's administration did not see it this way, however. They were not European and not accustomed to opera houses; they believed that their job was just to put on dances, the way their contract said. However much Alterman may have enjoyed watching Mortier play politics, he did not feel he had to play politics himself. He still wore his

Gérard Mortier and
Morris, 1988
(Tom Brazil)

jeans and his Yankees jacket to the theater. He still, at intermission, went backstage rather than circulating in the lobby and making himself agreeable to the press. As for Mortier, however much he may have been charmed by Alterman's down-to-earth ways during the setup period, he still expected, once the troupe arrived, that Alterman would put on a suit and start making phone calls. And as the company began encountering difficulties with the press, he expected this all the more. "He could have done very positive things," Mortier says, "so that Mark could acquire positive public relations to the television, to the newspapers. I know some people in Belgium that you can turn around your hand. He could have won them over completely." He was also unhappy that Alterman didn't learn French. "Maybe, in a certain way, Barry was best for Mark," says Mortier, "but he was not the best for Belgium . . . He didn't understand how to arrange people." In any case, he didn't choose to.

Mortier never spoke to Morris or Alterman about this. Presumably he decided that it would be easier to replace Morris's administration than to re-educate them. Until the summer of 1989, he gave no sign of trouble. Then, in June, when the company was on tour in the United States, he sent Morris a letter detailing what he now described as Alterman's and Umanoff's administrative failings. Soon afterward, the company secretary called from Brussels to say that in processing the contracts for the next season, Mortier had left two contracts aside, unsigned—Alterman's and Umanoff's. They were being fired.

For the moment, nothing could be done. Mortier had left on vacation. Furthermore, the company was still on the road. The tour limped forward. In Italy, at the Spoleto Festival, *New Love Song Waltzes* was danced for the first time with a mostly new cast. By all accounts, it was a terrible performance. After Spoleto, the troupe proceeded to Barcelona, then to Seville, the last stop of the tour. After that, the four dancers who were leaving would pack up and go. For their final performance in Seville, they ended with *Gloria*, which was still performed only by the old dancers. This was their theme song, their anthem, and now, with every one of its meanings called into question—equality, friendship, hope—they danced it together for the last time. They were already weeping, men and women, before the curtain went down. Alterman believed that this was the end of the troupe: "I felt that we had taken the Mark Morris Dance Group to Belgium and destroyed it." What they had left was an old company halved and demoralized and a new company that didn't know how to do the work. It seemed only a matter of time before it fell apart.

Instead, it came together. When the company returned to Belgium, Morris, Umanoff, and Alterman had a tense meeting with Mortier, after which he signed the two remaining contracts. ("Mark insisted," says Mortier, "and for me it was more important to have a compromise than to have a fight." Also, Mortier had just found out that he was leaving the Monnaie in about a year's time, so he now had far less investment in who ran Morris's company.) For the remainder of the Belgian period, Alterman and Mortier barely spoke; all dealings with the Monnaie went through Umanoff. Nevertheless, the company's administration was back in place. And gradually the company fell into place. The departure of the four older dancers, though it deprived the troupe of some of its finest talent, was actually beneficial. These were the people who had been most unhappy in Brussels, and their mood had darkened the whole operation during the first year. (It had also affected Morris's state of mind. Among those four were some of his closest friends, and he had listened to their complaints continually.) Once they were gone, and once it became clear—as it did, absolutely, after the *Mythologies* scandal and the break with Mortier— that the company was not going to stay beyond its three-year contract, so that all they had to do was stick it out for two more years, the dancers began trying to make the Monnaie Dance Group work. The new dancers slowly mastered Morris's style, and as they did, the old dancers started treating them like colleagues. "The first year was the tearing-apart year," says Alterman. "The second year was about trying to make something new."

Making peace with Brussels was harder. Almost all the dancers learned some French. A few of them made friends outside the company. (Four of them even found mates, who returned with them to the United States in 1991.) Most of them, including the Europeans, never ceased to dislike the city, but they found a way to cope. Essentially, they barricaded themselves at rue Bara, and what they did was work, all the time. Then, after work, they had dinner at each other's houses. Had they gotten out more, they might have been happier, but by isolating themselves together, they evolved a new community to replace the old one that had been destroyed by the move to Belgium. They closed the doors and huddled together. Every now and then Nancy Umanoff would post a sign on the bulletin board: "Only 365 days left," "Only 100 days left."

They had comforts—for example, their U.S. tours. *Dido*, which the Belgian critics so hated, had audiences leaping to their feet in Boston and New York in 1989 and 1990. *L'Allegro*, which the company performed in

New York in 1990, was even more rapturously received. And if the company's Belgian performances were still being reviled by Belgian critics, they were receiving loving attention from other critics, particularly the Americans. The American dance press's support of Morris during his Belgian years is hard to assess, for there is nothing to compare it with. This was the first time, ever, that an American dance company had picked up its entire operation and moved to Europe. But the response of the American journalists was remarkable. Under ordinary circumstances, the largest American papers may send their critics to a European dance event if it is something very special. But while Morris was in Belgium, many, many American critics—some (particularly after the *Mythologies* scandal) in search of a good story, some (again, after *Mythologies*) out of loyalty, others simply eager to see Morris's new work—persuaded their editors to send them to Brussels to attend Morris's regular seasons. In New York, Boston, Chicago, San Francisco, Los Angeles, and Seattle, daily papers published reports—in some cases, regular reports—on the company's Belgian performances. So did a number of American magazines. And most of these articles were not the same old feature story (American Bad Boy Meets Stuffy European Capital) but actual reviews, as if the company had never left. As a result, Morris managed, while a continent away, to remain the most prominent young choreographer in the United States. Many of London's dance critics were equally assiduous in their attendance.

While the company settled down, so did Morris. During the first few months in Brussels, when all was well, he was in a vile temper, but this was because he was making *L'Allegro*, that enormous work. Once he got *L'Allegro* onstage, his peace of mind returned, and the battle with the press never succeeded in shaking it. Morris has an extraordinarily thick hide. It is almost impossible to make him doubt his work, no matter what the attacks against him. In Belgium, those attacks were steady, ferocious, and personal. It was not just a matter of the booing and the bad reviews; the hostility seeped into his daily life outside the theater. Strangers, when they met him, would give him advice on how to improve his dances. Once, in a bar, a man came over and asked him if he was Mark Morris. When he said yes, the man poured his beer into Morris's lap. On the street Morris was repeatedly stopped by the police and asked for his identification papers. This was probably not because he was Mark Morris but because he has long, shaggy hair. Guillermo Resto, who has dreadlocks, got the same treatment.

Morris learned to cope. After a few encounters with the police, he kept off the streets. He stopped walking to the studio in the morning; he took cabs. Whenever a photographer came near him, he froze his face— no more mugging—so that the newspapers could not publish silly photographs of him. And he learned to be careful about what he said to journalists. Once, he forgot himself. He told a reporter from the The Times of London that Brussels was "highly racist, highly sexist, highly homophobic, and highly conservative, and there are certain aspects that are quite fascistic." After The Times published this, the story was picked up by Philippon in Le Soir—the headline was "Mark Morris Spits in the Soup Again"—and Morris received a letter from the president of the Monnaie inviting him, if he had so low an opinion of Belgium, to terminate his contract. (He replied that the injustices he had imputed to Belgium existed in every Western democracy, that he had protested against them in the United States as well, and that he would finish out his contract.) But otherwise he watched his mouth. At press conferences he would say, "I'm not good at talking," and then talk little. He became vigilant. "I think I get it now," he told Alan Kriegsman of The Washington Post. "I know who *not* to pass a message through. I've figured out how I can function, if I can just be left alone."

The booing he seems to have had a relatively easy time with. It made him "very sad," he says, but booing does not shock him. Like the Europeans, he respects it, as a legitimate form of protest: "I boo stuff that I hate. If you watch something and hate it, you *should* boo. I prefer that to polite applause." At curtain calls, the booing invariably doubled in volume when he came out, but he would stride to the middle of the stage and bow and smile, as if everyone were clapping. As for the reviews, the only reaction he betrayed was wonder at their violence. "Come on," as he commented to Thea Singer of The Boston Phoenix, "it's only a dance, it's not a machine gun." His attitude spread to the dancers, and comforted them. As Clarice Marshall puts it, "He swept us up into a feeling of 'Here we are and this is what we do and go ahead and say whatever you have to say.' "

He was not just putting up a brave front. Of all the people in the company, Morris was probably the least unhappy in Belgium. In part, this was simply a matter of temperament. Depression is not natural to him. But what really protected him was his utter devotion to his work. (As David Landis commented, "It was harder on the dancers—they had a life.") On workdays, he had to be dragged out of the studio. On days off,

Mikhail Baryshnikov
and Morris in re-
hearsal. Brussels. 1990
(Annie Leibovitz)

he tended to stay home and look out the window, waiting to get back to the studio. He took on extra assignments. During his vacation time, he worked extensively for Mikhail Baryshnikov's modern dance company, the White Oak Dance Project. Indeed, he helped organize that troupe. After the success of *Drink to Me Only with Thine Eyes*, which Baryshnikov had commissioned for American Ballet Theatre, both men wanted to work together again, and it was arranged that Baryshnikov, in his time off from ABT, would come to Brussels in the fall of 1989 to dance in Morris's new Schoenberg piece, *Wonderland*. By the time Baryshnikov arrived, however, he had quit his post at ABT. He was now footloose, casting about for what to do next, and during the rehearsal period for *Wonderland*, he cooked up with Morris the idea of a small modern dance troupe made up of mature dancers—no teenagers—with strong, individual personalities. (In this sense, White Oak was built on the model of the pre-Belgian Mark

Morris Dance Group, the troupe that Morris had just lost.) Morris helped pick the dancers, and for White Oak's first three tours, in 1990 and 1991, he supplied and rehearsed all the dances. For the third tour, he was also a member of the company. Fueled by Baryshnikov's immense fame, White Oak sold out large theaters across the United States. Indeed, it sold out basketball arenas, houses seating eight thousand and ten thousand people. Together with his U.S. tours, and the American dance press's willingness to trek to Europe to see his Belgian shows, White Oak was the major factor in keeping Morris's reputation alive in America while he was in Europe.

White Oak was what he did on vacation. In Brussels, he simply poured his whole soul into making dances for his company. Unhappy though he and his dancers might be, they still had the facilities of the Monnaie— the orchestra, the chorus, the set and costume shops—and would have them for only two more years. He wasted no time. During his Belgian period, in addition to five works for other companies or for productions directed by others, Morris made seven pieces for his own company. Of these, the majority—*Wonderland*, with an orchestra of ninety-five; *The Hard Nut*, with its $600,000 design budget; *L'Allegro*, with its huge choruses, its forty-eight silk chiffon costumes, its twenty-one scrims and drops—used the Monnaie resources to the hilt. And not only were they expensive; they were very good. Ironically, Morris's artistic achievement at the Monnaie was greater than in any other comparable period of his life. In Belgium, he rose to a wholly new level of mastery, creating a group of pieces—*L'Allegro, Dido, Love Song Waltzes, Wonderland, Behemoth, Going Away Party, The Hard Nut*—that together show a freedom and force of imagination rarely equaled in recent American dance. It was as if, all those years, he had just been waiting for the Monnaie offer. Once it happened, these dances burst out of him. No amount of sorrow or confusion or fear could stop them.

And except for *L'Allegro*, which was made before the trouble began, all of them have to do with sorrow or confusion or fear. They are consistent in this regard—a remarkable testament to the continuity of art and life. They are also a testament to the flexibility of that connection, for though all of them deal with pain, each deals with it differently. The brash, ugly, funny *Hard Nut*, the large-hearted *Love Song Waltzes*, the stark, terrible *Dido*: all are woven from the same thread. Morris will presumably go on working for many more years, but it is doubtful that he will ever again demonstrate the richness of his imagination in so pure a fashion as he did in his three years in Brussels. That city taught him sorrow in a new way. He responded by smiling and saying that everything was fine—and indeed, much of the time, by feeling fine. And then he went into the studio and, one after the other, created six completely different works about the darkness of life.

The most unusual of them was *Behemoth*, long (38 minutes), cold, abstract, and silent: the only full-scale piece Morris has ever made without music. The dance is in eleven sections, separated by slicing blackouts. In each section the dancers engage in strange, ritualistic maneuvers whose only emotion seems to be a quest for precision. Twisting their torsos, turning on the floor like the hands of a clock, the dancers get each angle

Jean-Guillaume Weis, bending, and Rachel Murray in *Behemoth* (Beatriz Schiller)

just right—38 degrees, not 37—as if they had worked out a system by which, against all odds, they might be able to survive, but any deviation from which would spell disaster. The disaster is already there, however. Again and again, one dancer will be set off at an angle to the group, in frightening isolation. Often, the dancers are headless; they lie on the floor upstage-downstage, so we can't see their heads. Elsewhere they are face-less. They look at each other without recognition. (They acknowledge us even less. They end the piece with their backs to us.) Now and then the terror implicit in all this is given some meager expression: the dancers fall to their knees, their hands shiver, they look upward. But for the most part the piece makes no emotional appeal whatsoever. It is modest and absolute, a *Rite of Spring* without the sacrifice.

This is the coldest, darkest dance Morris has ever made—next to it, *Stabat Mater* looks warm—and in it one can read Morris's feeling of danger during his years in Brussels. But the fear of life is there in the other Belgian works as well. In *Wonderland*, a sort of film noir piece to Schoenberg, stock characters—the boss, the blonde, the punk—enact or meditate some crime, but we never find out who killed whom, or why. The piece has a coming-upon-the-dead-body scene that is replayed five times, *Rashomon*-like, from five different angles. You see, but you don't know.

Even the lighter works in the Belgian group are full of darkness. In *Going Away Party* (1990), a comic essay on cow-town romance set to country-western music, there is a cast of seven: three male-female couples plus Morris. Partnerless, he tries to join the others, but he doesn't really understand what they're doing. At the end, he is left alone onstage, and the lights go out while he is still in motion. (This is the only piece by Morris that seems to contain self-pity. As usual, though, the emotions are mixed. The dance is as funny and raunchy as it is elegiac.) Morris has said that he began *Going Away Party* as a satire on heterosexual relations but found, as he designed the choreography for these brawling, horny couples, that he had come to like them. So the sense of isolation is balanced against a kind of forgiveness and affirmation—in a word, love. That same mix, painted in different hues, is the basis of *Love Song Waltzes* and *The Hard Nut*. All the Belgian works say one or both of two things: life is terrifying; to brave its terrors, you need others. And that is an exact re-flection of the life of the troupe in Brussels. "Almost unanimously," says Nancy Umanoff, "people were miserable, but they drew together. There was a tremendous sense of friendship. We knew each other, we depended on each other, and that's how we survived."

Opposite:
Rob Besserer (standing) and Mikhail Baryshni-kov in *Wonderland*
(Klaus Lefebvre)

The reviews of Morris's later Belgian shows were more subdued than those of the first year. After the explosion with *Mythologies*, the reviewers seem to have wearied of the whole business. Most of them still didn't like Morris's work, but they were no longer surprised by it. When, on occasion, he seemed to focus more on narrative and less on dancing, as in *Wonderland*, some of them liked him better. But most of the time he just did the same old dancing.

Nor, in their eyes, was the tedium of the dancing alleviated by any pleasure in looking at the dancers. Lacking a modern dance tradition, most of these critics thought of dancers as ballet dancers—thin, glamorous, high-bred. Morris's barefoot dancers, with their exposed, human look, performing, as he asked them to, with bluntness, weight, and effort, seemed to the critics clumsy and plain. "People in Brussels thought that the company Mark had in America was the way it was because he couldn't afford anything else," Clarice Marshall says. "And now that he was in Europe, why didn't he dump those cows and those guys who couldn't point their feet and get some people who could dance?" The company's technique was continually faulted. *Marble Halls*, wrote Nicole Verschoore in *Het Laatste Nieuws*, looked as though someone had "put a bunch of chimpanzees in shorts onstage to prove that they could hop to the beat." Running an eye over the company, "you find . . . maybe one girl and one boy who would have a sure chance of passing an entry exam to study for a professional ballet career," she said. Most of the dancers, however, were "pitiful." Furthermore, they were fat. "One girl," Verschoore wrote, "has to lose ten kilos, another five kilos. Three others have cellulite."

It was not just the critics who found the women glamorless. The complaint arose backstage as well. "In the costume department," Marshall remembers, "they were constantly trying to do something about my body, like puffing the fabric up to make my breasts look bigger. The first week I was there, the masseuse took me aside—she was trying to be helpful—and told me, 'You would look a lot prettier if you wore makeup.' They were always trying to get us to go on diets too. They were used to Béjart's dancers—slim, feminine women who never went anywhere without lipstick on. And here we were, a bunch of big, athletic-looking American women walking around in jeans and T-shirts, with no makeup. To them, we looked like men. That's what they kept saying to us, over and over: 'You look like a man.' " The "new androgyny" is not a popular concept in Belgium. Nor, for that matter, is feminism, relative to its status in the United States. When Nancy Umanoff's Monnaie contract was being prepared, a major struggle was required in order to obtain for her the title of administrator rather than secretary. In Belgium, women are still viewed as very different from men. They are *feminine*—hence, objects of reverence and of discrimination. This is an old story, and hardly unique to Belgium, but it must be factored into the critics' response to the troupe.

But while *Le Soir* and *Het Laatste Nieuws* went on pouring scorn on Morris's work, a small counteroffensive was growing, largely in the Flemish press. Actually, it began with *Mythologies*, when *Le Soir* printed its front-page "Mark Morris, go home!" article. The day after that piece appeared, *De Morgen* published a reply, an editorial entitled "Morris, please stay." The attacks on *Mythologies*, the writer said, had as much to do with Mortier and Béjart as with Morris. Morris might have his faults, but he was new and lively; he stirred things up. If he should leave the Monnaie, the writer concluded, "Belgium might well be a little more polite, a little less agitated, and a great deal less interesting. The old adage is truer than ever: he who eschews controversy will end in grayness."

This old adage, which no doubt sounds better in Flemish, was also the main thrust of the very few other articles defending *Mythologies*. For example, *Knack*, a respected Flemish weekly, ran a long essay entitled "The Satanic Verses of Dance: A Small Plea for Mark Morris, a Great Choreographer." The critics' outrage against Morris, says the author, Fons de Haas, is comparable to Islam's death curse on Salman Rushdie: the fury of a closed-minded people against anyone who dares speak the truth. Unlike Béjart, with his "sloppy rites of spring"—as I said, not everyone in Brussels was a Béjart fan—Morris deals in real situations, real emotions. And if not all his dancers are beauties, so what? "The beauty of a human being is not in his legs or his butt but in the nobility of his expressive action. It is to Morris's credit that that is all he takes into account." Finally, if these people are not ballet dancers, so much the better. "You can't sell toe shoes and tutus to Morris . . . He *dances*." Like others of Morris's Belgian defenders, de Haas identifies hostility to Morris with conservatism (and hence with ballet). The booing at *Mythologies*, he says, was simply "Béjart-sclerosis."

Increasingly, for the remainder of the company's stay in Brussels, journalists spoke out against the rough treatment Morris had been given, particularly by *Le Soir*. Such protests, understandably, were more common in non-Belgian publications. *La Repubblica*, the Rome daily, wrote of Morris's being "attacked with fury by the Belgian press." *The New York Times*'s Brussels correspondent, Paul Montgomery, targeted *Le Soir* specifically, describing Philippon as having been "scarifying and mean-spirited about the least of Mr. Morris's acts." René Sirvin of Paris's *Le Figaro* also wrote of the violence of the Béjart partisans. From the very beginning, actually, *Le Figaro* had reported on Morris's seasons with an almost determined sympathy, a sentiment in which contempt for Belgian conservatism may have played some part. Making fun of what Baudelaire called *l'esprit belge*—provincialism, small-mindedness—is old sport for the French.

But Belgian critics also protested. "How long is the Morris-go-home game going to last?" asked Stephan Moens in *De Morgen*. "And will we regret it later?" Nor were these critics just rushing to the aid of the wounded. A number of them, to judge from their reviews, were sincerely interested in the work that Morris was producing. They didn't write at length about the choreography; they had no tradition for doing so. But they wrote admiringly of Morris's complicated emotional world, and they praised him for his boldness. "Morris's only sacrilege," said Guy Cools in *De Morgen*, "is that in the Old World he openly dares to choose the New."

It is just possible that if Morris had stayed, he might have won the Belgians over. (As some critics pointed out, Béjart too was booed and harshly reviewed during his first years in Brussels.) The Monnaie was not asking him to renew his contract, however, and if it had, and if he had accepted, he probably would have lost at least half his company. They were counting the days; nothing could stop them from going home.

The adventure ended on an ironic note. Morris's last independent dance production in Brussels, *The Hard Nut*, was a triumphant success. It received rave reviews not just from the papers that were now leaning in his favor—"a milestone in dance history," wrote *De Morgen*—but also from those that had consistently vilified him. *The Hard Nut*, wrote Nicole Verschoore, was "dance theater at its best." As for *Le Soir*, Philippon called the ballet "a jewel of invention, humor, fantasy, and poetry." The writers were aware that this represented a reversal in their evaluation of Morris, but they could explain it. In *The Hard Nut*, wrote Philippon, Morris avoided "all the failings of kitsch and vulgarity" that had marred his earlier productions. (*The Hard Nut*, as noted, is chockablock with kitsch and vulgarity; in some measure, it is an essay on kitsch and vulgarity.) Verschoore had a simpler explanation. Of the lead dancers in *The Hard Nut*, she wrote, "not a single one belongs to the Mark Morris Group Brussels" except Kraig Patterson. In fact, of the eight lead dancers in *The*

Hard Nut, only two were hired from the outside, and the stars of the ballet, Clarice Marshall (Marie) and William Wagner (the Nutcracker), had danced in almost all the company's prior Belgian shows—shows that Verschoore had reviewed.

The *New York Times* correspondent offered a different interpretation of Morris's new popularity: "Several cynics attributed the glowing notice [in *Le Soir*] today to the unwillingness of the newspaper to take the blame for the company's departure." Such reasoning could apply to *Het Laatste Nieuws* as well. Actually, there are obvious artistic reasons why the Brussels critics would have preferred *The Hard Nut* to Morris's other work. It is markedly different from his other work. It deemphasizes dancing, the thing the critics were so bored with, and it has a story, an assertive "concept" (*Nutcracker* update), a surface iconoclasm, and a splashy decor— all the things they liked. So, again, the reviewers' motivation was not simply political. But it was no doubt political too. Morris was leaving; they could afford to be generous.

Finally, in June of 1991, the three-year contract expired. Four more members of the "old company" resigned from the troupe, and one member of the "new company" stayed in Europe. That left sixteen dancers who wanted to return to America with Morris. He took them all and went back to New York.

Much had changed for him in three years, above all his troupe. The old Mark Morris Dance Group, that idealistic gang of soulmates—people who had drunk from the same cup and learned, together, how to dance: this company no longer existed. In its place was a new company which, though it inherited the spirit and style of the old group, was nevertheless different—larger, younger, more technically skilled, and headed by a man who was no longer first among equals but simply first, the boss. This change in the company, which cost a thousand tears, was inevitable. It happens in every dance troupe that lasts longer than ten years. They start as a merry band; they end as an institution. In the case of the Mark Morris Dance Group, the transition was merely hastened by the move to Belgium.

Also hastened was a change in Morris's status, and not just within the troupe. As a result of the Belgian scandal and the White Oak tours— but above all, as a result of his Belgian works, which he had already toured in Europe and the United States—he was now a famous man. In 1991, shortly before his return, the MacArthur Foundation awarded him one of its prestigious five-year fellowships. When he left the United States in 1988, he was often described as America's foremost young choreographer. When he came back, the "young" was dropped. He was one of America's foremost artists.

In many ways, he was no longer young. If his period of troubles in 1985–86, the years leading up to *Stabat Mater*, had hardened him once, Belgium had hardened him again. He had become more sophisticated— his clothes less weird, his temper less volatile, his manner with strangers smoother, more discreet. And according to his friends, he had become less available emotionally. What he had had to give them before was now being routed, more and more, into the work.

The other big change was of course in repertory. The dances Morris had made for the Belgians he now took home with him, together with their sets and costumes, which the Monnaie sold him at a good price. (For the $600,000 production of *The Hard Nut*, the company paid $55,000.) He could now produce these works wherever he wished, and if his repertory had been rich before, with the addition of *L'Allegro* and *Dido* it was one of the finest repertories in American dance. "Brussels was fraught with difficulty, pain, and agony," Barry Alterman said to an interviewer soon after the company's return, "but it was not a mistake." Actually, it was a triumph.

Shortly after Morris left Belgium, Mortier left too. In 1992, at the young age of forty-eight, he succeeded the late Herbert von Karajan as director of the Salzburg Festival, probably the most important musical job in Europe. There, to the anguish of conservative Viennese critics, he now exercises his bold tastes and political skills. (He has invited the Mark Morris Dance Group to appear at the festival in 1995.) Mortier's appointment in Salzburg was no sooner announced, and Morris's departure from Belgium thereby assured, than people in the Belgian dance establishment began trying to lure Béjart back, but no agreement was reached. Béjart remained in Lausanne, and Morris was succeeded at the Monnaie by Anne Teresa de Keersmaeker.

THE HIDDEN SOUL

OF HARMONY

However the Brussels assignment ended, it had begun in joy. That job offer was a great validation for Morris, and a great opportunity. Whatever he had in him as an artist, he could at last find this out, and the hopefulness, the sheer relish, with which he faced this prospect is written all over his first Belgian work, *L'Allegro, il Penseroso ed il Moderato*, set to Handel's oratorio of the same name. *L'Allegro* is a great big dance, two hours long—three times longer than any piece Morris had made before—and with a cast of twenty-four, double the size of any of his previous company works. It uses an orchestra of thirty, a chorus of forty, a set (by Adrianne Lobel) consisting of twenty-one different scrims and drops, blue for the sky, green for the meadows, purple and gold for the towered cities that Morris tells of in this dance. The costumes are in every color of the spectrum, and each dancer has not one but two costumes: muted colors for Act I, bright greens and pinks and yellows and blues for Act II. The piece streaks like a rainbow across the stage. It blossoms and blooms, and stints on nothing.

This is in keeping with its text. The words to Handel's oratorio were spliced together, for the most part, from Milton's companion poems "L'Allegro" and "Il Penseroso." "L'Allegro" is a portrait of the joyful mind, "Il Penseroso" of the contemplative mind, but together they form a portrait of what, to Milton, was the known universe. L'Allegro, the joyful man, wakes at dawn and goes out into the world. He shows us the lark, the hunters, the plowmen, the grazing sheep. He goes to the city and attends the theater. He watches young people dancing and then, at nightfall, warming themselves with beer and stories. Il Penseroso, the contemplative man, offers us quieter pleasures but, again, plenty of them. With him we hear the nightingale, the cricket, the tolling curfew, the roaring tide. We walk in twilit groves, go to church, go home and make a fire and read all night.

Each speaker, furthermore, peoples his world with the gods and goddesses of antiquity—Vesta and Jove for Il Penseroso, Venus and Bacchus for L'Allegro—and fills it also with the history of literature: plays by Shakespeare and Ben Jonson for L'Allegro to watch, books by Aeschylus and Plato, Chaucer and Spenser, for Il Penseroso to read. Appropriate skies shine down on each: for L'Allegro, the sun robed in flames, for Il Penseroso, the cloud-hung heaven. Milton was only in his twenties when he wrote these poems, but with typical Renaissance confidence he has packed into them psychology, cosmology, astronomy, meteorology—the whole world, and the history of the world, with the human mind at its center.

When Handel, a century later, composed an oratorio on the text of "L'Allegro" and "Il Penseroso," he rivaled Milton's abundance. Charles Jennens, his librettist, had rearranged the two poems so that they no longer stood side by side but were interleaved, part with matching part: L'Allegro's invocation of Mirth followed by Il Penseroso's invocation of Melancholy, L'Allegro's hearing the lark followed by Il Penseroso's hearing the nightingale, and so on. So, in the oratorio what we get is a sort of debate in which the singers compete with one another in proclaiming the virtues of the active and the contemplative life.

This shuttling pattern only increases the bustle and fullness of the poems, and now, of course, that fullness is a matter not just of words but of music. Back and forth goes Handel, outdoing himself in finding musical equivalents for L'Allegro's delights, Il Penseroso's broodings. Mirth skims on the violins; Melancholy growls in the bass viols. The soaring mountain is pictured in great, blocklike chords; the rising moon by a slow, silvery modulation through the keys. Ben Jonson's genius is celebrated in a foursquare tune; "sweetest Shakespeare, fancy's child," in looping cantilenas and coloraturas. L'Allegro exits in a blaze of trumpets; Il Penseroso, with a majestic double fugue. Over Milton's world, Handel has laid another world, a universe of sound.

And over this Morris has constructed another, brimming world—

The female ensemble
in *L'Allegro*. Left to
right: Teri Weksler.
Olivia Maridjan-Koop.
Ruth Davidson. June
Omura. Alyce Bo-
chette. Penny
Hutchinson
(Klaus Lefebvre)

thirty-odd dances, all in different patterns, rhythms, and tones. As usual,
he has listened to his text. All of Milton's creatures are there—nymphs
and goddesses, plowmen and milkmaids, dogs and birds—and they do
what Milton says. When the text speaks of Vesta giving birth to Melancholy, the dancers take to the floor in frank, open-thighed birth throes.
When Il Penseroso sings of reading by the fire, the dancers, climbing on
one another's knees and shoulders, build a fireplace, and one dancer, with
shimmering arms, becomes the fire. There are dances about hunting,
dreaming, laughing, going to church; others about mountains, meadows,
cities, weddings, all in keeping with Milton's text. Needless to say, the
choreography also heeds the score. When the music runs, plods, skips,
sweeps, glides, meanders, so do the dancers.

But what is striking is not Morris's ability to mirror Milton's and Handel's bright, full worlds, but his matching that fullness on his own dance terms. The choreography bristles with patterns—circles and grids, laterals and diagonals, wedges and arcs and rosettes. The dancers move now like Isadora Duncan, now like courtiers or Balkan peasants. The stage lives a thousand lives, empty and full, open and layered, shallow and deeper and deeper still.

Every story seems to be told in a different way. At times the dance sticks very close to the text. When Milton speaks of the hunt, we get one of Morris's little memory-of-grade-school mime dramas, complete with trees and hedgerows, lords and ladies, and a pack of riotous dogs peeing on the bushes. Elsewhere, the imitative logic is indirect—Morris's usual half-narrative. At one point L'Allegro sings:

> And ever against eating cares,
> Lap me in soft Lydian airs;
> Soothe me with immortal verse,
> Such as the meeting soul may pierce
> In notes, with many a winding bout
> Of linkèd sweetness, long drawn out;
> With wanton heed, and giddy cunning,
> The melting voice, through mazes running,
> Untwisting all the chains that tie
> The hidden soul of harmony.

The subject here is song—specifically, how singing, while it may lead us through a thousand complications, still reveals itself in the end as something *rational*, with its basis in harmony. Milton tells this story by poetic means, Handel by musical means. Morris hears all that, but out of it he makes his own, dance story. Discarding the subject of song and going just for the point about reason and fancy, he arranges twelve women in a braided wreath and has them dance in and out among one another. The wreath winds and turns, twists and untwists—this is the "wanton heed," the "giddy cunning"—but always with the simple, rational circle (the "hidden soul of harmony") at its center. As the song nears its end, the drama intensifies. The women break into groups of three, and in each trio, one woman dips down while the two others join their hands over her head, imprisoning her. Then, on the final cadence, she bursts up through the barrier: the hidden soul of harmony, rising, sweet-faced, out of apparent confusion. So Milton's image is there, but it has become a dance image, a matter of hiding and revealing through dancing. The same is true in most of *L'Allegro*. Goddess, nymph, bird, dream: the thing is indicated, but then it begins to change. It sprouts new meanings, flows back into the dance.

Full as it is, however, *L'Allegro* is an organized world, where things relate to one another, predict and recall one another. When, at the beginning of the dance, L'Allegro invokes the goddess Mirth, she appears in the form of three women. Then Il Penseroso beckons his goddess, Melancholy, and she too appears in the form of three women. These latter three are the ones who lie down and give birth. But they are not the only ones who do so. Further along, there is a rambunctious sex dance—this is the song about weddings—and while that is going on in one part of the stage, a lone man in another part of the stage lies down and repeats the

goddesses' birth-throes move. (He is presumably giving birth to the babies being engendered on the other side of the stage.) Then, twenty minutes later, in the midst of a solemn dance about old age, the dancers echo, in muted form, a little step from the sex dance—and also one from the laughing dance and the dance about skipping through the meadows. Old now, they are remembering love, laughter, and meadows. You could do this same point-for-point tracking for almost every important motif in *L'Allegro*. It all ties together.

And nothing seems to occur alone. This is true, actually, in most of Morris's work. He is always doubling things. In *Lovey*, there are two mothers, two fathers, two babies. In *Dido* there are two Didos, Dido and the Sorceress. But Morris's doubling technique has never been more obvious than in *L'Allegro*. No matter how exalted or private the experience he is portraying, it is never wholly private; someone else is having it at the same time. For Il Penseroso's nightingale, Morris creates a beautiful, anguished solo, a sort of "Dying Swan." But it is not a solo. At the back of the stage, behind a scrim, there is a second nightingale doing much the same dance. Another of Il Penseroso's songs paints a quintessentially romantic scene—a solitary dreamer, on a cliff, gazing out over the sea at nightfall—and Morris portrays the same scene, except double: two dreamers, two seas, on two sides of the stage. In Il Penseroso's study, there are two fireplaces; in the hunt, two foxes; in the sky, two moons.

This double vision is probably just a facet of Morris's habitual ensemble vision. In any case, there is no clearer demonstration of that ensemble vision than *L'Allegro*. The piece is a classic Mark Morris product, a dance for the group, with little internal dances for smaller groups, but with the whole ensemble coming back again and again to remind us that they are the fundamental unit of meaning—this dance is about them. At the conclusion of Act I all twenty-four dancers are onstage, their hands joined, running in a circle, and then, as the chorus sings of nightfall, taking to the floor and going to sleep—the human family completing its daily round. At the end of Act II, we again see the entire company in a circle, but here the circle is multiplied: three concentric rings, spinning in alternating directions. This is not just the human family now but the cosmos.

So everything is there together, and bound together—the universe, the human race, and also the arts, for *L'Allegro* is a hymn to the unity of poetry, music, and dance: a story of how each, like L'Allegro and Il Penseroso, can follow its own laws and still harmonize with the others. The

The finale of L'Allegro
(Tom Brazil)

piece is also a hymn to the unity of history, for the poetry, music, and dance that are wedded in this piece are from the seventeenth, eighteenth, and twentieth centuries. The nineteenth century is there, too. William Blake made a series of watercolor illustrations of "L'Allegro" and "Il Penseroso," and Morris based a number of steps on those paintings. *L'Allegro* spans about 350 years—actually about 2,300 years, for this is a pastoral, that hallowed Greco-Roman form—and it says, basically, that things haven't changed.

A historical vision such as this was natural enough for Milton's Renaissance mind. It was also natural for Handel and even for Blake, who, though he helped bring about the nineteenth century's break with Renaissance humanism, still had one foot in the eighteenth century. The only odd participant in this celebration of the unity of the world is the one who organized it, Mark Morris. Coming long after romanticism's break with classicism, indeed, long after modernism's presumed break with romanticism, and also after postmodernism's break with modernism—a line of succession carrying us further and further away from the idea that the mind can understand the world or the past or anything other than its own solitude—Morris aligns himself with the classical position, claiming

245

that what Milton and Handel said is still true. And this assertion has been there in his work from the beginning, from the time of *Gloria* in 1981, with those modern-looking people reenacting the faith of Vivaldi. As I have said, he believes in the existence of human wisdom: that there are a fixed number of stories about human life and that we all still know them and care about them.

Such a position is not unheard of among contemporary artists, but it is normally a mark of conservatism. The remarkable thing about Morris's work is how unconservative it is, given this subject matter. *L'Allegro* is a serene piece, but most of Morris's dances are full of trouble, with different historical styles tumbling in on each other, with different moods and meanings banging up against one another. He is fully modern—in the eyes of some critics, fully postmodern: uneasy, ironical. Yet he never feels that this isolates him from the past.

Why not? Again, the answer may have to do with music. When he was young, he fell in love with old music. As he grew up and found out that life, and particularly modern life, offered plenty of challenges to the apparent certainties on which old music was built—God, love, "human wisdom," A-B-A form—he still could not bring himself to doubt the truth of that music. And so, instead of renouncing it or removing it to some historicist, "classical music" shelf of his mind, he hung on to it, probed it more deeply, and found in it a living relation to modern experience—found that within its tidy forms it too contained doubt, distress, living terror, even irony. Out of this discovery came his long series of new/old works, dances in which the meanings of old music are reenacted in emphatically up-to-date form: *Gloria, New Love Song Waltzes, Marble Halls, L'Allegro, Dido, Beautiful Day*. It's not that he found meaning in the Past. It's that he found meaning in Purcell and Handel. And since they made sense, history made sense.

This experience of unity with the past seems to have set up a kind of trend in his mind. His thought became governed by the idea of relatedness. All art is concerned with the relations of things. But in Morris's work this is not just a concern; it is a constant subject. Throughout his dances, everywhere you look—in the emphasis on the ensemble, in the choreography's dependence on the music, in the obsession with structure, in the focus on social questions—you see this same story being told: how things connect with one another, depend on one another, rise from a common source. And those are only the obvious manifestations. There are subtler ones—for example, his habit of making his dances half-narrative. Because he believes that the world contains a fixed number of stories and that we all know them, he can simply *indicate* a story—sketch it in with a gesture or two—and then proceed with the dance, trusting that we will understand what is going on. In the "Nicht wandel" section of *Love Song Waltzes*, where Jon Mensinger tries to break out of the circle, we don't know why he wants to leave, and we don't need to know. We can supply the details, from the times when we have wanted to leave, or have been left.

This technique, the art of omission, of course magnifies the power of Morris's symbol, but it does something else as well. It brings us closer to him. What he is saying is "You and I—we understand the same things," and once he says it, we feel it is true. One of the qualities that the audience seems to like most in Morris's work is what they perceive as its *warmth*. They feel included by it, loved by it, even. They feel that the dancers are not just good dancers but good people, whom they would like to know, indeed, whom they do know—a sentiment that has occasionally provoked ardent statements from reviewers. (Clives Barnes of the *New York Post*: "Somehow you feel that he and his dancers are just the sweetest people ever to step on stage." Deborah Jowitt of *The Village Voice*: "I feel . . . that if I ran down the aisle and climbed up on stage, they'd take my hand.") And if that is the way reviewers feel, it is no surprise that the audience, less skeptical, feels the same way. This reaction is certainly due in part to the whole-grain, sixties-type qualities of the work—the ensemble emphasis, the imperfect, laboring, "human" bodies—but it also has to do with the drier fact that because Morris believes in a fund of common experience, he is constantly appealing to it. It's not that he loves us; it's that he respects our emotional intelligence, treats us as fellows. And so, when we look at his dances, we feel the warmth of fellowship.

His faith in relatedness soaks down into his very method of choreographing a dance, his habit of motif development. Built up out of variations on a few themes, his dances are mirrors of his view of the world. Things fit; they have underlying principles; you can grasp them. And as in his half-narrative approach, this philosophical attitude becomes an emotional attitude. Because he thinks that the world is understandable, he believes that he can make us understand what he has to say, and so he is willing to work hard toward that end. That's what the motif development is about, as he once pointed out in an interview: "By using fewer themes, it's like a secret trick to enable people to remember how the dance is going. You remember the last time you saw that action for a second, and it makes [the dance] tie together." This effort to communicate is very endearing, particularly in those dances where he is going after darker and more complicated meanings, double meanings. That he should see so difficult a truth and, in response to it, not cloak himself in a haughty obscurity but instead try, point by point, to say what it is, make it clear, comes across as an act of friendship. No matter how strange and involving the thing that is happening to him, he is always, in the middle of it, holding out a hand to us. "Nicht wandel": don't go, stay. His habit of doubling—the need to have two nightingales, two fireplaces, two moons in the sky —is probably governed by the same impulse. The earth has only one moon. Why does he need two? Partly, I think, to keep each other company, but also to show that nothing in the world is a unique instance, a special case.

His overarching sense of the relatedness of things helps to explain one of the more remarkable traits of his work, the largeness of his vision: the range of music he has used, the range of his subject matter, the great sweep of his cultural references—his uncoy use of mass culture, his un-genteel use of high culture. Because he thinks that everything fits, he is always tempted to fit more things in. Of course, this is also owing to his temperament, above all to a kind of felicitous inconsistency in his personality. In the words of David White, the director of Dance Theater Workshop:

Mark is a sort of car crash of personalities. There's this working-class guy and there's this music scholar guy, and there's this folk-dance guy and this gay guy, and they've all washed up into the same body. That's why he can use all that old classical music and still have it be about ordinary things—because those two sides are already hooked up together in him. He's open to everything, because all that stuff is in him. He's like one of those evacuation centers you go to after a flood. You know, there's the milkman and the belly dancer and the bank president, and they're all sitting on the same bench. That's Mark, and that's his work.

Because he seems to have a connection with so many things outside him, he doesn't feel he has to take a course in something in order to make it his. If he likes it, he uses it. He is a big mouth, a maw: he eats up everything.

That is how he developed his choreographic style. In view of the fact that he is a modern dance choreographer, it is worth noting that he had very little training in modern dance—just a few short courses at his dance camp and some classes with First Chamber Dance Company when he was a teenager—and that he never studied modern dance composition. As he has said, "When I started making up modern dance, I wasn't sure what that was." Yet nothing looks more like American modern dance than his work. The focus on the ensemble, the positing of the ensemble as a symbol of humankind, the soul-of-man idealism, the willingness to show weight and effort, the music visualizing: all these are traits of "middle" modern dance, the modern dance of the thirties through the fifties. Doris Humphrey was as devoted to Baroque music as he. José Limón, like him, built up dances out of a few seminal phrases.

Where did he get these habits if not from his modern dance predecessors? Partly he acquired them from sources that also affected those predecessors. The main influences on his style were music and Balkan dance—all the traits listed above come primarily from these two sources—and the "middle moderns" were also influenced by music and folk dance. Nevertheless, once he saw the work of other modern dance choreographers, he imitated what he liked, sometimes after only brief contact. What he knows of Isadora Duncan is not much more than most people know. He has seen still photographs of her; he attended a few concerts of Duncan dances by Annabelle Gamson; in 1985 he took one class from a third-generation Duncan dancer, Madeleine Lytton, at Harvard's summer school, where he was teaching at the time. But the ghost of Duncan hovers over many of his works, and certain solos that he has made for himself look like actual tributes to Duncan. With others of his elders he had longer contact—with Paul Taylor, for example. Taylor is the one modern dance choreographer to whom he is most often compared, and the comparison is apt. The habit of setting plain-looking movement to grand Baroque scores, the melding of comedy with horror, the absorption of male-female love into a kind of group love: if Morris didn't acquire these traits from Taylor, he must still have been encouraged by Taylor's example. Other models too flit through his work—Graham, Humphrey, Laura Dean, Lucinda Childs, Trisha Brown. Balanchine is there not so much on the surface as in the deep principle of musical structure. That's where Hannah Kahn is too.

He doesn't cover his traces. You can see what he was looking at: in *Dido*, Indian and Indonesian dance; in *O Rangasayee*, Indian dance and Ted Shawn and Ruth St. Denis; in *L'Allegro*, Duncan and Humphrey and the Dalcroze dancers. If you can't see the model, he will point it out to you. *Behemoth*, as he has said repeatedly in interviews, was inspired by Merce Cunningham. In *Stabat Mater* he was thinking of Lucinda Childs.

("I love Lucinda's math mind. I copy it all the time.") The first movement of *Marble Halls*, he says, is "a total Trisha Brown *hommage*." So is one section of *Deck of Cards*; it is a Trisha Brown accumulation dance (A, AB, ABC, ABCD, et cetera). In *L'Allegro* there is a Thracian line dance that he learned in Koleda. In *Ten Suggestions* there is a digging-with-a-shovel step that he learned in the Japanese Bon Odori festivals of his youth. The history of dance is his shopping mart.

In keeping with this attitude, he generally speaks of his predecessors with great respect. (Only under provocation, as in the case of Béjart, will he openly disparage the work of an older choreographer.) Asked by an interviewer whether he was trying to develop his own technique, he answered, "There are four different dance techniques—ballet, in several different flavors, Humphrey/Limón, Graham, and Cunningham and that's it. There aren't any others." The makers of those techniques, in his opinion, worked out certain truths about dance that do not need to be reworked out. ("The nature of the proscenium, as Doris Humphrey will tell you, has strong places [and] weak places. That's perception, that's how it is set up.") He doesn't see himself as avant-garde. The avant-garde, he says, "doesn't exist and hasn't since 1917, with constructivism and the Russian revolution."

So Morris does not believe that he is creating dance *ex nihilo*. Beyond that, however, he feels all the same pride and singularity that any serious artist feels, and he works with the same independence. For all his tributes to his predecessors, his work does not look like theirs. You could never mistake *Behemoth* for Cunningham or *Stabat Mater* for Lucinda Childs. Whatever the inspiration, it has been absorbed into Morris's own way of dancing. The shaggy hair, the fleshy thighs, the little half-stories, the extreme tenderness, the dark cackle, the folk dances, the grand musical designs: this is his and no one else's. Because he believes so strongly in the reality of things besides himself—history, dance history—he is free to be himself.

Another thing to which he accords a separate reality is art. As we have seen, his imagination is in many ways anchored in the sixties. Above all, he shares with the sixties a certain naturalness of movement that reads, symbolically, as candor. But unlike the experimentalists of the sixties, he has no interest in extending that naturalism to the formal properties of theater. His work is not a Happening. He does not mix media. He does not use non-professional dancers, and his dancers do not generally do "ordinary movement," nor do they hop off the stage and engage the au-

Opposite top: Ruth Davidson and Alyce Bochette in L'Allegro (Klaus Lefebvre). Bottom: Students of the Dalcroze Institute, c. 1916 (Boissonas)

dience in conversation. There is no effort to break down the fourth wall. As he has said, "I don't want my experience in the theater to be the same one I had in the street, outside the theater. Some people think that if it takes four hours to get to the theater on the subway, the show should be a four-hour show about being trapped in the subway. But theater is not a situation from real life. It's different. It's a fantastical situation."

And the job of the artist is to make it so—to create a fantasy that the audience can enter into. If Morris is respectful toward his elders, he can be extremely rude about the anti-dance tendencies of his own generation. ("A guy sits alone onstage in a spotlit chair, tells you his life story, then flicks his hands a couple of times to let you know it's a dance.") A dance must be interesting to watch: "I have fabulous, brilliant ideas, and then I look at them, and they don't look like anything. Even though they're really complicated and intellectually satisfying, it's bullshit if it doesn't look like something." Accordingly, much of his time in the studio is spent not in creating steps but in deleting them. His usual practice is to make a dance that is far too complicated. Then, as he puts it, "I clear it out." He occasionally edits older works too (though he doesn't like to). According to Robert Bordo, the original, 1981 *Gloria* "had every little beggar girl and every little fallen angel and every little sinner and repentant person." In 1984 he cleared it out. He also likes to work on more than one dance at the same time. *Going Away Party* and *Behemoth*, one warm and funny, one cold and frightening, were choreographed simultaneously.

He is objective. He sees the world as something separate and real, and he attaches himself to it. Out of that comes the dance, which again is separate from him, as is the audience. He is aware of the audience's needs: the need for understanding, for variety, for relief. He is a repertory builder. He makes big works and small works, funny works and grim works, and assembles them into shows that look like shows, with openers and closers. His pieces have satisfying endings. The conclusion of *L'Allegro*, with its spinning cosmos, is the prime example—audiences jump to their feet, cheering, when it's over—but even *Behemoth* has a terrific finish. And lest all this seem unduly salesmanlike, it should be added that not just the most instinctively satisfying aspects of his work but also its most difficult and demanding qualities, such as his ability to operate in the realm of pure symbol, are based on this same distinction he makes between his own mind and the things outside it. You have to see the world as real in order to imagine it as symbol; that's what the symbol is symbolizing.

What I have pictured here—a mind that sees many things, all real, all separate, all related—is a happy formula for art making and, one might say, an innocent one. It is easy to see Morris as a naïf. The Belgian critics did. Some of his works (*Gloria*, *L'Allegro*) invite such an interpretation, and his life certainly does. Loved and encouraged by his mother and his first teacher, Verla Flowers; initiated into art making as a form of play, so that it seemed completely natural to him; learning from the very beginning—at home, in Koleda—to regard art as a group endeavor, so that the concept of interdependence, which is fundamental to dance (dependence of dance on music, of choreographer on dancers, of choreography on performance), was never strange to him; receiving his primary training in three forms of dance (Balkan, Spanish, ballet) based on the idea of a continuous tradition, so that he was never encouraged to feel a break with the past or, if he imitated the past, to feel the anxiety of influence; a professional dancer from age eleven, a professional choreographer from age fourteen, launched into the work force at age seventeen, unviolated by college—Morris sounds like a Renaissance guild artist, or perhaps like the nineteenth century's idea of Mozart or Shakespeare, an artist who became an artist not in the modern way, by feeling some estrangement from the world, but in the old, "innocent" way, by inheriting a tradition and bringing to it his own natural genius. His personality in many ways fits this childlike model: his love of fun, his huge self-confidence, his curiosity, his indiscretion. Above all, his attitude to dance—his lack of self-consciousness about its symbolic character, his absolute belief that it means something, his description of his work as "making up" dances, as if he were still back home, wrapped in a bedsheet, interpreting Saint-Saëns on the hi-fi—all of this seems to bespeak an uncomplicated nature, an unclouded brow. "Mark is innocent, tremendously," says Robert Bordo:

He's not an insider. He doesn't go through any of this sort of cultural mediation that you see today. He doesn't want to deconstruct Balanchine. He wants to be a great artist and make great human dances as he sees fit. He's not self-willed. He doesn't have a vehicle or an angle or a strategy. He has a gift. I don't believe in stuff like that, really, except when I see his work.

If not naïve in the usual sense, he would seem to be so in the sense of Schiller's famous distinction between the "naïve" and the "sentimental" poet, the one still in harmony with the universe and therefore objective, positing his vision as reality, the other jarred out of harmony by civilization and therefore subjective, offering his vision as an unreachable ideal. In some measure, Schiller was describing classicism and romanticism, and ever since the early 1980s critics have been describing Morris's work as classical. (So has he. Once the reviewers came up with this, he leapt on it eagerly, probably because it helped to counter the view of his work as "outrageous.") And his dances *are* classical, both in the special, dance meaning of that term—that is, pure dance, issuing out of its music—and in the more general meaning: harmoniously structured, grounded in history and tradition, and intent on the general, the universal truth. It would be hard to find a more classical-looking work than *L'Allegro*, but even *The Vacant Chair*, with Morris storming around in his underpants, has a discrete three-part structure.

Yet discussions of Morris's classicism tend to overstress its stability. What makes most classical art interesting is not an achieved balance but a struggle for balance, and this is true of Morris's work as well. Though everything in the world may be related, it is sometimes hard to discover the relations. Though the universe may have a soul of harmony, that soul is *hidden*; it must be found. In one part of his brain Morris may have an almost ecstatic vision of the unity of history, but in another part he knows full well that there is a problem with that unity. The difference between the difficult, disjunct, God-is-dead present and the image of the world offered by old music is not lost on him. If it were, he wouldn't present it so strikingly. He wouldn't have people crawling on the floor to Vivaldi, screwing on the floor to Brahms. What allows him to make these pairings is not innocence but hope, and that, in the end, is probably what is most moving about his work: that he entertains the hope that history can be healed, that he sees, shows, and then tries to bridge the gap between the modern and the old. It's not for nothing that the audience's favorite works are *Gloria, New Love Song Waltzes, L'Allegro,* and *Dido,* works in which he drags us bodily through this divide and hauls us up, winded, on the other side.

And then there are the works, like *The Vacant Chair*, where unity is not achieved, and others, such as *The Hard Nut*, where he seems almost to back off from such a conclusion. These are troubling pieces. But it's the same as with his mixing of irony and sincerity: the drama is in the push toward unity, the strenuous, muscular effort to bring things together, to find their relation. That's what all the toil is about on his stage, and all the double emotions. And for this task he takes the music as his model.

He does not see Handel as inhabiting a paradise of unity and himself knocking on the gates. He hears in Baroque music the same darkness and distress that he himself feels. In his mind, what Handel achieved was not a "life" solution but an artistic solution: acuity of image, comeliness of form. That is his example, and so a quality of struggle doesn't bother him, nor does it bother most of us as we look at the work. The sight of these flesh-and-blood bodies laboring under the dome of this beautiful music becomes a metaphor for the tragic meanings of his work. Or it becomes a source of wit, or of tragic wit.

The trend of his work has been toward a more classical image—more precisely articulated, more firmly structured, more intent on dance values as opposed to charm or effrontery. If his later work is occasionally over-structured, his early work was often underchoreographed. There was a great deal of sweeping and splatting, and too few actual steps. Today, there are not necessarily more steps per minute. (He claims there are fewer.) But the steps are more complicated, more subdivided, more "dig-ital," as Keith Sabado has described them. They are more likely to have internal accents, rhythmic hitches, things that must be done very exactly. Therefore they are both more legible and more abstract. They look more like steps and less like a bunch of attractive young people tearing around. As the choreography has changed, so has the look of the body. The torso is more pulled up, the limbs more "worked," as they say in ballet—that is, pushing harder toward a specific shape, a specific image. In 1992 Morris decided to revive the 1982 *Songs That Tell a Story*, and he asked Barry Alterman for an archival videotape that was made around the time of the premiere. Alterman, who had seen the tape, told Morris that he didn't think it would be of much help. "The dancers are marking," he said—in other words, sketching the steps, the way dancers sometimes do in re-hearsal, rather than performing them full out. "They weren't marking," Morris replied. "That's how we danced it."

One can explain these changes simply by saying that he grew up—became more mature, mastered his craft—but there were times when he grew up faster. The shift toward a more classical style becomes very pronounced in 1985–86. As we saw, these were years of crisis for Morris. He lost Erin Matthiessen, he broke his foot, he committed himself to his company, and he began his intensive study of Baroque music. All these things made him pull back, think more, invest himself more in the *formal* conquest of feeling. Of special importance is the foot injury. He had to stop dancing for five months. This was a great sorrow to him, and it was probably a great boon as well. At the very moment when he was at last throwing himself into the company—and when, because of the break with Matthiessen, he was looking more deeply into himself—he was forced to become wholly a choreographer rather than a dancer-choreographer. That is, he now had to think about his work not in terms of how it felt to do it but in terms of how it looked, on other people. Before, almost all his choreography was an extension of his own dancing. As Guillermo Resto has described it, "Mark would have an idea, he would work the steps out . . . and all you could really do was try to approximate what he would do as a dancer." Now, says Resto, "more and more, he actually choreographs on this group rather than on himself or in his mind." This has vastly increased his range. Wonderful dancer though he is, he is only one dancer, with one set of possibilities. Other dancers have other possibilities, which he could now develop, adding new colors to his palette. More than that, he became a *watcher*, a member of the audience. In 1992 he told an interviewer, "I realized a long time ago that just because it feels good doesn't mean it looks good." Chances are, he realized this only when it was forced on him.

Many first-class choreographers—indeed, in this country, most first-class modern dance choreographers: Martha Graham, Merce Cunningham, Paul Taylor, Twyla Tharp—begin as superb dancers and draw their choreographic style out of their own bodies. But in certain respects this is an unlucky combination. Dancing is a full-time job, as is choreography. It is hard to do both. And with the company standing there waiting to be told what to do and the next season booked and the clock ticking, the dancer-choreographer is likely to choose choreography over his or her own dancing, and then to resent the company as a result. Furthermore, when the dancing career ends, which it does between forty and fifty, this can precipitate a terrible crisis in the choreographic career (to say nothing of the life). Alternatively, the choreographer may simply refuse to give up dancing, and instead begin creating dances around his or her own diminished capacities, as Graham did, or about them, as Cunningham has done. This will probably not happen with Morris. He has already pulled himself out of a number of important roles. (He tends to put Keith Sabado in his place.) And though he still makes pieces for himself and dances superbly, he now uses himself judiciously, for very special things, such as Dido and the Erlking. Earlier and more deliberately than others, he has put choreography before dancing.

If his style changed in consequence of the events of 1985–86, it changed further, in the same direction, when he went to Belgium. With a studio at his disposal and with a group of new dancers who needed to learn his style, he began teaching company class, a ballet class, every morning. He had also begun making classical ballets; he staged three of them in the three years before he went to Brussels. As a result, more ballet steps began to creep into his modern-dance choreography—*A Lake* is full of them—and eventually he created two ballets, *The Hard Nut* and *Excursion to Grenada*, for his own company. But the real effect of ballet was on the spirit, not the letter. Ballet is the most precise and articulate of Western dance forms, and the whole trend of Morris's modern dance choreography in recent years has been toward greater precision. As he said to an interviewer while he was in Belgium, "We use ballet as a sort of Latin"—in other words, not as a spoken language but as a substructure. He probably would not have made that remark even three years earlier.

In Belgium he was also forced to live inside his work more than ever before and, more than before, to master sorrow artistically. If, in his more recent choreography, energy seems to resist its more obvious outlets and instead to collect inside the body's walls, molding it into severer shapes, the troupe's isolation in Brussels surely played some part in this, as did his own increasing isolation within the troupe. Again, the enlargement of the company was critical. The new dancers were younger, greener. With them, he *could* change his style, as he couldn't, beyond a certain point, with the older dancers. More important, the hiring of the new dancers and the departure of so many of the older dancers taught him that he was something other than his dancers. They could go; he would stay, and make new work on whoever was there. If, today, he tends to choreograph on the company rather than on himself, that is partly because he no longer sees the company as an extension of himself. This was the final act of separation-and-relation, and probably the hardest one.

As the work has become more exacting and more exact, it has deepened. It now depends less on shock value. This is not to say that it doesn't still contain shocks, but they are woven into a tighter web of meaning. When, in *Dido*, the Sorceress masturbates on the floor, this is not there to tell us what young people are up to these days—which, at least in part, is the meaning of the partner-swapping scene in *New Love Song Waltzes*—but to deepen our understanding of Dido's plight. In general, there appears to be less of a division in Morris's mind between himself and the public, less of an idea that he is showing us things about life that we refuse to see. He seems now to feel that we see them too. Accordingly, the meaning of the ensemble has changed. The "us" that we see in *Gloria* still has a hint of us-against-them; the "us" of *L'Allegro* is simply us. The relaxation of his gender politics is another part of this trend. He is still making unisex dances. Nothing he ever did before in that department is more extreme than *The Hard Nut*'s Waltz of the Snowflakes, with both men and women in tutus and on point. But the tone is different. As he said of the snowflakes in an interview with *The New York Times*, "This is not political. It's natural." Of course it's political too, but his politics now seem natural to him.

Morris did start out as an angry young man, and it is a fact worth remembering, for soon we will no longer see it onstage. (He is not sentimental about his early works. The only pre-1985 pieces that the company still dances with any frequency are *Gloria*, *New Love Song Waltzes*, and *Ten Suggestions*.) But as he grew older, that anger and its corollaries—his idealism, his powerful sense of irony, his vision of blackness—became yoked to other forces. We can see it happen. In 1984, in *O Rangasayee*, we watch a dark and private emotion being fed into what is now a fully developed drive for amalgamation, for the joining of opposites, the finding of relations. In that dance, male is joined to female, Eastern dance to Western, tradition to innovation, and in the process the grotesque is wedded to the sublime. Two years later, in *Stabat Mater*, we see a painful emotion being fed into what is now, in the midst of Morris's tutelage to Baroque music, a drive for structural clarity. His whole struggle in these years, the mid-eighties, is toward synthesis: bringing things together, making them make sense together.

Suddenly, in 1988, with *L'Allegro*, the struggles seem to end. *L'Allegro* is a burst of joy, a huge enlargement of vision. The piece is full of sight imagery: lights going on and off, scrims obscuring and revealing things, people covering and uncovering their eyes. If the meaning of that dance could be summed up in one sentence, it would be "I see." He sees everything in the world, and it all fits. Then, soon after, in *Behemoth*, we see what else he sees—pure, cold terror, the old blackness, coming now not with the old cackle and the snaking locks but neat and clean, like a blade. Clarity is not necessarily amelioration.

Since returning from Belgium, he has shown us other shades of dark and light: *Beautiful Day, Bedtime, Three Preludes*. In 1993 he premiered a thundering but severe primitivist work, *Grand Duo*, to Lou Harrison, that seemed a culmination of earlier trends in his choreography—"*Behemoth* goes to Macedonia," Barry Alterman called it—and another piece,

Megan Williams in
Mosaic and United
(Tom Brazil)

Mosaic and United, to Henry Cowell, that had an atmosphere wholly new to his work: eerie and deluxe, like a spider's web strung across a void. He has also made less successful pieces: the 1992 *Excursion to Grenada*, the 1993 *Jesu, Meine Freude*. Both were adventuresome ideas, though: a classical ballet to old calypso records (*Excursion to Grenada*), a dance of pure faith, faith beyond struggle, to Bach's purest, strictest motet (*Jesu, Meine Freude*). Even when he fails, it's interesting to watch.

The company is based in New York now. They operate out of a three-room office in SoHo, with desks wedged in among cartons full of costumes and old programs. This is a comedown from their lordly Belgian head-quarters but still a come-up from their pre-Belgian existence. From before-Brussels to after-Brussels, their budget went from $600,000 to $2 million; the administrative staff, from two to five; the number of dancers, from eleven to sixteen, excluding Morris. They are the fourth-largest modern dance troupe in the United States and, as *The Philadelphia Inquirer* recently put it, "the most talked-about company in the business."

At the same time, like almost every other American dance troupe, they are operating on the edge. The minute they knew they would be leaving Belgium—that is, in mid-1989, after *Mythologies* and the contract-signing crisis—they began looking for a development director, someone to stay in New York and raise money in anticipation of their return. That development director, Karen Hershey, was hired in early 1990, and by the time the company came home the following year, she had $2 million in the bank, most of it from corporations and foundations. The company now has three-year grants from the Lila Wallace–Reader's Digest Fund and the Andrew W. Mellon Foundation. With sixteen dancers, however, and with Morris's insistence on live music—but above all, with the sheer volume of new work that he produces, and the attendant rehearsal time —the money is quickly spent, and the scramble for grants is continuous. The company is once again working in rented studios.

Morris is not a poor artist anymore, and not a rich one. He lives off his MacArthur fellowship—about $45,000 a year before taxes. (He receives no salary from the company, and all his fees and royalties from outside projects go into the troupe's bank account.) After camping out for a year and a half in Baryshnikov's downtown loft, he finally found an apartment of his own, in a nondescript midtown neighborhood. The place is a sublet, though, and still has almost no furniture. The primary sign of occupation is a wall of shelves filled with little knickknacks—toy cars, figurines, a bust of Bach. There are also cabinets of records, shelves of CDs, drawers full of tapes.

With or without the company, Morris is on the road about half the year. At least once a year, he goes home to Seattle. At other times he brings Seattle to him. He flies Maxine and Maureen east to see his concerts. They also went four times to Brussels. (He had Verla Flowers come to Brussels too, for the opening of *L'Allegro*.) Most of his days are spent in the studio. At night, when the company is not performing, he has a few beers, eats dinner in a restaurant, and goes home and listens to music. Sometimes he rents a movie. More than ever, his life is his work.

That work may continue for a long time. Morris is only thirty-seven. He could go on making dances for another forty or fifty years, longer than he has now lived. If so, the smooth arc I have described here—angry young man to mature artist—will be only the first stage of a far more complicated itinerary and hence, perhaps, no longer an arc but a loop, a dip, a trajectory into some wholly new territory. This has been the portrait of a *young* artist. Later, other assessments will be needed. In any case, it is wonderful to think what he may do.

CHRONOLOGY OF WORKS
BY MARK MORRIS

————

SOURCE NOTES

————

INDEX

Morris and Teri Weksler in rehearsal, 1985 *(Beatriz Schiller)*

Chronology of Works

by Mark Morris

ABBREVIATIONS

M	Music by
DIR	Directed by
CH	Choreographed by
C	Costumes by
S	Sets by
L	Lighting by
PR	Premiere
D	Dancers
RV	Revisions
ST	Stagings on other companies
TV	Televised
N	Note
MMDG	Mark Morris Dance Group
MDG/MM	Monnaie Dance Group/Mark Morris

When the note specifies that the music was recorded ("rec."), this refers only to the first performance of the dance. Many works originally performed to recordings were later danced to live music.

Under new stagings: When a city is indicated after a company's name, this is where the company is based, not necessarily where the staging was premiered.

1971

BOXCAR BOOGIE (PIECE BY PIECE)
M Excerpts from Jacques Lasry (*Structures sonores*, c. 1964, for instruments by Bernard and François Baschet), Conlon Nancarrow, Harry Partch (*Castor and Pollux*, from *Plectra and Percussion Dances*, 1952), Steve Reich (*Violin Phase*, 1967), rec. **PR** 6/18/71, Verla Flowers Dance Arts, Seattle Center Playhouse. **D** 12 girls, 2 boys. **N** See *Castor and Pollux*, 1980.

CAPE DANCE
M Traditional Spanish, rec. **PR** 6/18/71, Verla Flowers Dance Arts, Seattle Center Playhouse. **D** 6 girls, 2 boys. **N** Probably a paso doble.

THE WIZARD'S GIFT
A Christmas Musical

M Jonathon Field, David Kiesel, Gary Lanz. Book and lyrics: R. Allen Paris. **DIR** Joan Galstaun. **CH** Mary Hoagland and Mark Morris. **PR** 12/71, Seattle Youth Theatre, Poncho Theatre, Seattle. **N** In addition to making dances, Morris played Top Elf. Penny Hutchinson was another elf, and this was how they met.

1972

RENAISSANCE

M Sixteenth-century French traditional music, rec. **PR** 4/29/72, Northwest Ballet Ensemble (Dance Theatre Seattle), Poncho Theatre, Seattle. **D** 3 women, 3 men.

MOURNING WITHOUT CLOUDS

M Mark Morris. **PR** 6/15/72, Verla Flowers Dance Arts, Seattle Center Playhouse. **D** 12 girls, 2 boys. **N** Morris's score was for 7-piece chamber orchestra (2 flutes, 2 clarinets, violin, viola, cello), plus 6-person chorus. Maureen Morris was one of the singers.

U.S.A.
TANGO, CHARLESTON

M Popular songs of 1900–29, rec. **DIR** Paul Nicholas. **PR** 11–12/72, Franklin High School, Seattle. **N** The show was based on John Dos Passos's *U.S.A.*

1973

IT'S ALMOST LIKE BEING ALIVE

M Phil Shallat, plus adaptations of popular songs. Book and lyrics: Shallat. **PR** 4/73 (?), One-Reel Vaudeville Show, Moore Theatre, Seattle. **N** For this musical comedy, Morris choreographed a dance and several brief entries for a trio of Non-Nutritive Foods: a hamburger, an order of french fries, and a Coke. He played the Coke.

CELEBRATION
DANCES

M Harvey Schmidt. Lyrics: Tom Jones. **DIR** Paul Nicholas. **PR** Spring, 1973, Franklin High School, Seattle.

[SPANISH DANCES]

For the Verla Flowers Dance Arts recital of 7/19/73 (Seattle Center Playhouse), Morris staged three Spanish dances: *Rain in Spain* (a sevillana for himself and another student), *Jota* (1 girl and 1 boy), and *Spain* (a solo for himself). All were adaptations of traditional dances, performed to recordings of traditional Spanish music.

THREE BY THREE

M Louis Moreau Gottschalk (*Grande Tarantelle*, 1868), rec. **CH** Gerald Teijelo, staged by Morris. **PR** 6/19/73, Verla Flowers Dance Arts, Seattle Center Playhouse. **D** 9 girls. **N** In 1972 Verla Flowers sent Morris, then fifteen, in her place to the annual Lucille Stoddart Dance Congress in New York so that he could learn how to stage a dance from notation. This ballet was one of the pieces he learned there.

BARSTOW
M Harry Partch (1941, rev. 1954), rec. **PR** 8/73, Summer Dance Laboratory, Fort Worden State Park, Port Townsend, Washington. **D** 6 students. **ST** 1974, First Chamber Junior Company, Seattle; 1980, MMDG. **N** Choreographed by Morris at his dance camp at age sixteen, *Barstow* was included without revision in the MMDG's debut concert seven years later.

1974

IN PRUNING MY ROSES
M Mark Morris (composition for cello and piano) and Dmitri Shostakovich (Sonata in D, op. 40, 1934, 2nd movement). **PR** 6/20/74, Verla Flowers Dance Arts, Seattle Center Playhouse. Cello: Page Smith. Piano: Kathryn Davis. **D** 4 girls, 1 boy. **N** See *Vestige*, 1984.

JOTA DE ALCAÑIZ
M Traditional Spanish, rec. **CH** Linda Mietzner and Mark Morris, after a traditional jota. **PR** 6/20/74, Verla Flowers Dance Arts, Seattle Center Playhouse. **D** Mietzner, Morris.

ŽENSKA
M Béla Bartók (String Quartet no. 4, 1928, 4th movement), rec. **PR** 1974 or 1975, First Chamber Junior Company, probably Seattle. **D** Penny Hutchinson. **ST** 1980, MMDG. **RV** In 1980, Morris added a second dancer (Hannah Kahn), attached a passage of traditional Bulgarian music, with new choreography, to the opening, and revised some of the remaining choreography. **N** "Ženska" is a Slavic word meaning "womanly."

1975

FARRUCA JEREZANA
M Traditional Spanish, rec. **PR** 6/19/75, Verla Flowers Dance Arts, Seattle Center Playhouse. **D** Kelsey Kara Ketterer. **N** Ketterer was one of Morris's advanced Spanish-dance students.

SPANISH
M Traditional Spanish, rec. **PR** 6/19/75, Verla Flowers Dance Arts, Seattle Center Playhouse. **D** 7 girls, 2 boys. **N** A medley of Spanish dances created by Morris for his Spanish-dance students.

SAINT GEORGE AND THE DRAGON
A Merry Christmas Entertainment
DRAGON'S SOLO
M John David Lamb. **DIR** Carole McCarthy. **PR** 12/20/75, Northwest Chamber Orchestra Young People's Concerts, Poncho Theatre, Seattle. **D** Penny Hutchinson.

1978

BRUMMAGEM
M Ludwig van Beethoven (Trio in B-flat major, op. 11, 1797, 2nd and 3rd movements), rec. **C** Alan Madsen. **L** Richard Moore. **PR** 7/22/78, Pacific Northwest Ballet, Meany Hall, University of Washington, Seattle. **D** Laura Bail, Cheryl Bruce, John Brudowsky, Jory Hancock, Melissa Lowe, Daniel Schwarz, Jerry Schwender, Leslie Vise. **ST** 1980, MMDG; 1981, Spo-

kane Ballet. **RV** 1980, MMDG: Reduced cast to 7. 1981, Spokane: Restored score's first movement and created choreography for it.

1980

RATTLESNAKE SONG
M "Old Joe Clark," "Shanty in the Hollow," "Unfortunate Man," "Rattlesnake Song," performed by Jimmy Driftwood, rec. **C** Robert Brand. **L** James McHugh. **PR** 4/19/80, Steffi Nossen Dance Company, Scarsdale Junior High School, Scarsdale, NY. **D** Lynne Cohen, Maria Erbacher, Elizabeth Gottlieb, Tara Keith, Donna Levine, Heather Manspeizer, Martha Perkins, Elizabeth Ross, Leslie Rossheim, Sharon Sahn, Christa Santangelo, Nancy Sutton, Jean Tostanoski, Margot Tohn, Charlotte Tsuyuki, Laura Weinstein.

CASTOR AND POLLUX
M Harry Partch (*Castor and Pollux*, from *Plectra and Percussion Dances*, 1952), rec. **L** William C. Yehle. **PR** 11/28/80, MMDG, Cunningham Studio, New York. **D** Ruth Davidson, Tina Fehlandt, Penny Hutchinson, Harry Laird, Donald Mouton, Elvira Psinas, Nora Reynolds, Jennifer Thienes. **N** Morris had previously used this music in *Boxcar Boogie*, 1971.

DAD'S CHARTS
M "Robbins Nest" (Charles Thompson and Illinois Jacquet, 1947), performed by Milt Buckner, rec. **L** William C. Yehle. **PR** 11/28/80, MMDG, Cunningham Studio, NY. **D** Mark Morris. **N** This solo began as a structured improvisation; over time, it became less improvised, more set.

1981

ÉTUDES MODERNES
PRELUDE, PATHÉTIQUE, ESPAGNOLE, HYSTÉRIQUE, PLASTIQUE
M Conlon Nancarrow (from Studies for Player Piano, 1950–68), rec. **PR** 2/13/81, MMDG, Jersey City Museum, Jersey City, NJ. **D** Tina Fehlandt, Peter Healey, Mark Morris, Donald Mouton. **RV** In 1982, Morris recast this work with all women, deleted its musical introduction ("Prelude"), and meshed its remaining four parts with the three parts of the 1982 *jr high*, an all-male dance also set to Nancarrow's player-piano studies. The cast of the final section, "Plastique," was expanded from 4 to 13.

TEN SUGGESTIONS
M Alexander Tcherepnin (Bagatelles, op. 5, 1913–18), rec. **PR** 2/13/81, MMDG, Jersey City Museum, Jersey City, NJ. **D** Mark Morris. **ST** 1990, White Oak Dance Project (NY); 1991, Peggy Baker/Solo Dance (Toronto). **N** This solo, like others that Morris has made for himself, contained substantial improvisation when it was first performed, and then gelled over the years. When Mikhail Baryshnikov danced it with the White Oak Dance Project, the shape of the steps was far more balletic than when Morris danced it.

SCHÖN ROSMARIN
M Fritz Kreisler (from *Alt Wiener Tanzweisen*, 1911), rec. **PR** 8/21/81, "Choreography by Mark Morris and Penny Hutchinson," Soundworks Hall, Seattle. **D** Tina Fehlandt. **N** Morris remembers this solo as either a study for or a derivative of *Brummagem*, 1978. He himself may have performed it prior to 1981.

I LOVE YOU DEARLY

M Three traditional Romanian songs, rec. **PR** 11/20/81, Kinetics Company, On the Boards, Washington Hall Performance Gallery, Seattle. **D** Michael Clawson. **ST** 1981, MMDG; 1982, Gregg Lizenbery.

GLORIA

M Antonio Vivaldi (Gloria in D, RV589), rec. **L** Donald Firestone. **PR** 12/12/81, MMDG, Bessie Schönberg Theater, Dance Theater Workshop, NY. **D** Ruth Davidson, Tina Fehlandt, Penny Hutchinson, Harry Laird, Elvira Psinas, Nora Reynolds, Jennifer Thienes, Douglas Varone, Teri Weksler, Holly Williams. **RV** In 1984, Morris created the walk-and-crawl duet to the first movement ("Gloria in excelsis"), which was unchoreographed in the 1981 version. He also changed the ending. In 1981 the dancers simply backed to the sides of the stage on the final "Amen." In 1984 they formed an X pattern, twirled, and fell. Elsewhere, he simplified the choreography. **TV** Abbrev. version, *Mark Morris*, Dance in America, PBS, 1986.

1982

CANONIC 3/4 STUDIES

M Carl Czerny and others, short piano pieces in 3/4 time, arr. Harriet Cavalli. **L** Terry Simpson. **PR** 7/29/82, "Jr High and Other Dances" (concert of works by Morris and Penny Hutchinson), On the Boards, Washington Hall Performance Gallery, Seattle. Piano: Harriet Cavalli. **D** Janice Bourdage, Rachel Brumer, Moya Devine, Janie Hostetter, Penny Hutchinson, Erin Matthiessen, Caroline Mayfield-Buchanan, Mark Morris, Kirsten Peterson, Liz Valauri. **ST** 1982, Five College Dance Department (Amherst, MA); 1983, University Dancers, University of Massachusetts (Amherst); 1983, MMDG; 1985, Batsheva Dance Company (Tel Aviv); 1985, Repertory Dance Company of Canada (Vancouver); 1986, Concert Dance Company of Boston; 1991, White Oak Dance Project (NY). **N** Originally *Canonic Waltz Studies*, the title was changed when Morris discovered that not all the musical selections were waltzes. He created it on the students of his summer workshop at On the Boards in Seattle. The piece was a workshop for him too; he was about to make *New Love Song Waltzes*, and he was practicing working with 3/4 time.

JR HIGH

A. MORNING, B. TEST, C. GYM

M Conlon Nancarrow (from Studies for Player Piano, 1950–68, nos. 10 and 7), rec. **L** Terry Simpson. **PR** 7/29/82, "Jr High and Other Dances" (concert of works by Morris and Penny Hutchinson), On the Boards, Washington Hall Performance Gallery, Seattle. **D** Mark Morris; Chris Davis, Chad Henry, Erin Matthiessen. **ST** 1982, MMDG. **RV** For the MMDG staging (11/82), Morris meshed this dance with the 1981 *Etudes Modernes*. With the women of *Etudes Modernes* in knee socks and pleated skirts, and the men of *jr high* in chinos and sneakers, the result looked something like a junior-high student body. **N** The second section, "test," is performed in silence. In the third section, "gym," three young men do athletic exercises while a fourth (Morris) tries to do the same, gets things wrong, and finally ends up dancing instead. Morris hated gym when he was in school.

SONGS THAT TELL A STORY

M "Insured beyond the Grave" (I. and C. Louvin, 1956), "I'll Live with God (To Die No More)" (I. and C. Louvin/Hill, 1956), "Robe of White" (I. and C. Louvin/Hill, 1956), "The

Great Atomic Power" (I and C. Louvin/Bain, 1956), performed by the Louvin Brothers, rec. **PR** 9/4(?)/82, Kinetics Company, Seattle Center Playhouse, Bumbershoot Festival, Seattle. **D** Peggy Hackney, Eric Johnson, Janice Meaden Reel. **ST** 1982, MMDG; 1986, CoDanceCo (NY). **TV** "Robe of White" on *Mark Morris*, Dance in America, PBS, 1986.

NEW LOVE SONG WALTZES

M Johannes Brahms (*Neue Liebeslieder*, op. 65, 1874), rec. **L** Phil Sandström. **PR** 11/4/82, MMDG, Bessie Schönberg Theater, Dance Theater Workshop, NY. **D** Rachel Brumer, Ruth Davidson, Tina Fehlandt, Penny Hutchinson, Harry Laird, Erin Matthiessen, Jon Mensinger, Jennifer Thienes, Teri Weksler, Holly Williams.

NOT GOODBYE

M Three traditional Tahitian songs, rec. **L** Phil Sandström. **PR** 11/4/82, MMDG, Bessie Schönberg Theater, Dance Theater Workshop, NY. **D** Rachel Brumer, Mark Morris, Teri Weksler. **N** All three performers danced bare-chested, in sarongs.

1983

PONCHIELLIANA

M Amilcare Ponchielli (Quartet in B), rec. **C** Charles Schoonmaker. **L** William C. Yehle. **PR** 7/19/83, Pillow Parade, Ted Shawn Theatre, Jacob's Pillow, Becket, MA. **D** Beth Freedman, Susan Gresko, Tracy Hahn, Bruce R. Harris, Daedra Nicola Kaehler, Cynthia Kommers, Laura Kray, Elizabeth Monaco, Orlando Pagan, Jennifer Perrone, Suzanne Polastri, Liz Young.

CARYATIDS

M Harold Budd (*Madrigals of the Rose Angel*, 1972), rec. **L** Pjay Guttierez. **PR** 9/29/83, "*Dogtown* and Other Dances: Choreography by Mark Morris," On the Boards, Washington Hall Performance Gallery, Seattle. **D** Tina Fehlandt; Joannie Anderson, Christy Dorman, Karen Gee, Gina Gibney, Lee Anne Hartley, Penny Hutchinson, Lodi McClellan, Katherine Mezur, Long Nguyen, Tim Tucker, Liz Valauri, Jennifer Walker. **ST** 1984, Jacob's Pillow Jazz Workshop (Becket, MA). **N** A study for what was to be *The Death of Socrates*, 1983.

CELESTIAL GREETINGS

M Thai popular music, rec. **L** Pjay Guttierez. **PR** 9/29/83, "*Dogtown* and Other Dances: Choreography by Mark Morris," On the Boards, Washington Hall Performance Gallery, Seattle. **D** Christy Dorman, Penny Hutchinson, Shannon Loch, Long Nguyen, Lory Wilson, Rachel Van Dessel. **ST** 1983, MMDG.

DECK OF CARDS

M "Gear Jammer" (J. Logsdon—S. Campbell, 1963), performed by Jimmy Logsdon; "Say It's Not You" (D. Frazier, 1967), performed by George Jones; "Deck of Cards" (1948), written and performed by T. Texas Tyler, all rec. **L** Pjay Guttierez. Truck designed by Glenn Horton. **PR** 9/29/83, "*Dogtown* and Other Dances: Choreography by Mark Morris," On the Boards, Washington Hall Performance Gallery, Seattle. **D** Pat Graney, Mark Morris. **ST** 1983, MMDG; 1991, White Oak Dance Project (NY). **N** The first dance, to Logsdon, was a solo for a computer-controlled toy truck. The second, to Jones, was a solo for Morris, in a dress. The third, to Tyler, was a solo for Graney in an army uniform minus trousers. The same basic gestures appeared in Morris's and Graney's solos, but Morris performed them legato whereas Graney performed them staccato, and in the form of an accumulation dance, as she mimed the story told by the song: how a soldier, brought before a military tribunal for playing cards in church, demonstrated that all the truths in the Bible were contained in a deck of cards. Graney's role has since been taken by men.

DOGTOWN

M Yoko Ono ("Toyboat," 1981; "Extension 33," 1981; "Dogtown," 1981; "Give Me Something," 1980), performed by Yoko Ono, rec. **L** Pjay Guttierez. **PR** 9/29/83, "*Dogtown* and Other Dances: Choreography by Mark Morris," On the Boards, Washington Hall Performance Gallery, Seattle. **D** Tina Fehlandt, Gina Gibney, Penny Hutchinson, Shannon Loch, Mark Morris, Lory Wilson, Rachel Van Dessel. **ST** 1983, MMDG. **RV** In late 1983, for the MMDG staging, Morris added an additional Yoko Ono song, "No, No, No" (1981), to the opening and choreographed a dance to it. **TV** "No, No, No," "Dogtown," and "Give Me Something" on *Mark Morris*, Dance in America, PBS, 1986.

BIJOUX

M Erik Satie (*Quatre petites mélodies*, 1920; *Ludions*, 1923), rec. **L** Phil Sandström. **PR** 12/8/83, MMDG, Bessie Schönberg Theater, Dance Theater Workshop, NY. **D** Teri Weksler. **ST** 1984, Rhonda Martin (NY). **N** This solo has also been performed by Morris, in a skirt and blouse.

THE DEATH OF SOCRATES

M Erik Satie (*Socrate*, 1918), rec. **S** Robert Bordo. **C** Karen Strand. **L** Phil Sandström. **PR** 12/15/83, MMDG, Bessie Schönberg Theater, NY. **D** Rob Besserer, David Landis, Erin Matthiessen, Jon Mensinger, Donald Mouton, Guillermo Resto. **N** See *Caryatids*, 1983.

MINUET AND ALLEGRO IN G

M Ludwig van Beethoven (Allegro and Minuet in G, WoO 26, 1792, order of two movements reversed), rec. **L** Phil Sandström. **PR** 12/15/83, MMDG, Bessie Schönberg Theater, Dance Theater Workshop, NY. **D** Tina Fehlandt, Jennifer Thienes.

THE "TAMIL FILM SONGS IN STEREO" PAS DE DEUX

M Contemporary Indian, rec. **L** Phil Sandström. **PR** 12/15/83, MMDG, Bessie Schönberg Theater, Dance Theater Workshop, NY. **D** Mark Morris, Nora Reynolds. **TV** *Mark Morris*, Dance in America, PBS, 1986. **N** In 1983, in Singapore, Morris bought a tape labeled only "Tamil Film Songs in Stereo" from a street vendor. To three excerpts from that tape he created this little comic drama of a tyrannical dance teacher and his beleaguered student.

1984

VESTIGE

M Dmitri Shostakovich (Sonata in D, op. 40, 1934, 1st movement omitted). **C** Mark Morris. **PR** 2/4/84, Spokane Ballet, Whitworth College Auditorium, Spokane. Cello: Helen Fitch. Piano: Linda Siverts. **D** Alfonso Adame Acosta, Melissa Earl, Margaret Goodner, Mary Frances Johnson, Pamela Kawai, Gene M. Kendrick, Wendy Long, Julie E. Stocker, Linnea B. Zwiesler. **ST** 1985, MMDG. **N** A modern dance piece, performed barefoot. Morris had already used this music for *in pruning my roses*, 1974.

O RANGASAYEE

M Sri Tyagaraja ("O Rangasayee"), performed by Smt. M. S. Subbulakshmi, rec. **PR** 3/15/84, Danséchange Montréal–New York, Tangente Danse-Actuelle, Montreal. **D** Mark Morris. **ST** 1984, MMDG. **N** Previewed 2/26/84, Washington Performance Hall, Seattle. Morris danced bare-chested, with the soles of his feet and the palms of his hands stained red, in the Indian manner. In Seattle and Montreal, he wore white shorts; in New York, in 11/84, he wore an Indian *dhoti*, or loincloth.

LOVE, YOU HAVE WON

M Antonio Vivaldi (Solo cantata "Amor hai vinto," RV651). **L** Jeff Bickford. **PR** 6/7/84, MMDG, On the Boards, Washington Hall Performance Gallery, Seattle. Harpsichord: Randall J. McCarty. Cello: Page Smith-Weaver. Soprano: Nancy Zylstra. **D** Mark Morris, Guillermo Resto. **TV** *Mark Morris*, Dance in America, PBS, 1986.

MY PARTY

M Jean Françaix (Trio in C, 1933). **L** Jeff Bickford. **PR** 6/7/84, MMDG, On the Boards, Washington Hall Performance Gallery, Seattle. Violin: Stacy Phelps. Viola: Ron Strauss. Cello: Page Smith-Weaver. **D** Tina Fehlandt, Penny Hutchinson, David Landis, Shannon Loch, Erin Matthiessen, Lodi McClellan, Long Nguyen, Guillermo Resto. **ST** 1988, Second Avenue Dance Company, New York University.

PRELUDE AND PRELUDE

M Henry Cowell (*Set of Two*, 1955, 1st movement). **L** Jeff Bickford. **PR** 6/7/84, MMDG, On the Boards, Washington Hall Performance Gallery, Seattle. Violin: Stacy Phelps. Harpsichord: Randall J. McCarty. **D** Tina Fehlandt, Penny Hutchinson, Shannon Loch, Erin Matthiessen, Lodi McClellan, Long Nguyen. **RV** 1985, cast increased to 9. **N** The music is played twice. The first time, one dancer (always chosen by Morris just as the dance is about to go on) performs a traveling solo while the others remain in a line, doing a stationary dance in canon. When the music is repeated, the assignments are reversed: the soloist does the stationary dance while the others do the traveling dance, in canon. Morris asked the dancers to wear as little as possible in this piece. At various performances, some of the women danced bare-breasted, and some of the men wore only dance belts. **TV** First half of dance (retitled *Prelude*), *Mark Morris*, Dance in America, PBS, 1986.

SHE CAME FROM THERE

M Ernst von Dohnányi (Serenade in C, op. 10, 1902). **L** Jeff Bickford. **PR** 6/7/84, MMDG, On the Boards, Washington Hall Performance Gallery, Seattle. Violin: Stacy Phelps. Viola: Ron Strauss. Cello: Page Smith-Weaver. **D** Tina Fehlandt, Penny Hutchinson, David Landis, Shannon Loch, Long Nguyen, Guillermo Resto.

FORTY ARMS, TWENTY NECKS, ONE WREATHING
I. CHACONY, II. RETURN, III. ECHO SONG, IV. DANCE

M Herschel Garfein (*One Wreathing*, 1984). **L** Mark Litvin. **PR** 7/10/84, American Dance Festival, Young Choreographers and Composers in Residence Program, Reynolds Theatre, Duke University, Durham, NC. Flute: Ann Randolf. Clarinet: Brett Wery. Cello: Virginia Hudson. Horn: Barbara Hadfield. Percussion: Eric Lecain. Piano: Mary Fleming. **D** Penny Hutchinson, Erin Matthiessen, Mark Morris, Guillermo Resto, Betsy Babcock, David Beadle, Monica D'Agostino, Emily Fraenkel, Orna Frankl, Sarah Johnson, Lara Kohn, Jennifer Kinnier, Kaela Lee, Gabriel Masson, Amy McCall, Mark Nimkoff, Fairfax O'Riley, Marsha Pabalis, Vanessa Player, Debbie Warner. **ST** 1986, MMDG.

COME ON HOME

M "Come on Home" (H. Silver), "The New ABC" (D. Lambert), "Bijou" (J. Hendricks—R. Burns), "Summertime" (G. Gershwin—D. Heyward), "Cloudburst" (L. Kirkland—J. Harris), "With Malice Toward None" (J. Hendricks—F. McIntosh), performed by Dave Lambert, Jon Hendricks, and Annie Ross, with Ike Isaacs Trio, rec. **C** Charles Schoonmaker. **L** William C. Yehle. **PR** 8/21/84, Pillow Jazz Parade, Ted Shawn Theatre, Jacob's Pillow, Becket, MA. **D** Scott Cunningham, Nobuko Horibe, Dan Joyce, Nikki McGlynn, Hunter Mills, Rachel Murray, Iku Nishida, Noni Petersen, Sue Ellen Peterson, Amelia Rudolph, Gretchen Sherman.

SLUGFEST

PR 10/3/84, MMDG, Dance Umbrella, The Place, London. **D** Penny Hutchinson, Guillermo Resto. **N** Performed in silence, with the dancers "socking it to each other according to certain abstruse rules" (Clement Crisp, *The Financial Times*, 10/5/84), this piece was a study for *Championship Wrestling after Roland Barthes*, 1984.

THE VACANT CHAIR

M "The Vacant Chair" (G. F. Root/H. S. Washburn, 1861), "Trees" (O. Rasbach/J. Kilmer, 1922), "A Perfect Day" (C. Jacobs-Bond, 1910), rec. **PR** 10/3/84, MMDG, Dance Umbrella, The Place, London. **D** Mark Morris.

CHAMPIONSHIP WRESTLING AFTER ROLAND BARTHES

M Herschel Garfein, rec. **L** Phil Sandström. **PR** 11/28/84, MMDG, Lepercq Space, Brooklyn Academy of Music, NY. **D** Rob Besserer, Scott Cunningham, Ruth Davidson, Tina Fehlandt, Penny Hutchinson, David Landis, Donald Mouton, Guillermo Resto, Jennifer Thienes, Teri Weksler. **N** Based on Roland Barthes's essay "The World of Wrestling." The score combines computer-synthesized music with sounds taped at live wrestling matches and from television wrestling. In 1986, when the dance became part of *Mythologies* (q.v.), its title was shortened to *Championship Wrestling*. See also *Slugfest*, 1984.

[CAPRI SUN TELEVISION COMMERCIAL]

In 1984 Morris choreographed a television commercial for a fruit drink called Capri Sun. In it, a dull day in the school cafeteria is redeemed when a group of cooler students arrives, drinking Capri Sun. "They slid down the counters, they knocked over fruit baskets," says Morris. "It was a revolution scene—*La Muette de Portici* in a school lunchroom."

1985

MARBLE HALLS

M Johann Sebastian Bach (Concerto in C minor, BWV1060), rec. **C** Oded Gera. **L** Kevin McAlister. **PR** 3/14/85, Batsheva Dance Company, Jerusalem Theater, Jerusalem. **D** Shula Botney, Ofra Doudai-Mizrahi, David Dvir, Natan Gardah, Graciela Kozak, Erez Levy, Bruno de Saint Chauffray, Daniela Slavik, Liat Steiner, Nira Triffon. **ST** 1985, MMDG; 1991, Second Avenue Dance Company, New York University; 1991, University Dance Company, Ohio State University (Columbus); 1992, URepCo, University of Minnesota–Twin Cities (Minneapolis).

LOVEY

M Gordon Gano ("I Hear the Rain," 1984; "Blister in the Sun," 1983; "Country Death Song," 1984; "Kiss Off," 1983; "I Know It's True, But I'm Sorry to Say," 1984), performed by the Violent Femmes, rec. **L** Jeff Bickford. **PR** 5/9/85, MMDG, On the Boards, Washington Hall Performance Gallery, Seattle. **D** Tina Fehlandt (baby), Ruth Davidson (mother), Long Nguyen ("interlocutor"), Guillermo Resto (father); Lodi McClellan, Penny Hutchinson, Keith Sabado, Erin Matthiessen. **N** A core group of 4 performs "Blister in the Sun," "Country Death Song," and "I Know It's True." Normally, they are joined by 4 others, as their doubles, for the two remaining songs. But the doubles may be omitted (hence total cast of 4) or increased to triples (hence total cast of 12). There is some improvisation in "Kiss Off" and "I Know It's True."

JEALOUSY

M George Frideric Handel (*Hercules*, 1745, no. 36, chorus: "Jealousy"), rec. **L** Phil Sandström. **PR** 9/6/85, MMDG, Stephen Foster Theater, Pittsburgh. **D** Mark Morris. **N** Became part of *Handel Choruses* (q.v.), 1985, but was premiered earlier and was often performed by itself. **TV** *Mark Morris*, Dance in America, PBS, 1986.

SWEENEY TODD

The Demon Barber of Fleet Street

M and lyrics: Stephen Sondheim. Book: Hugh Wheeler. **DIR** Anne Denise Ford. Movement consultant: Mark Morris. **PR** 10/4/85, Civic Light Opera, Jane Addams Theatre, Seattle. **N** Morris simply coached the performers in how to move. He did not create actual dances.

RETREAT FROM MADRID

M Luigi Boccherini (Quintet no. 9, "La Ritirata di Madrid," 4th movement), rec. **PR** 10/9/85, MMDG, American Center, Paris. **D** Tina Fehlandt, Penny Hutchinson, Mark Morris, Donald Mouton.

HANDEL CHORUSES

M George Frideric Handel ("All we like sheep have gone astray," from *Messiah*, 1742; "Jealousy," from *Hercules*, 1745; "He sent thick darkness," from *Israel in Egypt*, 1739; "Crown with festal pomp the day," from *Hercules*), rec. **L** Phil Sandström. **PR** 12/6/85, MMDG, Bessie Schönberg Theater, Dance Theater Workshop, NY. **D** Keith Sabado ("All we like sheep"), Mark Morris ("Jealousy"), Penny Hutchinson ("He sent thick darkness"), Susan Hadley ("Crown with festal pomp"). **N** Both "Jealousy" and "He sent thick darkness" have been performed by both male and female dancers. See *Jealousy*, 1985. **TV** "Jealousy" on *Mark Morris*, Dance in America, PBS, 1986.

FRISSON

M Igor Stravinsky (*Symphonies of Wind Instruments*, 1920, rev. 1945–47), rec. **L** Phil Sandström. **PR** 12/7/85, MMDG, Bessie Schönberg Theater, Dance Theater Workshop, NY. **D** Tina Fehlandt, David Landis, Donald Mouton, Jennifer Thienes, Teri Weksler.

ONE CHARMING NIGHT

M Henry Purcell ("Be Welcome, Then, Great Sir," from "Fly, Bold Rebellion," 1683; "One Charming Night" and "Hark! The Ech'ing Air," from *The Fairy Queen*, 1692; "Lord, What Is Man?" 1693), rec. **L** Phil Sandström. **PR** 12/7/85, MMDG, Bessie Schönberg Theater, Dance Theater Workshop, NY. **D** Mark Morris, Teri Weksler.

1986

MORT SUBITE

M Francis Poulenc (Concerto in G minor, 1938). **C** Mark Morris. **L** Craig Miller. **PR** 2/5/86, Boston Ballet, Wang Center, Boston. Conductor: Myron Romanul. Organ: James David Christie. **D** Christopher Adams, Elaine Bauer, Devon Carney, Leslie Jonas, Victor Lacasse, Dierdre Myles, Marie-Christine Mouis, William Pizzuto, Denise Pons, Anamarie Sazarin, Kyra Strasberg, Alexander Van Alstyne, Andrew Ward, Susan Williams, Stewart Yaros, Christian Zimmerman.

MYTHOLOGIES

Dances Based on the Essays of Roland Barthes

M and text: Herschel Garfein (*Championship Wrestling after Roland Barthes*, 1984; *Soap-Powders and Detergents* and *Striptease*, 1986). **L** Phil Sandström. **PR** 2/27/86, MMDG, Dance Umbrella, Northeastern University Alumni Auditorium, Boston. Alea III. Conductor: Theodore Antoniou. Singers: Judith Kellock, Nan Hughes, Richard Kennedy, Michael O'Brian. **D** *Soap-Powders and Detergents*: Scott Cunningham, Tina Fehlandt, Susan Hadley, Penny Hutchinson, David Landis, Donald Mouton, Guillermo Resto, Keith Sabado, Jennifer Thienes, Teri Weksler. *Striptease*: Rob Besserer, Ruth Davidson, Tina Fehlandt, Susan Hadley, Mark Morris, Donald Mouton, Keith Sabado, Jennifer Thienes. *Championship Wrestling*: Rob Besserer, Scott Cunningham, Ruth Davidson, Tina Fehlandt, Penny Hutchinson, David Landis, Donald Mouton, Guillermo Resto, Jennifer Thienes, Teri Weksler. **N** See *Championship Wrestling*, 1984. *Soap-Powders and Detergents* and *Striptease* are based on essays of the same names in Roland Barthes's *Mythologies*, 1957. The score for *Soap-Powders* is a cantata (loosely based on Bach's Coffee Cantata) in praise of laundry detergents. The score for *Striptease* combines taped synthesizer music with strip club–type music for a small instrumental ensemble.

SALOME

SALOME'S DANCE

M Richard Strauss, 1905. Libretto after Oscar Wilde. **DIR** Sonja Frisell. **C** Sarah Nash Gates. **L** Joan Sullivan. **PR** 3/22/86, Seattle Opera, Seattle Opera House. Conductor: Stefan Minde. **D** Josephine Barstow. **N** The dance was performed by the soprano, Barstow, and she did remove seven veils.

BALLABILI

M Giuseppe Verdi (*Aida*, 1871, Act II, Scene 2, "Triumphal Scene," nos. 20–22). **L** Joan Sullivan. **PR** 6/10/86, MMDG, Seattle Opera, Seattle Opera House. Seattle Symphony Musicians. Conductor: Gerald Schwarz. **D** Tina Fehlandt, Penny Hutchinson, Erin Matthiessen, Mark Morris, Long Nguyen, Jennifer Thienes. **N** This faux-Egyptian number was first danced at a Seattle Opera benefit concert, where it appeared, untitled, as part of the Triumphal Scene from *Aida*. A month later, when it was first performed at a MMDG concert, it was given the title *Ballabili* ("dances").

THE SHEPHERD ON THE ROCK

M Franz Schubert (*Der Hirt auf dem Felsen*, D965, 1828), rec. **C** Sarah Nash Gates. **L** Phil Sandström. **PR** 7/11/86, MMDG, Bagley Wright Theater, Seattle. **D** Ruth Davidson, David Landis, Donald Mouton, Long Nguyen, Jennifer Thienes, Teri Weksler.

ESTEEMED GUESTS
M Carl Philipp Emanuel Bach (Concerto in A, W172, 1753?). **C** Santo Loquasto. **L** Phil Sandström. **PR** 9/24/86, Joffrey Ballet, Dorothy Chandler Pavilion, Los Angeles. Conductor: Allan Lewis. Cello: Stephen Erdody. **D** Julie Janus; Jennifer Habig, Jerel Hilding, Tom Mossbrucker, Beatriz Rodriguez; Dominique Angel, Beth Bartholomew, Linda Bechtold, Carl Corry, Peter Narbutas, Elizabeth Parkinson, Victoria Pasquale, Raymond Perrin, Roger Plaut, Edward Stierle.

PIÈCES EN CONCERT
M François Couperin (*Pièces en concert*, arr. Paul Bazelaire: "Prelude," from Suite no. 14; "Sicilienne," from Suite no. 7; "Tromba" and "Plainte" from Suite no. 10; "Air de diable," from Suite no. 6). **L** Phil Sandström. **PR** 11/12/86, MMDG, Opera House, Brooklyn Academy of Music, NY. Cello: Myron Lutzke. Harpsichord: Robert Wolinsky. **D** Rob Besserer, Susan Hadley, Mark Morris.

STABAT MATER
M Giovanni Battista Pergolesi, 1736. **S** Robert Bordo. **L** Phil Sandström. **PR** 11/12/86, MMDG, Opera House, Brooklyn Academy of Music, NY. St. Luke's Chamber Ensemble. Conductor: Michael Feldman. Soprano: Julianne Baird. Countertenor: Drew Minter. **D** Rob Besserer, Ruth Davidson, Tina Fehlandt, Susan Hadley, Larry Hahn, David Landis, Donald Mouton, Long Nguyen, Guillermo Resto, Keith Sabado, Jennifer Thienes, Teri Weksler.

1987

SONATA FOR CLARINET AND PIANO
M Francis Poulenc, 1962. **L** Thomas Hines. **PR** 3/6/87, University of Washington School of Music and Division of Dance, Meany Hall, University of Washington, Seattle. Clarinet: William O. Smith. Piano: Anne Marie Scotto. **D** Terrence Grizzell; Tasha Cook, Gretchen Junker, Nancy Kadel, McLaurin Layh, Lara McIntosh, Lori McKim, Erin Smith, Anne Solseng, Lauren Tolle, Nancy Widen. **ST** 1987, MMDG.

STRICT SONGS
M and text: Lou Harrison (*Four Strict Songs*, 1955). **L** Phil Sandström. **PR** 3/19/87, Seattle Men's Chorus and MMDG, Meany Hall, University of Washington, Seattle. Conductor: Dennis Coleman. Vocal soloist: Rob Hard. **D** Ruth Davidson, Tina Fehlandt, Susan Hadley, Penny Hutchinson, David Landis, Jon Mensinger, Donald Mouton, Guillermo Resto, Keith Sabado, Jennifer Thienes.

LA FOLIA
M Antonio Vivaldi (Trio Sonata in D minor, RV63: "Variations on 'La Folia' "), rec. **C** Alan Madsen. **L** David Saxton. **PR** 4/10/87, Cornish Dance Theater (Cornish College of the Arts), Broadway Performance Hall, Seattle Central Community College. **D** John Carlson, Nanette Cresto, Paul Dew, Tom Dickerson, Kathleen Kelly, Nancy Salisbury, Lara Turner.

THE FANTASY
M Wolfgang Amadeus Mozart (Fantasia in C minor, K475), rec. **L** Phil Sandström. **PR** 7/23/87, MMDG, Meany Hall, University of Washington, Seattle. **D** Ruth Davidson, Susan

Hadley, Jon Mensinger, Donald Mouton, Keith Sabado. **N** Became second movement of *Fugue and Fantasy*, 1988.

NIXON IN CHINA

M John Adams. Libretto: Alice Goodman. **DIR** Peter Sellars. **S** Adrianne Lobel. **C** Dunya Ramicova. **L** James F. Ingalls. **PR** 10/22/87, Houston Grand Opera, Brown Theater, Wortham Theater Center, Houston. Conductor: John DeMain. **D** THE RED DETACHMENT OF WOMEN: Steven Ochoa (Hung Ch'ang-ching), Heather Toma (Wu Ching-hua); Homer Avila, Miguel Aviles, Pamela Giardino, Michael Ing, Andrew Pacho, Cristina Perera, Pamela Semmler, Kelly Slough. DREAM BALLET: Ochoa, Toma. **N** Morris contributed two dances: in Act II, Scene 2, a takeoff on the Chinese Communist agitprop ballet *The Red Detachment of Women*; in Act II, Scene 3, a dream ballet for the hero and heroine of *The Red Detachment*. **TV** *Nixon in China*, Great Performances, PBS, 1988.

[SCARLATTI SOLOS]

M Domenico Scarlatti (Sonata in D, K491), rec. **L** John Vadino. **PR** 10/27/87, MMDG, Campbell Hall, University of California, Santa Barbara. **D** Mark Morris. **N** This solo was completely improvised, different at every performance, and differently titled at every performance. At its premiere it was *Lies*. Later, it was *More Lies*; *Big Lies*; *Utter Lies*; *Fraud*; *Run, Children, Run*; *Copperhead*; *Always*; and *Never*.

1988

ORPHEUS AND EURYDICE

M Christoph Willibald Gluck (Paris version, 1774). Libretto: Pierre-Louis Moline after Raniero de Calzabigi. **DIR** Stephen Wadsworth. **S** Thomas Lynch. **C** Martin Paklodinaz. **L** Peter Kaczorowski. **PR** 1/16/88, Seattle Opera, Seattle Opera House. Conductor: George Manahan. **D** Mark Morris; Stephen Brown, Ruth Davidson, Tina Fehlandt, Susan Hadley, Penny Hutchinson, David Landis, Erin Matthiessen, Jon Mensinger, Donald Mouton, Kraig Patterson, Keith Sabado, Teri Weksler. **N** Morris choreographed dances to the following numbers: Act I, Scene 1, *Pantomime*; Act II, *Air de furie*; Act III, Scene 3, *Ballet, Gavotte, Chaconne, Menuet*. He also created a Duncanesque solo for himself to the Dance of the Furies.

OFFERTORIUM

M Franz Schubert (*Salve Regina* [*Offertorium*], 1819), rec. **L** David Ferri. **PR** 2/4/88, P.S. 122 benefit concert, P.S. 122, NY. **D** Mark Morris. **ST** 1988, MMDG.

DIE FLEDERMAUS

M Johann Strauss the Younger, 1874. Libretto: Richard Genée and Karl Haffner, after Henri Meilhac and Ludovic Halévy. **DIR** Mark Morris. **S** Zack Brown. **C** Andrew Marley. **L** Joan Sullivan. **PR** 5/7/88, Seattle Opera, Seattle Opera House. Conductor: Hermann Michael. Cast: Kathryn Gamberoni (Adele), Beverly Morgan (Rosalinda), Dale Deusing (von Eisenstein), Erich Parce (Dr. Falke), Emily Golden (Orlovsky), others. **N** The cast included no professional dancers. All dancing was done by the singers.

FUGUE AND FANTASY

M Wolfgang Amadeus Mozart (Fugue in C minor, K426; Fantasia in C minor, K475). **L** Phil Sandström. **PR** 5/17/88, MMDG, Opera House, Brooklyn Academy of Music, NY. Orchestra of St. Luke's. Conductor: Michael Feldman. Piano: David Oei. **D** FUGUE: Tina Fehlandt,

David Landis, Kraig Patterson, Teri Weksler. FANTASY: Ruth Davidson, Susan Hadley, Jon Mensinger, Donald Mouton, Keith Sabado. N In this piece's first season, at BAM, "Fugue" was danced to the second movement of Adagio and Fugue for String Quartet, K546, which Mozart adapted from the Fugue for Two Pianos, K426. But the dance was choreographed to K426, and thereafter it was always performed to K426. See *The Fantasy*, 1987.

DRINK TO ME ONLY WITH THINE EYES
M Virgil Thomson (from Nine Etudes, 1940 and 1951, and Ten Etudes, 1943: "Chromatic Double Harmonies," "Repeating Tremolo," "Fingered Fifths," "Double Glissando," "Oscillating Arm," "Pivoting on the Thumb," "Alternating Octaves," "Double Sevenths," "Broken Arpeggios," "Parallel Chords," "Ragtime Bass," "For the Weaker Fingers," "Tenor Lead"). **C** Santo Loquasto. **L** Phil Sandström. **PR** 5/31/88, American Ballet Theatre, Metropolitan Opera House, NY. Piano: Michael Boriskin. **D** Mikhail Baryshnikov, Shawn Black, Julio Bocca, Isabella Padovani, Robert Hill, Susan Jaffe, Carld Jonassaint, Lucette Katerndahl, Kathleen Moore, Martine van Hamel, Robert Wallace, Ross Yearsley.

LE NOZZE DI FIGARO
FANDANGO
M Wolfgang Amadeus Mozart, K492. Libretto: Lorenzo da Ponte, after Beaumarchais. **DIR** Peter Sellars. **S** Adrianne Lobel. **C** Dunya Ramicova. **L** James F. Ingalls. **PR** 7/13/88, PepsiCo Summerfare, Theatre B, Performing Arts Center, State University of New York, Purchase. Conductor: Craig Smith. **D** Michael Ing, Steven Ochoa, Heather Toma. **N** Morris choreographed a rock 'n' roll dance to the fandango in the Act III wedding scene. **TV** *Peter Sellars Directs: The Marriage of Figaro*, Great Performances, PBS, 1990.

L'ALLEGRO, IL PENSEROSO ED IL MODERATO
M George Frideric Handel, 1740. Text: Charles Jennens, compiled in part from Milton. Act I overture: Handel, Concerto Grosso, op. 6, no. 1, movements 1–3. Act II overture: same, movements 4 and 5. **S** Adrianne Lobel. **C** Christine Van Loon. **L** James F. Ingalls. **PR** 11/23/88, MDG/MM, Théâtre Royal de la Monnaie, Brussels. Monnaie Symphony Orchestra and Chorus. Conductor: Craig Smith. Vocal soloists: Lorraine Hunt, Jeanne Ommerlé, Jayne West, Frederick Urrey, James Maddalena. **D** Alyce Bochette, Raphael Brand, Ruth Davidson, Tina Fehlandt, Michael Gallo, Susan Hadley, Penny Hutchinson, Dan Joyce, David Landis, Paul Lorenger, Olivia Maridjan-Koop, Clarice Marshall, Erin Matthiessen, Jon Mensinger, Donald Mouton, Rachel Murray, June Omura, Kraig Patterson, Mireille Radwan-Dana, Keith Sabado, Joachim Schlömer, William Wagner, Teri Weksler, Megan Williams. **N** Handel's score is in three parts. Each of the first two parts is devoted to the alternating arguments of L'Allegro and Il Penseroso. The third is devoted to a third voice, Il Moderato, intermediate between Mirth and Melancholy. In later performances of the oratorio, Handel deleted Part 3, and Morris followed his example, but he salvaged two numbers from "Il Moderato": "Each action will derive new grace," which he inserted into Act I, and "As steals the morn upon the night," which he inserted into Act II. He also deleted one of L'Allegro's arias ("Straight mine eye") and reversed the order of Il Penseroso's and L'Allegro's concluding arguments, ending with L'Allegro where Handel ended with Il Penseroso. **RV** 1989, Act I overture shortened to include only movements 1 and 2 of Concerto Grosso; Act II overture deleted. **TV** Scenes from rehearsal and performance, *The Hidden Soul of Harmony*, South Bank Show, London Weekend Television, 1990.

1989

DIDO AND AENEAS
M Henry Purcell, 1689. Libretto: Nahum Tate. **S** Robert Bordo. **C** Christine Van Loon. **L** James F. Ingalls. **PR** 3/11/89, MDG/MM, Théâtre Varia, Brussels. Emmanuel Music. Conductor: Craig Smith. Vocal soloists: Mary Westbrook-Geha (Dido), William Hite (Sorceress), James Maddalena (Aeneas), Jayne West (Belinda), Lynn Torgove (Second Woman), Mark Kagan (Sailor). **D** Mark Morris (Dido/Sorceress), Guillermo Resto (Aeneas), Penny Hutchinson (Belinda), Susan Hadley (Second Woman), Ruth Davidson and Jon Mensinger (Witches), Teri Weksler (Sailor); Olivia Maridjan-Koop, Clarice Marshall, Rachel Murray, Kraig Patterson, Keith Sabado. **N** Morris planned *Dido and Aeneas* as a solo for himself: he would dance all the roles, all the choruses. Only when he began to work on the piece did he decide to add the other dancers. **TV** Scenes from rehearsal and performance, *Opéra* (French television), FR3 and Twincom, 1992.

LOVE SONG WALTZES
M Johannes Brahms (*Liebeslieder*, op. 52, 1868–69). **L** James F. Ingalls. **PR** 11/4/89, MDG/MM, Théâtre Royal de la Monnaie, Brussels. Piano: Udo Gefe, Ann Eckman. Singers: Deborah Voigt, Elzbieta Ardam, Norbert Orth, Johan Tilli. **D** Joe Bowie, Tina Fehlandt, Penny Hutchinson, Olivia Maridjan-Koop, Clarice Marshall, Jon Mensinger, Kraig Patterson, Mireille Radwan Dana, Keith Sabado, Joachim Schlömer, Jean-Guillaume Weis, Holly Williams.

WONDERLAND
M Arnold Schoenberg (*Accompaniment-Music for a Motion Picture*, op. 34, 1930; Five Orchestral Pieces, op. 16, 1909). **C** Martin Pakledinaz. **L** James F. Ingalls. **PR** 11/4/89, MDG/MM, Théâtre Royal de la Monnaie, Brussels. Monnaie Symphony Orchestra. Conductor: Ingo Metzmacher. **D** Mikhail Baryshnikov, Rob Besserer, Ruth Davidson, Olivia Maridjan-Koop, Keith Sabado. **TV** Rehearsal scenes, *The Hidden Soul of Harmony*, South Bank Show, London Weekend Television, 1990.

1990

BEHEMOTH
C Christine Van Loon. **L** James F. Ingalls. **PR** 4/14/90, MDG/MM, Halles de Schaerbeek, Brussels. **D** Katharina Bader, Alyce Bochette, Ruth Davidson, Penny Hutchinson, Dan Joyce, Hans-Georg Lenhart, Olivia Maridjan-Koop, Erin Matthiessen, Rachel Murray, June Omura, Kraig Patterson, Mireille Radwan-Dana, Joachim Schlömer, William Wagner, Jean-Guillaume Weis.

GOING AWAY PARTY
M "Playboy Theme" (T. A. Dorsey—B. Wills), "Yearning" (B. Davis—J. A. Burke), "My Shoes Keep Walking Back to You" (B. Wills—L. Ross), "Goin' Away Party" (C. Walker), "Baby, That Sure Would Go Good" (C. Walker), "Milk Cow Blues" (K. Arnold), "Crippled Turkey" (arr. H. Nix), "When You Leave Amarillo, Turn Out the Lights" (C. Walker), performed by Bob Wills and His Texas Playboys, rec. **C** Christine Van Loon. **L** Phil Sandström. **PR** 4/14/90, MDG/MM, Halles de Schaerbeek, Brussels. **D** Clarice Marshall, Jon Mensinger, Mark Morris, Rachel Murray, Guillermo Resto, Keith Sabado, Holly Williams. **ST** 1990, White Oak Dance Project (NY).

EIN HERZ

M Johann Sebastian Bach (Cantata BWV134, 1724, "Ein Herz, das seinem Jesum lebend weiss"). **C** Martin Pakledinaz. **L** James F. Ingalls. **PR** 6/6/90, Paris Opera Ballet, Paris Opera. Conductor: André Presser. Countertenor: James Bowman. Tenor: Martyn Hill. **D** Françoise Legrée and Olivier Patey, Fanny Gaida and Hervé Dirmann, Delphine Moussin and Félix Vivian; Eric Camillo, Nicolas Le Riche, José Martinez, Jean-François Créteaux, Arnaud Dreyfus; Olivier Ageorges, Delphine Baey, Mirentchu Battut, Aurélie Dupont, Christophe Duquenne, Cyril Fleury, Jean-Christophe Guerri, Carole Maison, Eric Monin, Stéphane Phavorin, Anne Rebeschini, Sylvie Ton Nu, José Valls.

PAS DE POISSON

M Erik Satie (*Cinéma*, symphonic interlude from *Relâche*, 1924, piano reduction for four hands by Darius Milhaud). **L** James F. Ingalls. **PR** 10/7/90, MDG/MM, Opera House, Brooklyn Academy of Music, NY. Piano: Linda Dowdell, Mizue Murakami. **D** Mikhail Baryshnikov, Penny Hutchinson, Mark Morris. **ST** 1990, White Oak Dance Project (NY).

MOTORCADE

M Camille Saint-Saëns (Septet in E-flat major, op. 65, 1881). **C** Santo Loquasto. **L** James F. Ingalls. **PR** 10/24/90, White Oak Dance Project, Wang Center, Boston. Trumpet: Susan Radcliff. Violins: Ron Oakland, Charles Barker. Viola: Karie Prescott. Cello: Armen Ksajikian. Bass: Judith Sugarman. Piano: Linda Dowdell. **D** Peggy Baker, Mikhail Baryshnikov, Rob Besserer, Jamie Bishton, Nancy Colahan, Kate Johnson, William Pizzuto, Denise Pons. **ST** 1992, London Contemporary Dance Theatre.

1991

THE HARD NUT

M Pyotr Il'yich Tchaikovsky, 1892. Libretto after "Nutcracker and Mouse King" by E.T.A. Hoffmann. Production based on the work of Charles Burns. **S** Adrianne Lobel. **C** Martin Pakledinaz. **L** James F. Ingalls. **PR** 1/12/91, MDG/MM, Théâtre Royal de la Monnaie, Brussels. Monnaie Symphony Orchestra and Chorus. Conductor: Sylvain Cambreling. **D** Clarice Marshall (Marie); Marianne Moore (Fritz); Tina Fehlandt (Louise/Princess Pirlipat); Erin Matthiessen (Dr. Stahlbaum/King); Peter Wing Healey (Mrs. Stahlbaum/Queen); Kraig Patterson (Housekeeper/Nurse); Rob Besserer (Drosselmeier); William Wagner (Nutcracker/Young Drosselmeier); Ruth Davidson (Barbie Doll); Joachim Schlömer (Robot); Joe Bowie, Penny Hutchinson, Mark Morris, Mireille Radwan-Dana, Guillermo Resto, Keith Sabado, William Wagner, Holly Williams, Megan Williams (Party Guests); Hans-Georg Lenhart, Olivia Maridjan-Koop, June Omura (Rat King); 5 women (Rat Soldiers); 5 men (G.I. Joe Soldiers); 11 women, 11 men (Snow); Dan Joyce, Mark Nimkoff (Suitors); Nathaniel Lee (Dentist); Rachel Murray (Rat Queen); Sam Louwyck, Gene Reddick (Changers); Guillermo Resto, Mireille Radwan-Dana (Spanish); Mark Morris and Dan Joyce, Mark Nimkoff, Gene Reddick, Joachim Schlömer (Arabian); Olivia Maridjan-Koop, June Omura, Keith Sabado (Chinese); Katharina Bader, Ruth Davidson, Penny Hutchinson, Hans-Georg Lenhart, Jean-Guillaume Weis, Holly Williams (Russian); Alyce Bochette, Joe Bowie, Keith Sabado, Megan Williams (French); 9 women, 5 men (Flowers). **RV** In 11/91, for the second season of *The Hard Nut*, Morris revised the battle of the rats and the G.I. Joes and reconceived the role of the Rat King. Formerly three dancers in one costume, the Rat King became a single dancer with three heads, all resembling Elvis Presley. **TV** *The Hard Nut*, Dance in America, PBS, 1992 (distributed by Electra Nonesuch, 1992).

THE DEATH OF KLINGHOFFER

M John Adams. Libretto: Alice Goodman. **DIR** Peter Sellars. **S** George Tsypin. **C** Dunya Ramicova. **L** James F. Ingalls. **PR** 3/19/91, Théâtre Royal de la Monnaie, Brussels. Monnaie Symphony Orchestra and Chorus. Conductor: Kent Nagano. **D** Alyce Bochette, Joe Bowie, Ruth Davidson, Tina Fehlandt, Penny Hutchinson, Dan Joyce, Hans-Georg Lenhart, Olivia Maridjan-Koop, Clarice Marshall, Erin Matthiessen, Jon Mensinger, Rachel Murray, Mark Nimkoff, June Omura, Kraig Patterson, Mireille Radwan-Dana, Guillermo Resto, Keith Sabado, William Wagner, Jean-Guillaume Weis, Megan Williams. **N** Morris created ensemble dances for the following choruses: "Ocean," "Night," "Hagar and the Angel," "Desert," and "Day." He also choreographed dances to accompany the Captain's solo (Act I, Scene 1), the highjacking (Act I, Scene 1), Mamoud's bird aria (Act I, Scene 2), and the British Dancing Girl's aria (Act II, Scene 1). **RV** 1991, added new material to end of "Hagar" chorus; 1992, deleted dance to British Dancing Girl's aria.

A LAKE

M Joseph Haydn (Horn Concerto no. 2 in D), rec. **C** Martin Pakledinaz. **L** James F. Ingalls. **PR** 7/30/91, White Oak Dance Project, Filene Center, Wolf Trap Farm Park, Vienna, Virginia. **D** Mikhail Baryshnikov, Rob Besserer, Nancy Colahan, Tina Fehlandt, Kate Johnson, Clarice Marshall, Donald Mouton, Carol Parker, Kraig Patterson, Guillermo Resto. **ST** 1992, MMDG.

LE NOZZE DI FIGARO

M Wolfgang Amadeus Mozart, K492. Libretto: Lorenzo da Ponte, after Beaumarchais. **DIR** Mark Morris. **S** Adrianne Lobel. **C** Martin Pakledinaz. **L** James F. Ingalls. **PR** 12/17/91, Théâtre Royal de la Monnaie, Brussels. Monnaie Symphony Orchestra and Chorus. Conductor: Sylvain Cambreling. Cast: Dale Deusing (Almaviva), Hillevi Martinpelto (Countess), Elzbieta Szmytka (Susanna), José van Dam (Figaro), Ugo Benelli (Basilio), Jules Bastin (Bartolo), Magali Chalmeau Damonte (Marcellina), Monica Bacelli (Cherubino), Georg Paucker (Antonio), Laura Cherici (Barbarina), Luc De Meulenaere (Curzio), Qilian Chen, Beata Morawska (Two Women). **N** In addition to directing the production, Morris choreographed a Spanish-style dance for Penny Hutchinson to the Act III fandango.

1992

PAUKENSCHLAG

M Franz Joseph Haydn (Symphony no. 94, 1791). **S/C** Robert Bordo. **L** Nicholas Cernovitch. **PR** 3/14/92, Les Grands Ballets Canadiens, O'Keefe Centre, Toronto. Conductor: Richard Hoenich. **D** Marcello Angelini, Andrea Boardman, Nathalie Buisson, David Michael Cohen, Yvonne Cutaran, Nicolo Fonte, Suzanne Gagnon, Andrew Giday, Jennifer Habig, Benjamin Hatcher, Geoffrey Hipps, Kevin Irving, Edmond Kilpatrick, Sylvain Lafortune, Rosemary Neville. **N** What English speakers call the "Surprise" Symphony is known to German speakers as "mit dem Paukenschlag," or "with the drumbeat." **TV** Scenes from rehearsal and performance, *Mark Morris, Choreographer*, Adrienne Clarkson Presents, CBC, 1992.

BEAUTIFUL DAY

M Attrib. to Johann Sebastian Bach (Cantata BWV53, 1757, "Schlage doch, gewünschte Stunde"), probably by Georg-Melchior Hoffmann. **C** Susan Ruddie. **L** James F. Ingalls. **PR** 4/7/92, MMDG, Manhattan Center Grand Ballroom, NY. Orchestra of St. Luke's. Conductor: Michael Feldman. Mezzo-soprano: Mary Westbrook-Geha. **D** Clarice Marshall, Keith Sabado.

ST 1992, Peggy Baker/Solo Dance (Toronto). **TV** Scenes from rehearsal and performance, *Mark Morris, Choreographer*, Adrienne Clarkson Presents, CBC, 1992.

POLKA

M Lou Harrison (Grand Duo, 1988, 5th movement). **C** Susan Ruddie. **L** James F. Ingalls. **PR** 4/7/92, MMDG, Manhattan Center Grand Ballroom, NY. Violin: Eriko Sato. Piano: Linda Dowdell. **D** Alyce Bochette, Joe Bowie, Ruth Davidson, Tina Fehlandt, Dan Joyce, Olivia Maridjan-Koop, Clarice Marshall, Rachel Murray, June Omura, Kraig Patterson, Mireille Radwan-Dana, Guillermo Resto, Keith Sabado, William Wagner, Jean-Guillaume Weis, Megan Williams. **RV** 1992, cast reduced to 14. **N** *Polka* became the last movement of *Grand Duo*, 1993.

BEDTIME

M Franz Schubert ("Wiegenlied," D498, 1816; "Ständchen," D920, first version, 1827; "Erlkönig," D328, fourth version, 1815?). **C** Susan Ruddie. **L** James F. Ingalls. **PR** 6/2/92, MMDG, Dance Umbrella, Emerson Majestic Theatre, Boston. Mezzo-soprano: Lorraine Hunt. Piano: Linda Dowdell. **D** Alyce Bochette, Ruth Davidson, Tina Fehlandt, Olivia Maridjan-Koop, Clarice Marshall, Mark Morris, Rachel Murray, June Omura, Kraig Patterson, Mireille Radwan-Dana, Guillermo Resto, Megan Williams.

THREE PRELUDES

M George Gershwin (Preludes, 1926). **C** Isaac Mizrahi. **L** James F. Ingalls. **PR** 6/2/92, MMDG, Dance Umbrella, Emerson Majestic Theatre, Boston. Piano: Linda Dowdell. **D** Mark Morris. **ST** 1992, White Oak Dance Project (NY). **N** This solo was created to be danced either by Morris or by Mikhail Baryshnikov. Baryshnikov danced it as a guest artist with New York City Ballet before performing it with his own White Oak Dance Project.

EXCURSION TO GRENADA
A Calypso Ballet

M Lionel Belasco and His Orchestra, "Carmencita"; The Growler, "An Excursion to Grenada"; Lord Executor, "Seven Skeletons Found in the Yard"; Sam Manning, "Lieutenant Julian," all rec. **C** Susan Ruddie. **L** Michael Chybowski. **PR** 7/7/92, MMDG, Ted Shawn Theatre, Jacob's Pillow, Becket, MA. **D** Alyce Bochette, Ruth Davidson, Tina Fehlandt, Dan Joyce, June Omura, Mireille Radwan-Dana, William Wagner, Jean-Guillaume Weis, Megan Williams.

1993

GRAND DUO
PRELUDE, STAMPEDE, A ROUND, POLKA

M Lou Harrison, 1988. **C** Susan Ruddie. **L** Michael Chybowski. **PR** 2/16/93, MMDG, Fine Arts Center, University of Massachusetts, Amherst. **D** Alyce Bochette, Joe Bowie, Ruth Davidson, Tina Fehlandt, Dan Joyce, Olivia Maridjan-Koop, Rachel Murray, June Omura, Kraig Patterson, Mireille Radwan-Dana, Guillermo Resto, Keith Sabado, William Wagner, Megan Williams. **N** See *Polka*, 1992.

MOSAIC AND UNITED

M Henry Cowell (String Quartet no. 3, "Mosaic," 1935; String Quartet no. 4, "United," 1936). **C** Isaac Mizrahi **L** Michael Chybowski **PR** 4/29/93, MMDG and White Oak Dance Project,

Opera House, Brooklyn Academy of Music, NY. Violins: Lynn Chang, Diane Monroe. Viola: Misha Amory. Cello: Yo-Yo Ma. **D** Mikhail Baryshnikov, Rob Besserer, Tina Fehlandt, John Gardner, Kate Johnson, Dan Joyce, Marianne Moore, Keith Sabado, William Wagner, Megan Williams. **N** The five movements of "Mosaic," according to Cowell, could be ordered and repeated in various different patterns. Morris arranged them as follows: 1-2-3-4-5-3-1, each with different choreography. *Mosaic and United* was created for both the MMDG and the White Oak Dance Project, to be danced by five people. In its first performances, however, it had a cast of ten, two groups of five (each combining White Oak dancers and MMDG dancers) that more or less alternated in the twelve sections of the dance.

HOME

M Michelle Shocked ("Homestead," "Stillborn," "Custom Cutter," all 1993) and Rob Wasserman (instrumental music, 1993). **C** Susan Ruddie **L** Michael Chybowski **PR** 4/29/93, MMDG, Opera House, Brooklyn Academy of Music, NY. Guitar, mandolin, and vocals: Michelle Shocked. Upright basses and fiddle: Rob Wasserman. **D** SONG SECTIONS: Alyce Bochette, Ruth Davidson, Olivia Maridjan-Koop, Clarice Marshall, Rachel Murray, Mireille Radwan-Dana, Guillermo Resto. STEP-DANCING: Tina Fehlandt, Mark Morris, June Omura, Kraig Patterson, Guillermo Resto, Megan Williams. **N** The dances to the first and second songs were followed by interludes of step-dancing, to a fiddle tune. The piece ended with an instrumental section danced by the entire cast.

JESU, MEINE FREUDE

M Johann Sebastian Bach (Motet BWV227, 1723?). **L** Michael Chybowski. **PR** 6/8/93, MMDG, Dance Umbrella, Emerson Majestic Theatre, Boston. Conductor: Craig Smith. Cello: Michael Curry. Organ: Michael Beattie. Chorus of Emmanuel Music. **D** Alyce Bochette, Joe Bowie, Ruth Davidson, Clarice Marshall, June Omura, Kraig Patterson, Mireille Radwan-Dana, Guillermo Resto, William Wagner, Megan Williams. **N** The men wore loose white pants, no tops. The women wore white nylon nightgowns, bought off the rack at Filene's department store in Boston. As usual when there is no costume credit, Morris gave Nancy Umanoff an idea of what he wanted and she did the shopping.

Megan Williams in *Love Song Waltzes (Tom Brazil)*

Source Notes

Recent quotations for which no source is given are from interviews with Joan Acocella

MARK MORRIS

Page

6   "I thought they meant me": Quoted in Christine Temin, "The Triumph of Mark Morris," *The Boston Globe Magazine*, February 19, 1989.

6   part diva, part truck driver: Marcelle Michel, "Mark Morris, allegro vivace," *Libération* (Paris), May 23, 1991.

6   "the Peter Martins record collection festival," "that lecture-demonstration": Quoted in Laura Shapiro, "Cheers for Mark Morris," *Newsweek*, May 30, 1988.

7   "Wonderful BAM!" "He can be": Quoted in Janice Berman, "No Time for Rules," *Newsday*, May 15, 1988.

7   "All you have to do": Quoted in Charles Siebert, "Morris Dances," *Vanity Fair*, April 1989.

7   "In work and in life": Quoted in Berman, op. cit.

8   "I hand out money": Quoted in Joan Dupont, "An American in Brussels," *The New York Times Magazine*, January 22, 1989.

CHILDHOOD

27   "a very wild bunch indeed": Quoted in Roger Downey, "Looking Back at Mark Morris," *Seattle Weekly*, May 4, 1988.

30   "We sang and drank": Quoted in Tobi Tobias, "Manchild in the Promised Land: Mark Morris," *Dance Magazine*, December 1984.

A COMPANY

45   "how to flatten": Quoted in Jennifer Dunning, "Mark Morris, a Choreographer Who Makes Things Happen," *The New York Times*, November 5, 1982.

50   "When I came to New York": Ibid.

54   "you could only walk": Twyla Tharp, *Push Comes to Shove: An Autobiography* (New York: Bantam, 1992), pp. 86–88.

55 "This mastery of mimetic implication," "the raw gift of choreography": Arlene Croce, "Mark Morris Comes to Town," *The New Yorker*, January 2, 1984.

56 "the most solidly promising heir": Jennifer Dunning, "Mark Morris at Brooklyn Academy," *The New York Times*, November 29, 1984.

56 "Had Doris Humphrey": Deborah Jowitt, "New Stars and That Old Glow," *The Village Voice*, December 18, 1984.

56 "What might have been": Dale Harris, "The Avant-Garde Grows in Brooklyn," *The Wall Street Journal*, December 12, 1984.

56 "the clearest illustration": Arlene Croce, "Championship Form," *The New Yorker*, December 17, 1984.

56 "Pessimists who announced": Tobi Tobias, "Dance," *New York*, December 17, 1984.

61 "You come in like a commando": Quoted in Allen Robertson, "Mark Morris in Brussels: An American Dream," *Los Angeles Times*, December 11, 1988.

65 "Often my things look clichéd": Quoted in John Gruen, "Mark Morris: He's Here," *Dance Magazine*, September 1986.

66 "you can't be corny": Quoted in Dunning, "Mark Morris, a Choreographer Who Makes Things Happen," November 5, 1982.

67 "The use of a genuine talent": Anna Kisselgoff, "Divining the Mystique of Mark Morris," *The New York Times*, November 11, 1990.

67 getting caught in his lipstick: Tobi Tobias, "Dance: Mark Morris Brings His Extravagant Style into the Big Time," *New York*, September 15, 1986.

67 "effeminate to a degree": Eva Resnikova, "Mark Morris Superstar," January 1987.

67 "What cigarettes I smoke": Lori Brungard, with Michael Corsetino, "Choreographer Mark Morris: Interview," *MOA* (Purchase, NY), Fall 1986.

68 "Why . . . is there the feeling": Kisselgoff, op. cit.

68 "Mark Morris is not a great choreographer": Anna Kisselgoff, "Emphasis on Music by Mark Morris Troupe," *The New York Times*, May 19, 1988.

68 "He is far from being": Clive Barnes, "Mark Morris in Musical Maze," *New York Post* May 20, 1988.

68 "In the end": Anna Kisselgoff, "Purcell's 'Dido and Aeneas' as Mark Morris Sees It," *The New York Times*, June 9, 1989.

64 "commonplace, and totally irrelevant": Clive Barnes, "Avant Darling's Hard to Handel," *New York Post*, October 8, 1990.

69 "The other day," "Or perhaps it is," "The idea that some": Kisselgoff, "Divining the Mystique of Mark Morris."

72 "I was so moved": Quoted in Siebert, op. cit.

THE BODY

75 "Big bottoms": Quoted in Daryl Jung, "Mark Morris," *NOW* (Toronto), March 12–18, 1992.

76 "Gravity is our friend": Quoted in Dupont, op. cit.

76 used his feet as if they were webbed: Laura Jacobs, "Indulgences of the Flesh," *7 Days* (New York), June 1, 1988.

76 "People have always said": Quoted in Temin, op. cit.

79 "It's like we all pull our pants down": Quoted in Alan Kriegsman, "On the Road with Misha and Mark," *The Washington Post*, July 28, 1991.

81 "so they can't do imitations": Quoted in Dupont, op. cit.

81 "Abandon hope of rescue": Georg Friedrich Daumer, translated by Lionel Salter, Monnaie Dance Group/Mark Morris souvenir program, Théâtre Royal de la Monnaie, fall 1989.

85 "I hate, more than anything": Quoted in Jung, op. cit.

85 "The big thing": Macaulay, "Morris Makes His Move," *Interview*, May 1989.

86 "got tired of pretending": Quoted in Tobias, "Manchild in the Promised Land."

LOVE AND SEX

92 "the bassoon and the French horns": Tobias Schneebaum, "Encountering Mark Morris," *Christopher Street*, December 1987.

92 "In rehearsal I say": Macaulay, op. cit.

94 *"What do you think"*: Schneebaum, op. cit.

101 "What is put before us": Thierry Lassence, "Mark Morris danse l'amour incarné par Didon," *La Libre Belgique* (Brussels), March 13, 1989.

107 "should set the anti-child-porn movement": Carole Beers, "They're Turning Dancing on Its Ear," *The Seattle Times*, May 10, 1985.

113 "Do not stray": Daumer, op. cit.

115 "I won't live that long," "AIDS": Macaulay, op. cit.

116 "People often complain": Monnaie Dance Group/Mark Morris souvenir program, Théâtre des Champs-Elysées, Paris, May 21–25, 1991.

HEAVEN AND HELL

118 "an expression of degeneration": Isadora Duncan, "The Dance of the Future," in *The Art of the Dance* (New York: Theatre Arts, 1928), p. 56.

118 "Man, arrived at the end": Ibid., p. 55.

118 "I demand of the dance": Ruth St. Denis, Folder 216, Denishawn Collection, New York Public Library, quoted in Deborah Jowitt, *Time and the Dancing Image* (New York: William Morrow, 1988), p. 128.

118 "the great goal of healing": Quoted in Hedwig Müller and Norbert Servos, "From Isadora Duncan to Leni Riefenstahl," *Ballett International* (Cologne), April 1982.

118 "The modern dance is not a system": John Martin, *The Modern Dance*, 1933 (rept. New York: Dance Horizons, 1965), p. 20.

119 "like organized religion": Thea Singer, "Mark Morris: Beautiful Dancers," *Stuff* (Boston), June 1992.

120 "From my earliest childhood": Isadora Duncan, *My Life* (New York: Liveright, 1927), p. 276.

122 "I love seeing people naked": "Afterword," in Philip Trager, *Dancers* (Boston: Little, Brown, 1992), p. 157.

122 "You know, barefoot": Quoted in Luisa Moffett, "Mark Morris and the Monnaie," *The Bulletin* (Brussels), January 24, 1991.

127 "I'm not part of any club": David Vaughan, "A Conversation with Mark Morris," *Ballet Review*, Summer 1986.

127 "My mother's family": Schneebaum, op. cit.

THE STORY

137 "Art can certainly be very ugly": *Mark Morris*, directed by Thomas Grimm, Dance in America, PBS, 1986.

137 "I can defend every single measure": Quoted in Kriegsman, op. cit.

138 "Neighbor, guard," "From the mountains," "Before you stands," "No, beloved": Translated by Lionel Salter, Monnaie Dance Group/Mark Morris souvenir program, Théâtre Royal de la Monnaie, fall 1989.

140 "hardly gives a thought": Eva-Elisabeth Fischer, "Brightness and Gloom—Baryshnikov and Morris," *Ballett International*, February 1990.

143 "He always hates it": Quoted in Nancy Dalva, "Misha and Mark: Out on a Limb," *Dance Magazine*, January 1991.

144 "The architecture of music": Quoted in Tobias, "Manchild in the Promised Land."

150 "never drooly": Quoted in Pope Brock, "Mark Morris," *People*, December 21, 1992.

152 "Once he has got hold": Arlene Croce, "Choreographer of the Year," *The New Yorker*, December 1, 1986.

157 "Put a man and a girl": *By George Balanchine* (New York: San Marco Press, 1984), p. 23.

MUSIC

163 "I love Mozart": Thierry Lassence and Yannick Vermeirsch, "*L'Allegro, il Penseroso ed il Moderato*: Interview Mark Morris," *La Monnaie/De Munt Magazine* (Brussels), November 1988.

163 "dance rhythms and dance tempi," "perfect architecture": Quoted in Thea Singer, "Singing the Body Electric," *The Boston Phoenix*, June 1, 1990.

164 "Beauty for me is usually structure": Quoted in Michael Crabb, "Bad Boy," *Dance Connection*, June/July/August 1992.

164 "Bach is God's favorite composer": Quoted in Singer, "Singing the Body Electric."

168 he may have wanted to stamp: Alastair Macaulay, "While the Music Lasts," *The New Yorker*, May 11, 1992.

168 "You can't just choose": Lassence and Vermeirsch, op. cit.

169 "The more you listen": *The Hidden Soul of Harmony*, directed by Nigel Wattis, South Bank Show, London Weekend Television, 1990. An edited transcription of Morris's comments on this show appears as "The Hidden Soul of Harmony" in Selma Jeanne Cohen and Katy Matheson, eds., *Dance as a Theatre Art*, 2nd ed. (Princeton, NJ: Princeton Book Company, 1992).

176 "Too often his choreography": Shapiro, op. cit.

176 "He usually choreographs": "Amazing Grace, Morris Makes His Mark," April 16, 1992.

176 "all the musical sensibility": Barnes, "Morris in Musical Maze."

176 "step-to-note style": Anna Kisselgoff, "Who Does What to Whom, or, A Kinetic Wit at Play," June 29, 1990.

178 "It is the rhythm": *The Mary Wigman Book: Her Writings*, ed. and trans. Walter Sorrell (Middletown, CT: Wesleyan University Press, 1975), p. 122.

179 "frame to the picture": Quoted in Janet Soares, *Louis Horst: Musician in a Dancer's World* (Durham, NC: Duke University Press, 1992), p. 93.

179 "The music dominates": John Martin, *The New York Times*, January 17, 1943; quoted in Marcia B. Siegel, *Days on Earth: The Dance of Doris Humphrey* (New Haven: Yale University Press, 1987), p. 212.

179 "matter": *The New York Times*, March 8, 1945, quoted in Nancy Reynolds, *Repertory in Review: 40 Years of the New York City Ballet* (New York: Dial Press, 1977), p. 44.

179 "abstract patterns": Hanna Rubin, "The Shock of the Old," *The Village Voice*, June 30, 1992.

IRONY AND SINCERITY

189 "smash": Quoted in Iris Fanger, "Dancing to a Different Beat," *The Boston Herald*, June 8, 1990.

191 "Morris' Peter Sellars ballet": Uncut version of "Le nozze di Figaro," Alastair Macaulay, *The Financial Times*, February 10, 1992, quoted by permission.

194 "the *Nutcracker* ballet," "the romantic love": Marcia B. Siegel, "Decomposing Sugar Plums & Robot Mice," *Ballet Review*, Spring 1991.

195 "Evil is *advertised*": Roland Barthes, "Striptease," in *Mythologies*, trans. Annette Lavers (New York: Hill and Wang, 1972), p. 84.

196 "Look at Tommy's uniform": Herschel Garfein, libretto, *Soap-Powders and Detergents*, Monnaie Dance Group/Mark Morris souvenir program, Théâtre Royal de la Monnaie, April 19–23, 1989.

198 "There's not a lot": Quoted in Rudy Kikel, "Taking Notes for a Boston 'Striptease' with Morris and Co.," *The Advocate*, May 13, 1986.

198 "I have absolutely no sense": Quoted in David Daniel, "Dance," *Vogue*, November 1990.

200 "dead virgins": Quoted in Brock, op. cit.

201 "Ballet dancers are antigravity": Quoted in Dupont, op. cit.

BRUSSELS

206 "Like emperor-for-life": Quoted in Robertson, op. cit.

207 "If you dare to take one step": Birgit Kirchner, "Dancing Really Does Make Sense: Interview with Susanne Linke," *Ballett International*, December 1983.

208 "I don't work": Quoted in Deborah Jowitt, "When Worlds Collide," *The Village Voice*, December 5, 1989.

209 "the standard by which": Luisa Moffett, "Mark Morris and the Monnaie," *The Bulletin*, January 24, 1991.

209 "Brussels was never a city": *The Hidden Soul of Harmony*, op. cit.

210 "Béjart was Belgium's most important export": Quoted in Robert Greskovic, "Mark Morris on 'Farewell Tour,'" *Los Angeles Times*, October 11, 1987.

210 "No, I don't like Béjart": Quoted in Laurence Bertels, "Non, je n'aime pas Béjart!" *La Dernière Heure*, September 29, 1988.

212 "a new era": Charles Philippon, *Le Soir*, November 23, 1988.

213 "Morris is musical?"' Nicole Verschoore, "Morris maakt geen grote indruk," *Het Laatste Nieuws*, November 25, 1988.

213 "The hour of existential meditations": Reinhard Beuth, "Mit Frischem Wind das Pastoral durchpustet," *Die Welt*, November 25, 1988.

213 "Where is the profundity?": Claire Diez, "L'homme qui visualise les intentions musicales," *La Libre Belgique*, December 6, 1988.

213 "dumbfounding simplicity": Clair Diez, "Pour sa première à la Monnaie le public a adopté Mark Morris," *La Libre Belgique*, November 25, 1988.

213 "the expression of the wellsprings": Charles Philippon, "Le corps relaxé, la tendresse et l'humour de Mark Morris pour le gala de la presse," *Le Soir*, December 5, 1988.

213 "All of Belgium," "hideous spectacle": Nicole Verschoore, "Mark Morris en het Nederlands Dans Theater, *Het Laatste Nieuws*, March 13, 1989.

214 "tasteless," "debased": Charles Philippon, "Monnaie n'est pas or, Morris n'est pas bon Didon," *Le Soir*, March 13, 1989.

214 "vulgar parody and syrupy pathos": Verschoore, "Mark Morris en het Nederlands Dans Theater."

214 "The art of Mark Morris": René Sirvin, "Un Baryshnikov new-look," *Le Figaro*, November 6, 1989.

214 "Queen of what?": Philippon, "Monnaie n'est pas or."

214 "just competent enough": Verschoore, "Mark Morris en het Nederlands Dans Theater."

214 "pulls aside his little black skirt," "a lack of respect for Woman": Philippon, "Monnaie n'est pas or."

215 "Provocation or suicidal anti-performance?": "Mark Morris, go home!" *Le Soir*, April 21, 1989.

215 "sordid display": Charles Philippon, "Les tristes supercheries de Mark Morris: assez!" April 21, 1989.

215 "Perhaps in the U.S.A.": Jacques de Decker, "Bas les Barthes!" *Le Soir*, April 21, 1989.

215 "Obviously, Mark Morris's choreographic inspiration": Martine DuBois, "Pitié!" *Le Drapeau Rouge*, April 26, 1989.

216 "painful images": Ibid.

216 "there remains nothing": Philippon, "Les tristes supercheries."

218 "It's a three-ring circus": Allen Robertson, "Blunderland for the Morris men," *The Daily Mail*, November 14, 1989.

218 "How much longer": Verschoore, "Mark Morris en het Nederlands Dans Theater."

219 "Yes, things have changed," "Béjart's work is shit," "de Tearjerker," "It was empty," "Maggie Thatcher": Quoted in Siebert, op. cit.

220 "Mark Morris: 'Béjart is shit' ": *De Morgen*, April 25, 1989.

224 "I am a Machiavellian": Quoted in Rupert Christiansen, "Salzburg Supremo," *Vanity Fair*, March 1990.

228 "highly racist": quoted in Debra Craine, "Controversy stalks a Morris dancer," *The Times* (London), March 24, 1990.

228 "Mark Morris Spits in the Soup Again": Charles Philippon, "Mark Morris continue à cracher dans la soupe," *Le Soir*, March 29, 1990.

228 "I think I get it now": Quoted in Alan Kriegsman, "Rocking and Rolling in the Monnaie," *The Washington Post*, November 21, 1990.

228 "Come on": Quoted in Singer, "Singing the Body Electric."

234 "put a bunch of chimpanzees," "you find": Nicole Verschoore, "Morris waardeloos maar Herreweghe schittert in Munt," *Het Laatste Nieuws*, December 19, 1989.

234 "pitiful," "One girl": Nicole Verschoore, " 'Gloria' redt Mark Morris," *Het Laatste Nieuws*, December 5, 1988.

235 "Belgium might well be": "Morris, please stay," *De Morgen*, April 22, 1989.

235 "sloppy rites of spring," "The beauty of a human being," "You can't sell toe shoes," "Béjart-sclerosis": Fons de Haas, "De duivelsverzen van de dans," *Knack*, May 3, 1989.

235 "attacked with fury": Leonetta Bentivoglio, "Impazza Schiaccianoci tra sbronze e fumetti," *La Repubblica*, January 17, 1991.

236 "scarifying and mean-spirited": Paul Montgomery, "Sugar-Free 'Nutcracker' with Men in Tutus," *The New York Times*, January 12, 1991.

236 "How long is the Morris-go-home game": Stephan Moens, "Het Gewone Morris-Rantsoen," *De Morgen*, November 6, 1989.

236 "Morris's only sacrilege": Guy Cools, "Lichtvoetigheid, helderheid en maaterk," *De Morgen*, December 19, 1989.

236 "a milestone in dance history": Paul Verduyckt, "Een poppy lovesong," *De Morgen*, January 14, 1991.

236 "dance theater at its best": Nicole Verschoore, " 'Notenkraker' is heerlijk gek," *Het Laatste Nieuws*, January 25, 1991.

236 "a jewel of invention," "all the failings": Charles Philippon, "Invention, humour, poésie: Morris au pays des merveilles," *Le Soir*, January 14, 1991.

236 "not a single one": Verschoore, " 'Notenkraker' is heerlijk gek."

237 "Several cynics": Montgomery, op. cit.

238 "Brussels was fraught": Quoted in Nancy Dalva, "Mark Morris Comes Home," *Dance Ink*, July/August, 1991.

THE HIDDEN SOUL OF HARMONY

247 "Somehow you feel": Clive Barnes, "Bad, but So Good," *New York Post*, April 18, 1992.

247 "I feel": Jowitt, "When Worlds Collide."

247 "By using fewer themes": Brungard, op. cit.

251 "There are four different dance techniques," "The nature of the proscenium," "doesn't exist and hasn't": Ibid.

252 "A guy sits alone": Quoted in Charles Siebert, "Footloose!" *Esquire*, December 1985.

252 "I have fabulous, brilliant ideas": Brungard, op. cit.

256 "Mark would have an idea," "more and more," "I realized a long time ago": Singer, "Mark Morris: Beautiful Dancers."

257 "We use ballet": *The Hidden Soul of Harmony*, op. cit.

258 "This is not political": Quoted in Jennifer Dunning, "Mark Morris Gives 'The Nutcracker' a Twist," *The New York Times*, December 6, 1992.

259 "the most talked-about company": Nancy Goldner, "Mark Morris at Annenberg," *The Philadelphia Inquirer*, February 10, 1993.

Donald Mouton and Jon Mensinger in
L'Allegro, il Penseroso ed il Moderato (Klaus Lefebvre)

Index

Numbers in italics refer to illustrations.